SCHOOLS AND URBAN REVITALIZATION

New research in community development shows that institutions matter. Where the private sector disinvests from the inner city, public and nonprofit institutions step in and provide engines to economic revitalization and promote greater equity in society. *Schools and Urban Revitalization* collects emerging research in this field, with special interest in new school–neighborhood partnerships that lead today's most vibrant policy responses to urban blight.

Adapted from a recent issue of *Community Development*, Patterson and Silverman collect some of the emerging literature on anchor institutions like schools, universities, churches and cultural centers, and offer a new paradigm for neighborhood revitalization, exploring its advantages and challenges. While many scholars have come to criticize the "meds and eds" model of organizing around schools and hospitals, the essays show the unique role public schools play in urban revitalization. With case studies from across the United States, including large and mid-sized cities, *Schools and Urban Revitalization* shows the vital role that schools play in bridging citizens to larger institutions, and more importantly, connecting disenfranchised residents to society.

Kelly L. Patterson is an Assistant Professor in the School of Social Work at the University at Buffalo. She holds a Ph.D. in Urban Studies from the University of Wisconsin-Milwaukee, a Masters in Public Affairs from the University at Buffalo, and a B.A. in Sociology from North Carolina Central University. Her research focuses on rent vouchers, fair housing, discrimination, social policy, and the African-American experience. She has published in *Housing Policy Debate*, *Housing and Society*, *Journal of Black Psychology*, and other peer reviewed journals. She is co-editor of *Fair and Affordable Housing in the US: Trends, Outcomes, Future Directions* (Brill, 2011).

Robert Mark Silverman is an Associate Professor in the Department of Urban and Regional Planning at the University at Buffalo. He holds a Ph.D. in Urban Studies from the University of Wisconsin-Milwaukee. He also holds a B.S. in Political Science and a Masters in Public Administration from Arizona State University. His research focuses on community development, the nonprofit sector, community-based organizations, education reform, and inequality in inner city housing markets. He has published in *Urban Affairs Review*, *Urban Studies*, *National Civic Review*, *Action Research*, *Community Development*, *Journal of Black Studies*, *Journal of Social History*, and other peer reviewed journals. He is co-editor of *Fair and Affordable Housing in the US: Trends, Outcomes, Future Directions* (Brill, 2011).

The Community Development Research and Practice Series

Volume 1

Series Editor:

RHONDA G. PHILLIPS
Arizona State University, USA

Editorial Board:

MARK BRENNAN
Pennsylvania State University, USA

JAN FLORA
Iowa State University, USA

GARY P. GREEN
University of Wisconsin, USA

BRIAN MCGRATH
National University of Ireland

NORMAN WALZER
Northern Illinois University, USA

This series serves community developers, planners, public administrators and others involved in practice and policy making in the realm of community development. The series provides timely and applied information for researchers, students, and practitioners. Building on a 40 year history of publishing the Community Development Society's journal, *Community Development* (www.comm-dev.org), the book series contributes to a growing and rapidly changing knowledge base as a resource for practitioners and researchers alike.

For additional information please see the series page at www.routledge.com

Community development as reflected in both theory and practice is continually evolving. This comes as no surprise as our communities and regions constantly change. As a practice focused discipline, change is the only constant in the community development realm. The need to integrate theory, practice, research, teaching and training is even more pressing now than ever given uncertain and rapidly transforming economic, social, environmental and cultural climates. Current and applicable information and insights about effective community development research and practice are needed.

In partnership with Routledge, the Community Development Society is delighted to present this new book series serving community developers, planners, public administrators, citizen activists and others involved in community development practice, research and policy making. The series is designed to integrate innovative thinking on tools, strategies, experiences as a resource especially well-suited for bridging the gaps between theory, research, and practice. It is our intent that the series will provide timely and useful information for responding to the rapidly changing environment in which community development researchers and practitioners operate. The Community Development Society was formed in 1970 as a professional association to serve the needs of both researchers and practitioners. That same year, the Society began publishing *Community Development*, its journal promoting exchange of ideas, experiences and approaches between practice and research. *Community Development Research and Practice* builds on this rich legacy of scholarship by offering contributions to the growing knowledge base.

The Community Development Society actively promotes the continued advancement of the practice and theory of community development. Fundamental to this mission is adherence to the following core Principles of Good Practice. This new book series is a reflection of many of these core principles.

- Promote active and representative participation toward enabling all community members to meaningfully influence the decisions that affect their lives.
- Engage community members in learning about and understanding community issues, and the economic, social, environmental, political, psychological and other impacts associated with alternative courses of action.
- Incorporate the diverse interest and cultures of the community in the community development process; and disengage from support of any effort that is likely to adversely affect the disadvantaged members of a community.
- Work actively to enhance the leadership capacity of community members, leaders, and groups within the community.
- Be open to using the full range of action strategies to work toward the long-term sustainability and well being of the community.

On behalf of the Community Development Society, and the editorial board of the series, I invite you to explore this volume. Further, continue to explore the series as new volumes are added, and we do hope you will find it a valuable resource for supporting community development research and practice.

Rhonda Phillips
Editor, *Community Development Research and Practice Series*

SCHOOLS AND URBAN REVITALIZATION

Rethinking Institutions and Community Development

Kelly L. Patterson and Robert Mark Silverman

Routledge
Taylor & Francis Group

NEW YORK AND LONDON

First published 2014
by Routledge
711 Third Avenue, New York, NY 10017

Simultaneously published in the UK
by Routledge
2 Park Square, Milton Park, Abingdon, Oxon OX14 4RN

Routledge is an imprint of the Taylor & Francis Group, an informa business

Library of Congress Cataloging-in-Publication Data
A catalog record has been requested for this book

ISBN13: 978-0-415-64423-5 (hbk)
ISBN13: 978-0-415-64424-2 (pbk)
ISBN13: 978-0-203-07966-9 (ebk)

Typeset in Bembo
by HWA Text and Data Management, London

Printed and bound in the United States of America by Publishers Graphics, LLC on sustainably sourced paper.

CONTENTS

CONTRIBUTORS

Janice Bockmeyer is an associate professor of political science in the John Jay College of Criminal Justice at the City University of New York. She received a B.A. from the University of Michigan and an M.A. and Ph.D. from the Graduate Center of the City University of New York. Professor Bockmeyer's primary research interests are comparative urban politics, global migration and immigrant urban participation, federalism and urban politics, community revitalization and housing policies. Her publications include articles in *German Politics and Society*, *Urban Studies*, *Urban Affairs Review*, *The Social Science Journal*, and *Forschungsjournal Neue Soziale Bewegnung*. Her research on immigrant political incorporation also appears in *Governing Cities in a Global Era* (eds. R. Hambleton and J. Gross, Palgrave Macmillan, 2007) and *Toward a New Metropolitanism* (eds. G. Lenz, F. Ulfers and A. Dallman, Winter Verlag, 2006).

Greta Kirschenbaum Brownlow holds a Masters degree in Urban Planning from the University of California, Los Angeles and a Doctorate in Education from the Graduate School of Education at the University of California, Berkeley. Dr. Brownlow's primary interests are in the forms and benefits of school–community connections, including youth involvement in community planning, and in the potential for school and community change that emerges from community organizing for school reform. Dr. Brownlow currently works as a program manager in community development at a consulting firm in Oakland, California specializing in environmental and land use planning. She is also an adjunct faculty member in the Department of Geography and Environmental Studies at California State University, East Bay.

Brian D. Christens is an Assistant Professor in the School of Human Ecology at the University of Wisconsin–Madison. He conducts research on efforts by nonprofits and grassroots organizations to effect change in policies and systems, and the psychosocial predictors and effects of participation in these efforts, with applications to community development, youth development, and health promotion.

Jessica J. Collura is a Ph.D. candidate in Civil Society and Community Research in the School of Human Ecology at the University of Wisconsin–Madison. A former Teach for America corps member, her work focuses on youth civic engagement, youth–adult relationships, and community development.

Margaret Cowell is an Assistant Professor of Urban Affairs and Planning at Virginia Tech. She received her Doctorate in City and Regional Planning from Cornell University. Margaret is a member of the John D. and Catherine T. MacArthur Foundation-funded research project, "Building Resilient Regions" and is also part of a team of researchers assessing the potential of the homeland security economy for community economic development at the St. Elizabeths Hospital site in Southeast Washington, DC. Dr. Cowell's research has been funded by the MacArthur Foundation, National Association of Counties, and the United States Economic Development Administration.

Michael A. Kopish is an Assistant Professor in the Department of History and Philosophy and the Program Coordinator for Social Studies Teacher Certification at Plymouth State University. His areas of specialization for teaching and research include curriculum and instruction in social studies, pre-service teacher education, and youth civic engagement.

D. Gavin Luter is a Ph.D. student in Educational Administration at the University at Buffalo and also serves as Coordinator of the Perry Choice Neighborhood Mini-Education Pipeline strategy. As a practitioner-scholar, he has experience working in and with educational nonprofits, school systems, and universities to both run programs and build systems-wide service coordination and reform capacity. This work links to his research interest of how universities can catalyze school and neighborhood transformation. His recent work is as Co-Guest Editor of a themed issue of the *Peabody Journal of Education*, "Higher Education's Role and Capacity to Assist with Public School Reform."

Heike Mayer is Professor of Economic Geography and Deputy Director of the Center for Regional Economic Development at the University of Bern in Switzerland. Her primary area of research is in local and regional economic development with a particular focus on dynamics of innovation and entrepreneurship, place making and sustainability. Heike started her career in the United States, where she completed a Ph.D. in Urban Studies (Portland State University) and held a tenured professorship at Virginia Tech University. She is the author of the book *Entrepreneurship and Innovation in Second Tier Regions* (Edward Elgar) and co-author of the book *Small Town Sustainability* (with Prof. Paul L. Knox, Birkhäuser Press).

Linda McGlynn received her M.S.W. and Ph.D. from the School of Social Welfare, State University of New York at Albany. Twenty-five years of clinical work has been devoted to both community and school related services: developing and implementing programs for vulnerable children, youth, and families. These have included health–social services and positive youth development opportunities, many working within the context of reducing risk and increasing resiliency and protection for minority and immigrant children and families. The emphasis of her most recent work has been on globalization's effects on child well-being and educational equity, most particularly for vulnerable populations. In addition to her private practice, Dr. McGlynn is a Senior Research Associate in the Center for Urban Studies at the University at Buffalo.

Kelly L. Patterson is an Assistant Professor in the School of Social Work at the University at Buffalo. She holds a Ph.D. in Urban Studies from the University of Wisconsin-Milwaukee, a Masters in Public Affairs from the University at Buffalo, and a B.A. in Sociology from North Carolina Central University. Her research focuses on rent vouchers, fair housing, discrimination, social policy, and the African American experience. She has published in *Housing Policy Debate*, *Housing and Society*, *Journal of Black Psychology*, and other peer reviewed journals. She is co-editor of *Fair and Affordable Housing in the US: Trends, Outcomes, Future Directions* (Brill, 2011).

Robert Mark Silverman is an Associate Professor in the Department of Urban and Regional Planning at the University at Buffalo. He holds a Ph.D. in Urban Studies from the University of Wisconsin-Milwaukee. He also holds a B.S. in Political Science and a Masters in Public Administration from Arizona State University. His research focuses on community development, the nonprofit sector, community-based organizations, education reform, and inequality in inner city housing markets. He has published in *Urban Affairs Review*, *Urban Studies*, *National Civic Review*, *Action Research*, *Community Development*, *Journal of Black Studies*, *Journal of Social History*, and other peer reviewed journals. He is co-editor of *Fair and Affordable Housing in the US: Trends, Outcomes, Future Directions* (Brill, 2011).

Henry Louis Taylor, Jr. is a Professor in the Department of Urban and Regional Planning at the University at Buffalo and founding director of the U.B. Center for Urban Studies. He is the author of more than 80 articles, essays and technical reports and has written and edited five books and monographs. His latest book is *Inside El Barrio: A Bottom-Up View of Life in Castro's Cuba*. Taylor is currently working on a manuscript that examines the relationship between the city planning movement and black residential development in the urban metropolis.

Samantha N. Teixeira is in the Doctoral Program in Social Work at the University of Pittsburgh. Her research is focused on how housing and neighborhood environmental conditions affect children and youth. Samantha's recent work has focused on engaging youth as research assistants and using data to drive community organizing efforts. Samantha's diverse practice experience includes work in child protective services, community organizing and development and local government initiatives.

Matea Varvodić earned her Masters degree in Art Education from The School of the Art Institute of Chicago, where she focused on social justice activism through community based art. She has since worked on reproductive rights advocacy with planned parenthood and education equity initiatives with Teach for America. Her interests include community engagement, development, and empowerment.

Avis C. Vidal is Professor of Urban Planning at Wayne State University. Her research analyzes alternative approaches to strengthening poor neighborhoods. She is best known for her seminal research on community development corporations (CDCs), but has also analyzed the potential of such varied approaches as the federal Empowerment Zone and Enterprise Community program and university–community partnerships. Prior to joining Wayne State University, she served as Principal Research Associate at the Urban Institute; Director of the Community Development Research Center at the New School for Social Research; Senior Analyst on the Urban Policy Staff at HUD; and Associate Professor at Harvard's Kennedy School of Government.

John M. Wallace, Jr. Ph.D. is the Philip Hallen Chair in Community Health and Social Justice at the University of Pittsburgh's School of Social Work and a Faculty Associate at the Institute for Social Research at the University of Michigan. He earned his B.A. from the University of Chicago in 1987 and his Ph.D. from the University of Michigan in 1991. From 1992 to 1994 he was a National Science Foundation Postdoctoral Fellow. His research has appeared in numerous professional journals, books and monographs. His current research focuses on racial/ethnic and gender disparities in drug use; and community-based participatory research methods and comprehensive community initiatives to improve the life chances of poor children growing up in inner-city environments.

Mark R. Warren is associate professor of public policy and public affairs at the University of Massachusetts Boston. He is a sociologist who studies efforts to strengthen institutions that anchor low-income communities—public schools, religious congregations, and other community-based organizations—and to build broad-based alliances among these institutions and across race and social class. He is the author of several books, including *A Match on Dry Grass: Community Organizing as a Catalyst for School Reform* (Oxford University Press, 2011), *Fire in the Heart: How White Activists Embrace Racial Justice* (Oxford University Press, 2010) and *Dry Bones Rattling: Community Building to Revitalize American Democracy* (Princeton University Press, 2001).

Bethany J. Welch, Ph.D. is the founding director of the Aquinas Center in Philadelphia, PA, a former convent repurposed to house culturally competent outreach programs for local residents as well as service learning experiences for high school and college students. Dr. Welch has worked in research and practice capacities in community development, program evaluation, and human services. She has an M.S. in Higher Education Administration from the University of Rochester, and a Ph.D. in Urban Affairs and Public Policy from the University of Delaware.

PREFACE

Reconsidering the Role of Public Schools in Inner-City Revitalization

As urban scholars we have always been intrigued by the problem of dying cities. Although every urban area is the product of its unique historical context, most find it easy to identify declining places and offer explanations for the death of American cities. Customarily, Detroit tops the list as the quintessential dying city plagued by population decline, racial segregation, income inequality, blighted neighborhoods, and an industrial base hemorrhaging jobs. Other rust belt cities, like Buffalo and Cleveland, share a similar designation. In the contemporary period, coastal cities like New Orleans have moved up the list of dying cities as the impacts of climate change have compounded earlier challenges brought on by deindustrialization.

Yet, the downward trajectory of these places is only half the story. Most dying cities do not completely collapse. Many have remained in limbo for decades and repeatedly attempt to reinvent themselves. The latest incarnation of these efforts has involved a focus on transforming older industrial cities into centers for higher education and medicine. This model for urban revitalization is based on pursuing development around "eds and meds" in declining core cities. This model is based on the assumption that focused development around large universities, hospitals, and other place-based anchor institutions will increase wealth in these communities and spillover into urban neighborhoods. Frequently, the eds and meds economy has been cited as a stabilizing factor in slumping cities like Cleveland and Pittsburgh. A growing number of cities have replicated these efforts to promote urban revitalization by leveraging anchor institutions.

Despite the merits of the eds and meds approach, critics argue that this model suffers from some of the same shortcomings of past urban renewal processes driven by the interests of larger institutions. It is argued that strategies based on anchor institutions have the potential to unfold in a vacuum, with little transparency and accountability to the general public. As a result, low-income residents have a limited voice in anchor-based local economic development strategies, see minimal benefits from economic multipliers and other spillovers, and risk being displaced by anchor-driven gentrification. In response to these critiques, there have been increased calls for mechanisms to counterbalance the negative externalities of anchor-based development strategies.

One response was the growing movement for the adoption of community benefits agreements (CBAs). In these agreements, grassroots interests negotiate for concessions in the development process. CBAs include provisions for: set asides for minority and local procurement, workforce development programs, local hiring in distressed communities that surround anchor institutions, and development of community amenities that enrich the quality of life for residents.

Another response to anchor-based development involves grassroots capacity building in inner-city neighborhoods. The influence of large anchor institutions can be counterbalanced by block clubs, neighborhood associations, community development corporations, churches, and other grassroots organizations. However, this is only possible if these organizations have access to resources to support capacity building and a formal role in the decision-making processes that drive anchor-based development. Strengthening neighborhood-based institutions is a critical component of efforts to promote balanced community development.

In this volume, we argue that public schools are critical bridging institutions between larger anchor institutions and grassroots organizations in the urban revitalization process. Public schools are uniquely positioned at the neighborhood level and relatively accessible to neighborhood residents. In distressed urban neighborhoods, public schools remain one of the primary links between inner-city residents and the broader society. Repositioning public schools as neighborhood-based anchor institutions advances efforts to use community development as a mechanism to empower residents and augment community control in the urban revitalization process.

The purpose of this edited book is to better understand the role of larger anchor institutions in the urban revitalization process and the potential for public schools to serve as bridging institutions. This book is divided into two parts. The first part considers the urban context where anchor institutions are embedded. This context is examined conceptually, and through the analysis of anchor-based development in Detroit, Philadelphia, and Washington, DC. The second part focuses on the potential for the development of public schools as bridging institutions in the inner-city revitalization process. The role of public schools in the community development process is examined through case studies in Buffalo, Pittsburgh, Philadelphia, Chicago, and Los Angeles.

We hope that this edited book will inform the debate about the role of public schools in the urban revitalization process. We encourage policy makers, individuals engaged in community development practice and grassroots reformers to draw from this collection when planning for urban revitalization in the future. We also encourage members of the academic community to expand on the framework laid out here and continue to pursue scholarship that promotes social justice and empowerment in America's dying cities.

Kelly L. Patterson and Robert Mark Silverman
University at Buffalo

ACKNOWLEDGMENTS

We would like to thank a number of people who supported the development of this edited book. First and foremost, we must acknowledge Rhonda Phillips for her support of this project. The early framework for this project was an outgrowth of our co-edited themed issue of *Community Development* focusing on "inner-city empowerment and revitalization". At the time, Rhonda was the editor of the journal and she encouraged us to pursue the theme of our co-edited issue further as an edited book for Routledge's *Community Development Research and Practice Series*.

We also would like to acknowledge each of the contributors who wrote chapters for this edited book. Their work represents a snapshot of collective knowledge related to the intersection of anchor institutions, public schools, and inner-city revitalization in declining cities. We hope to continue our dialogue related to this important topic with them and other researchers in the future.

Finally, we would like to thank Fritz Brantley, Nicole Solano, and other members of the Routledge team for their invaluable assistance during the development of this project.

PART I

Institutions, Revitalization, and Inner-City Neighborhoods

1

INSTITUTIONS AND THE NEW NORMAL FOR COMMUNITY DEVELOPMENT

Kelly L. Patterson and Robert Mark Silverman,
University at Buffalo

Community Development and Urban Social Institutions

The central argument of this edited book is that community development processes are intimately linked to the institutional contexts in which they are embedded. Today, more than ever, working in an institutional context has become the new norm for community development practitioners. Increasingly, urban revitalization policies are shaped and driven by large anchor institutions like hospitals, universities, and cultural centers. These anchor institutions often solicit cooperation from other urban social institutions like churches, community development corporations, neighborhood associations, and block clubs as they pursue neighborhood revitalization efforts. However, relationships between larger anchor institutions and grassroots organizations are often unequal. Anchor institutions bring greater resources to local development initiatives and tend to dominate them. Consequently, grassroots organizations that represent the interests of inner-city residents run the risk of being co-opted or being muted in the local community development process. In the most extreme cases, inner-city neighborhoods fall victim to what Worthy (1977) labeled *institutional rape*, which occurs when unaccountable anchor institutions pursue expansion without restraint and to the detriment of inner-city residents.

Given the potential for urban revitalization efforts led by anchor institutions to produce negative externalities, we argue that it is essential for scholars, policy makers, and professional practitioners to understand the manner in which urban social institutions influence community development. This understanding will allow them to design policies and programs that are equitable and empower residents in inner-city neighborhoods. With this argument in mind, we conceptualized this book as a resource for those interested in the role of urban social institutions in the revitalization of inner-city neighborhoods. Scholars and students will find our framework for conceptualizing urban social institutions useful when developing new research to understand the role of anchor institutions in urban revitalization processes. Policy makers and individuals engaged in community development practice can apply concepts from this book to the formulation and implementation of local policies and programs. Moreover, leaders of grassroots organizations can use the framework of this book to inform local efforts to remove obstacles to local control and empower neighborhoods in the community development process.

This book is written in response to the growing consensus that urban social institutions have a substantial impact on the degree to which community development initiatives succeed. In addition to being a source of financial support, institutions provide leadership and capacity to urban revitalization efforts. Despite the benefits that urban social institutions bring to the table, tensions often exist between larger agencies and grassroots organizations engaged in inner-city revitalization. For example, community development initiatives led by large anchor institutions like hospitals, universities, and cultural centers are sometimes met with distrust by grassroots organizations that fear inner-city revitalization will entail gentrification and residential displacement. These concerns are often aggravated by a lack of transparency and community representation in planning processes. Examples of this type of tension are found in the history of neighborhood revitalization in the US, particularly during the urban renewal era (Anderson, 1964; Worthy, 1977; Etienne, 2012).

In the contemporary period there has been a shift away from traditional urban renewal strategies, and some anchor institutions have diligently forged partnerships with community-based organizations to pursue neighborhood revitalization that is equitable and sustainable. This shift is reflected in the growing literature on university–community partnerships (Maurrasse, 2001; Perry & Wiewel, 2005; Rodin, 2007; Wiewel & Perry, 2008). The emerging emphasis on partnerships between larger anchor institutions – like hospitals and universities – and their surrounding communities is encouraging. However, there is a tendency for these partnerships to remain driven by the development needs of larger anchor institutions at the expense of grassroots organizations. We argue that communities need to reassert themselves and demand greater control over neighborhood development processes. This entails gaining access to decision-making roles in anchor institutions, as well as other urban social institutions. A rationale for elevating the role of communities in urban revitalization can be found in the community development literature dealing with urban social institutions and community empowerment.

Connecting Anchor Institutions to their Radical Roots

The community development literature focusing on urban social institutions and community empowerment is informative to those interested in promoting equitable and sustainable neighborhood revitalization. At its core is the assumption that inner-city residents and grassroots organizations that represent their interests should control development decisions that impact the trajectory of urban neighborhoods. We discussed the theoretical foundations for this assumption in our guest editors' introduction to the themed issue on "inner-city empowerment and revitalization" of *Community Development* (Silverman & Patterson, 2012). The framework we outlined has a specific focus on addressing the needs of black, Latino, and other historically disenfranchised groups living in inner-city neighborhoods. Historically, these groups have absorbed the negative externalities of urban renewal and linked development by anchor institutions. To varying degrees, contemporary efforts to forge community partnerships attempt to address these externalities as anchor institutions pursue urban revitalization. However, disparities in power and capacity tend to place residents and smaller grassroots organizations at a disadvantage during the development process.

Our emphasis on urban social institutions highlights how disenfranchised groups interface with larger education, health care, business, and nonprofit organizations. The framework we adopt is rooted in seminal works focused on the nexus between race, inequality and community development. Among these works are Blauner's (1969, 1972) writings on racial oppression in America. His work is central to our framework because it accounted for power relations between majority and minority groups in society. Blauner argued that urban, black neighborhoods in the US faced multiple barriers to community development rooted in institutional relationships with schools, social welfare agencies, local businesses, and the police. He recommended that community empowerment and control of neighborhood institutions was essential to address inequality in society. This sentiment is echoed in contemporary calls for empowering African Americans in community development processes (Harris, 2012).

We bring themes examined by Blauner and others into the contemporary milieu, and argue that urban development driven by anchor institutions remains laden with underlying institutional inequalities. In order to remedy this problem, community-based organizations need to assume a more central role in the planning and implementation of neighborhood revitalization initiatives. Moreover, members of historically disenfranchised groups must be incorporated into the governance structure of larger anchor institutions as a mechanism to facilitate the promotion of equitable and sustainable neighborhood revitalization.

One component of incorporating historically disenfranchised groups into the governance structure of anchor institutions entails targeted capacity building and technical assistance aimed at leveling the playing field among actors in urban social institutions. This type of assistance is within the tradition of advocacy planning (Davidoff, 1965; Needleman & Needleman, 1974; Krumholz & Forester, 1990). It also exemplifies how community development practitioners can play a transformative role in inner-city neighborhoods by empowering residents to fully participate in urban revitalization processes. In some cases, these forms of advocacy and technical assistance by community planners have led to linked development agreements (DAs) and community benefit agreements (CBAs) which guarantee long-term benefits to residents of inner-city neighborhoods impacted by the expansion of anchor institutions (Lowe & Morton, 2008; Dobbie, 2009).

The adoption of DAs and CBAs serve as mechanisms to bring about a comprehensive anchor strategy focused on community capacity building and the redistribution of development resources to historically disempowered groups. This strategy entails the integration of three pillars: physical redevelopment, local procurement, and local hiring. Anchor-led physical redevelopment allows for the use of institutional resources to leverage new development. DAs and CBAs allow grassroots interests to negotiate for concessions in the development process. These concessions include amenities like affordable housing, improvements to schools and community facilities, public parks, enhanced public access, and other design elements that enrich the quality of life for residents. In addition to physical redevelopment, DAs and CBAs allow grassroots interests to negotiate for set-asides related to procurement. Negotiated agreements would include provisions for set-asides for minority and local procurement agreements directly related to construction projects, as well as agreements to contract with vendors that provide anchor institutions with services that support the operation of their core activities. Finally, negotiated DAs and CBAs create pipelines for education and workforce development in distressed communities. Through these agreements, anchors provide local education and training organizations with resources to develop human resources in distressed communities. Resources provided by anchors for workforce development are targeted in a manner that links local skill development with jobs in anchor institutions. Making DAs and CBAs the norm in urban revitalization is one goal of an anchor-based strategy to community development guided by our urban social institutions framework.

Another component of incorporating historically disenfranchised groups into the governance structure of anchor institutions entails capacity building in community-based organizations and expanding the scope of resident control. In part, this involves strengthening traditional grassroots organizations that residents have access to. These organizations include block clubs, neighborhood associations, and community development corporations. However, it also encompasses expanded resident control of neighborhood-based anchor institutions like churches, libraries, community centers, and public schools. This approach is grounded in Alinsky's (1969, 1971) model for community development which emphasized organizing through neighborhood-based urban social institutions. Mobilizing residents through community-based organizations produces a number of benefits to inner-city neighborhoods. Resident engagement in these organizations serves as a platform for the development of organizational skills and grassroots leadership. Enhanced resident participation also elevates the capacity of these organizations and their legitimacy in the eyes of elected officials and representatives of larger anchor institutions.

The presence of resident controlled community-based organizations with strong grassroots leadership and the capacity to engage at all levels in neighborhood revitalization processes alters the dynamics of inner-city community development. The presence of organizations with these characteristics strengthens the degree to which inner-city residents achieve equal partnerships with larger anchor institutions. Resident controlled community-based organizations can also emerge as viable alternatives for the implementation of urban development policies and community development programs. There is an urgent need for the development of resident controlled community-based organizations in the contemporary period, since in their absence anchor institutions have the potential to usurp power from residents. In some instances, larger anchor institutions initiate urban revitalization or form their own nonprofit development organizations which pursue initiatives in the name of the broader community. However, development organizations that are sponsored by larger anchor institutions tend to have less direct resident control and accountability. In order to maintain resident voice in the neighborhood development process, it is essential to incorporate historically disenfranchised groups into the governance structure of anchor institutions and foster the development of autonomous community-based organizations.

Countering New Urban Regimes with Neighborhood-Based Anchors

The need for resident controlled organizations is greater today, since anchor institutions do not operate as autonomously as they did in the past. Instead, they have begun to work collectively to shape the urban environments where they are located and form new urban regimes. By themselves, anchor institutions are distinct since they are historically and geographically tied to inner-cities. Hospitals, universities, and cultural centers have substantial capital investments in their physical plants and campuses. They also lack the geographic mobility often attributed to private businesses and other enterprises. Consequently, the fate of anchor institutions is closely tied to that of the inner-city neighborhoods where they are located.

Built on their shared interests, anchor institutions form new urban regimes. These regimes fill the vacuum left as traditional urban growth machines composed of private businesses, local government, and public service unions have been weakened in the contemporary period. In the wake of this shift, new urban regimes led by anchor institutions have now assumed an expanded role in urban revitalization processes. Contemporary scholars argue that the emergence of new urban regimes is pronounced in declining industrial cities. For example, Rae (2006) argues that new urban regimes have emerged to replace older growth regimes composed of private industry, commercial interests, and public service unions in rust belt cities. His new urban regimes consist of well-capitalized nonprofits and public sector institutions such as hospitals, universities, and cultural centers. Rae further argues that anchor institutions have replaced heavy industry as engines for economic development. Silverman, Yin and Patterson (2013) reached similar conclusions about new urban regimes, and added that their proximity to declining inner-city neighborhoods heightens concerns about displacement and the aggravation of social inequality resulting from regime-led urban revitalization.

In declining cities with few options for economic development, new urban regimes represent formidable hegemons that can drive urban renewal. The agenda of new urban regimes extends beyond physical redevelopment and is often driven by an ideology that recasts inner-city neighborhoods as centers of art, culture, health, and learning. In part, this ideology is an outgrowth of the composition of new urban regimes, since they are made up of large cultural, healthcare, and educational institutions. However, the ideology of new urban regimes is fed by chic economic development strategies that link inner-city revitalization to the attraction of highly skilled professionals and technical workers collectively referred to as the "creative class" (Florida, 2004). At a more macro level, the policies of new urban regimes are guided by a neoliberal ethos that calls for substantial public subsidies to support the activities of private and nonprofit anchor institutions (Purcell, 2008).

The reach of new urban regimes has moved beyond the boundaries of the physical plants and campuses that anchor institutions occupy. Through philanthropic activities and government lobbying, the agenda of anchor institutions has expanded. They are no longer restricted to a focus on reshaping the built environment. New urban regimes are now actively engaged in campaigns to reorganize and privatize the public institutions in the neighborhoods that surround them. This is evident in the area of public education, where members of new urban regimes sponsor and advocate for a variety of reforms. Many of these reforms complement the ideology of new urban regimes which is built on the creation of enclaves for the creative class and transferring public resources to private and nonprofit organizations (Lipman, 2011).

As the momentum of new urban regimes grows, scholars have begun to critically assess their impact on inner-city neighborhoods. At the heart of this analysis is an emerging critique of the ideological underpinnings of new urban regimes. For instance, Zimmerman's (2008) analysis of Milwaukee highlighted the inherent conflict between pursuing economic development based on the propagation of the creative class and promoting social equity. His research suggests that Milwaukee's efforts to become a creative city exacerbated class and race inequality. In a similar vein, Lipman (2009) argued that school reforms pursued in Chicago's gentrifying neighborhoods during the early 2000s were laden with racial stereotypes and grounded in "culture of poverty" theories. This framework served as a mechanism to accelerate the privatization of public schools and hindered historically disenfranchised groups' access to newly formed charter schools. Fabricant and Fine (2012) and Silverman (2013) raise similar concerns about inequality that stems from educational reforms driven by neoliberal policy.

The growing influence of new urban regimes on the content of state and federal policies is visible in all areas of community development, particularly those related to neighborhood revitalization and education reform. The design of many new state and federal policies has been heavily influenced by privately funded philanthropic initiatives and local demonstration projects. In the area of housing policy, the influence of new urban regimes is ubiquitous. For instance, applicants for funding under the Department of Housing and Urban Development's (HUD's) Choice Neighborhood program are required to demonstrate that they are collaborating with nonprofits and anchor institutions. Those criteria have been incorporated into scoring matrixes for funding of the Choice Neighborhood and other initiatives.[1] Similarly, percentages of funds in programs like the federal HOME program and the Low-Income Housing Tax Credit program have also been set-aside for nonprofit implementation. A parallel development has occurred in education policies where anchor institutions are central actors in state and federal initiatives. For instance, the Department of Education's (DOE's) Promise Neighborhood program, in part, grew out of policy advocacy by philanthropic organizations that promoted initiatives like the Harlem Children's Zone.

In many respects, public schools have become a focal point of efforts to revitalize inner-city neighborhoods. These efforts are heavily influenced by local anchor institutions and philanthropic organizations that represent their interests when lobbying for supportive federal and state policy. Absent from much of this dialogue are residents of communities where these public schools are located. We argue that there is an urgent need to augment the voice of residents in the debate about school reform and reestablish public schools as neighborhood-based and community controlled anchor institutions. We believe public schools are central to inner-city revitalization since they are one of the most prevalent urban social institutions found in distressed neighborhoods. Despite resource disparities between urban and suburban school districts, public schools remain one of the primary links between inner-city neighborhoods and the broader society. Public schools have traditionally been perceived as one of the most accessible neighborhood-based institutions, particularly for youth and families. Because of their embeddedness at the neighborhood level, public schools are increasingly identified by scholars and policy makers as pivotal to inner-city revitalization. Repositioning public schools as neighborhood-based anchor institutions advances efforts to use community development as a mechanism to empower residents and augment community control of urban social institutions.

Plan for the Book

This edited book intends to build on existing theory and inform the development of policy and practice aimed at promoting resident empowerment and community control of neighborhood revitalization processes. From a theoretical perspective, we elaborate on the emerging literature dealing with anchor institutions and school–neighborhood revitalization strategies. From a policy perspective, this book reasserts the role of community development principles in emerging neighborhood revitalization processes with a particular emphasis on establishing public schools as neighborhood-based anchor institutions.

This book is divided into two parts. The first part considers the urban context in which anchor institutions are embedded. This context and its influence on nonprofit partnerships, public accountability, and neighborhood revitalization is examined in the next five chapters. The second part of this book focuses on public schools as neighborhood-based anchor institutions. Through the last five chapters, we develop a broader understanding of the potential for public schools to emerge as community controlled anchor institutions in inner-cities.

Chapters 2 through 6 contextualize the scope of activities in which anchor institutions are currently engaged in inner-city neighborhoods. Part I of the book begins with an overview of contemporary anchor institutions and then elaborates on the rationale for focusing community development activities on schools and neighborhoods. In Chapter 2, Robert Mark Silverman reviews the existing literature on anchor institutions and links it to advocacy planning. This discussion is followed by Chapter 3, where Janice Bockmeyer discusses how tensions between anchor institutions and grassroots organizations are shaped by the constraints of pursuing neighborhood revitalization initiatives in shrinking cities. This chapter is followed by a case study of the efforts of anchor institutions to pursue urban revitalization against the backdrop of wholesale urban decline. In Chapter 4, Avis Vidal examines the case of urban revitalization efforts led by a collaboration between university, medical, and cultural anchor institutions in Detroit. Chapter 5, by Bethany Welch, focuses on another type of anchor institution, the Roman Catholic Church. Her analysis examines the challenges that the Church faces in attempting to balance its interests against those of residents when pursuing neighborhood revitalization in Philadelphia's inner-city. Finally, in Chapter 6, Margaret Cowell and Heike Mayer examine the role of the US Department of Homeland Security (DHS) in driving inner-city revitalization. They examine how best practices in anchor institution-led development are applied to the development of the new DHS headquarters on the campus of a former psychiatric hospital in Washington, DC.

Part II of this book explores the potential for public schools to emerge as neighborhood-based anchor institutions. The chapters in this part of the book have a particular emphasis on examining models for school–neighborhood revitalization and community organizing as it relates to youth enrolled in public schools, residents of surrounding neighborhoods, and institutional actors engaged in progressive coalition building. In Chapter 7, Henry Taylor, Linda McGlynn and Gavin Luter analyze the development of the Promise Neighborhood and Choice Neighborhood models in Buffalo. Their analysis offers insights into how anchor institutions interface with residents in inner-city neighborhoods during planning for neighborhood revitalization and school reform. In Chapter 8, John Wallace and Samantha Teixeira examine the case of the Homewood Children's Village (HCV), a collaborative comprehensive community initiative in an inner-city neighborhood of Pittsburgh. They describe how participatory action research was used to give residents voice in that initiative. In Chapter 9, Brian Christens, Matea Varvodić, Jessica Collura and Michael A. Kopish discuss how the youth organizing model can be applied to revitalization efforts led by anchor institutions. They argue that the integration of youth organizing with the activities of larger anchor institutions can enhance community input in the neighborhood revitalization and school reform processes. Chapter 10, by Mark Warren, adds a discussion of the benefits of collaborations between public schools and community organizing groups to improve school outcomes and foster neighborhood development. It draws upon data collected on a case study of initiatives in Chicago. Finally, Chapter 11, by Greta Kirschenbaum Brownlow, examines the Los Angeles Unified School District's (LAUSD's) school construction program. Her research looks at the forms of community participation used in the LAUSD school planning process to understand their impact on the production of sustained school–community partnerships in southeast Los Angeles.

Through the chapters in this book we frame two critical insights about inner-city revitalization in the contemporary period. Part I highlights that despite progress made in the field of community development, unchecked activities of anchor institutions continue to exhibit the potential for detrimental effects on inner-city neighborhoods. This is particularly problematic for residents of inner-city communities. In essence, Worthy's (1977) concerns about the threat posed by institutional rape are still salient in the contemporary period. Given this threat, part II of this book highlights strategies to empower grassroots organizations and place them on a more even playing field with anchor institutions in the community development process. In particular, the chapters in the second part of this book focus on the potential for public schools to emerge as neighborhood-based anchor institutions.

Note

1 For example, HUD's fiscal year 2012 notice of funding availability (NOFA) for the Choice Neighborhood implementation grant defined anchor institutions as "place-based entities that have regional significance and are permanently rooted, economic drivers in specific locales – generating jobs, creating local business opportunities, and contributing in significant ways to the development of human, social and cultural capital. They include universities, hospitals, sports facilities, performing arts and other major cultural facilities (like museums and libraries) public utilities and some very large churches and corporations." The NOFA also included "anchor institution engagement" as a rating factor in the grant review process, worth three points out of a total of 240 points.

References

Alinsky, S.D. (1969). *Reveille for radicals*. New York: Vintage.
Alinsky, S.D. (1971). *Rules for radicals*. New York: Random House.
Anderson, M. (1964). *The federal bulldozer: A critical analysis of urban renewal, 1949–1962*. Cambridge: MIT Press.
Blauner R. (1969). Internal colonialism and ghetto revolt. *Social Problems*, 16(4): 393–408.
Blauner, R. (1972). *Racial oppression in America*. New York: Harper and Row.
Davidoff, P. (1965). Advocacy and pluralism in planning. *Journal of the American Institute of Planners*, 31(4): 331–338.
Dobbie, D. (2009). Evolving strategies of labor-community-coalition building. *Journal of Community Practice*, 17: 107–119.
Etienne, H.F. (2012). *Pushing back the gates: Neighborhood-driven perspectives on university-driven revitalization in West Philadelphia*. Philadelphia: Temple University Press.
Fabricant, M. and Fine, M. (2012). *Charter schools and the corporate makeover of public education: What's at stake?* New York: Teachers College Press.
Florida, R. (2004). *The rise of the creative class: And how it's transforming work, leisure, community, and everyday life*. New York: Basic Books.
Harris, W.M. (2012). *African American community development (with twelve case studies): A plan for self-determination*. Lewiston: Edwin Mellon Press.
Krumholz, N. and Forester, J. (1990). *Making equity planning work: Leadership in the public sector*. Philadelphia: Temple University Press.
Lipman, P. (2009). The cultural politics of mixed-income schools and housing: A racialized discourse of displacement, exclusion, and control. *Anthropology and Education Quarterly*, 40(3): 215–236.
Lipman, P. (2011). *The new political economy of urban education: Neoliberalism, race, and the right to the city*. New York: Routledge.
Lowe, N. and Morton, B.J. (2008). Developing standards: The role of community benefits agreements in enhancing job quality, *Community Development*, 39(2): 23–35.

Maurrasse, D.J. (2001). *Beyond the campus: How colleges and universities form partnerships with their communities*. New York: Routledge.

Needleman, M.L. and Needleman, C.E. (1974). *Guerrillas in the bureaucracy: The community planning experiment in the United States*. New York: John Wiley & Sons.

Perry, D.C. and Wiewel, W. (2005). *The university as urban developer: Case studies and analysis*. New York: M.E. Sharpe.

Purcell, M. (2008). *Recapturing democracy: Neoliberalization and the struggle for alternative urban futures*. New York: Taylor and Francis.

Rae, D.W. (2006). Making life work in crowded places. *Urban Affairs Review* 41(3): 271–291.

Rodin, J. (2007). *The university and urban revival: Out of the ivory tower and into the streets*. Philadelphia: University of Pennsylvania Press.

Silverman, R.M. (2013). Making waves or treading water?: An analysis of charter schools in New York State. *Urban Education*, 48(2): 257–288.

Silverman, R.M. and Patterson, K.L. (2012). Guest editors' introduction: Themed issue on inner- city empowerment and revitalization. *Community Development*, 43(4): 411–415.

Silverman, R.M., Yin, L. and Patterson, K.L. (2013). Dawn of the dead city: An exploratory analysis of vacant addresses in Buffalo, NY 2008–2010. *Journal of Urban Affairs*, 35(2): 131–152.

Wiewel, W. and Perry, D.C. (2008). *Global universities and urban development: Case studies and Analysis*, New York: Routledge.

Worthy, W. (1977). *The rape of our neighborhoods: And how communities are resisting takeovers by colleges, hospitals, churches, businesses, and public agencies*. New York: William Morrow.

Zimmerman, J. (2008). From brew town to cool town: Neoliberalism and the creative city development strategy in Milwaukee. *Cities*, 25: 230–242.

2

ANCHORING COMMUNITY DEVELOPMENT TO SCHOOLS AND NEIGHBORHOODS

A Renewed Tradition of Putting People First

Robert Mark Silverman, University at Buffalo

The New Age of Anchor Institutions

There is a growing consensus among community development practitioners and scholars that anchor institutions are a critical component of inner-city revitalization strategies. A variety of organizations are identified as anchor institutions, including universities, hospitals, museums, and an assortment of other cultural and religious institutions. Despite their diversity, anchors share a common connection to the neighborhoods where they are located. They have substantial investments in their campuses and physical plants, and lack the geographic mobility typically associated with organizations in the private sector. In contrast to foot-loose organizations that operate under the logic of private capitalism, anchor institutions are place-based and have missions linked to the communities where they are located. They are also relatively autonomous organizations, since many anchors are nonprofits. Their nonprofit status allows anchor institutions to benefit from tax exemptions and other regulatory constraints related to land-use policies. Nonprofit status also provides anchor institutions with insulation from local politics and relative degrees of autonomy to pursue their missions.

Anchor institutions fill a number of functional roles in urban communities. They account for a substantial proportion of the job base in inner-cities, and they are employers of noticeable numbers of skilled professionals. In addition to employing skilled professionals, anchor institutions augment human capital through educational and research activities that take place within their walls. Along with the development of human capital, anchor institutions are important locations for the cultivation and development of cultural capital. This is particularly relevant to the work done by museums and other civic institutions. In addition to human and cultural resources, anchor institutions have the ability to leverage fiscal resources in inner-cities and add capacity to urban revitalization efforts. They have become important contributors to inner-city revitalization in the contemporary period, as public sector resources have contracted and the use of these resources increasingly requires collaboration across the public, private and nonprofit sectors.

Anchor institutions bring many benefits to inner-cities; however, they also have the potential to aggravate existing inequalities in the urban landscape. In an early analysis of the impact of anchor institutions on inner-city neighborhoods, Worthy (1977) described how the expansion of colleges, hospitals and other anchors resulted in the disruption of communities. He labeled conflicts associated with institutionally driven neighborhood revitalization efforts *institutional rape*, because of the victimization that these activities entailed for inner-city residents. To a large extent, the critical framework that was applied to anchor institutions in the past has become less pronounced in the contemporary period. Today, a great deal of the academic and professional dialogue about anchor-based development focuses on the potential for anchor institutions to transform neighborhoods. The more extreme expressions of this perspective lack a critique and simply couch boosterism in reports and studies of anchor institutions. This literature is tempered by emergent empirical scholarship measuring the effects of anchor institutions on urban revitalization processes. Despite the growing volume of scholarship, broader questions of social redistribution and equity in inner-city revitalization are largely absent from the current literature on anchor institutions.

Anchors Aweigh

The current movement advocating for the use of anchor institutions to leverage inner-city revitalization emerged from university-based policy centers and nonprofit research institutes. One of the more visible centers is the Penn Institute for Urban Research (Penn IUR) at the University of Pennsylvania which sponsors studies of anchor institutions and serves as lead organization for the national Anchor Institution Taskforce (http://www.margainc.com/initiatives/aitf/). The Penn IUR has published white papers and other reports advocating for anchor institutions to take a lead role in inner-city revitalization efforts (Birch, 2010; Penn IUR, 2009). At a more pragmatic level, the University of Pennsylvania has developed how-to manuals for anchor institutions in order to facilitate expanded activities related to inner-city revitalization (Netter Center for Community Partnership, 2008). Similar reports that include guidelines for anchor institutions to follow when pursuing community development activities have been produced at the University of Chicago (Webber & Karlström, 2009). In addition to university-based advocacy, nonprofit research institutes like the Urban Land Institute and the Initiative for a Competitive Inner City

(ICIC) have become proponents of increased anchor institution activity in urban revitalization (ICIC, 2011; Murphy, 2011). In a recent ICIC publication, anchors were identified as critical to urban economic development (ICIC, 2011). It was argued that partnerships between anchor institutions, the public sector, and businesses in the private sector could be forged to leverage inner-city development. In part, the argument forwarded by the ICIC is that the presence of anchor institutions adds to other factors identified by Michael Porter that create a competitive advantage for inner-cities in relation to economic development (Porter, 1995; ICIC, 2011).

Anchors and New Urban Regimes

Discussions of anchor institutions have appeared with increased frequency in academic literature. Much of this literature focuses on the transformation of institutions and the built environment in the modern city. Perry, Wiewel, and Menendez (2009) describe the emerging role of universities as anchor institutions in the urban development process. Universities are described as intermediary organizations that bring leadership, resources, and expertise to neighborhood revitalization initiatives. Birch (2009) offers one of the clearest articulations of the central role of anchor institutions in the transformation of inner-city communities. She argues that the revitalization of downtowns in older American cities has been driven by anchor institutions. This process has created a new paradigm for downtown revitalization. According to Birch (2009: 149):

> The new paradigm for downtown (dense, walkable, mixed use with a heavy component of housing) is quite established in many of the nation's cities. While this downtown still has considerable commercial activity, its employment base is more diverse, with jobs in anchor institutions (universities; hospitals; and entertainment including arts, culture, and sports) rising as a proportion of the total. The residential component has become significant and is shaping the demand for neighborhood-serving retail, schools, and open space.

This stream of research places anchor institutions at the center of the contemporary urban revitalization process. The current process is distinct from the past. It entails an emergent downtown comprised of anchor-based employment centers, gentrifying residential neighborhoods, linked entertainment and recreational amenities, and supportive infrastructure.

While Birch's (2009) paradigm for anchor institutions is set in a framework based on American cities, Gaffikin and Perry (2012) apply the concept of anchor-based revitalization to the global context. They argue that the emergence of anchor institutions as core actors in urban revitalization is a global phenomenon.

According to Gaffikin and Perry, anchors are uniquely positioned to lead inner-city revitalization efforts due to their substantial investments in urban real estate and their vested interest in promoting redevelopment. A unifying theme across these works is the portrayal of anchors as relatively benevolent institutions. For instance, Gaffikin and Perry (2012: 18) portray anchor institutions as "civic ambassadors" with an "interdisciplinary capacity that permits a multidimensional civic participation". Analyses of the impact of hospitals and universities on urban economic development have also focused on the employment and wage benefits that these anchor institutions bring to metropolitan areas (Harkavy & Zuckerman,1999; Bartik & Erickcek, 2008). Absent from many of these studies is a critical assessment of the impact of anchor institutions on the distribution of costs and benefits resulting from contemporary urban revitalization processes. This is particularly noticeable where costs and benefits to inner-city residents are concerned. Many applied studies and reports dealing with anchor institutions assume that the benefits from anchor-based development trickle down to inner-city residents. In essence, it is argued that the rising tide generated by anchor-based revitalization will lift all boats in the inner-city.

Eds and Meds to the Rescue?

Recent scholarship has begun to address this deficiency. Some empirical researchers have attempted to measure the impact of anchor institutions on inner-city revitalization and identify community-wide effects. Daniel and Schons (2010) attempted to measure the impact that Yale University's community investments had on economic and social conditions in New Haven, CT. They concluded that in the absence of three decades of university-led initiatives, Yale and New Haven would have been worse off. However, their analysis fell short of developing measures to calculate the exact impact of these investments on the community. Nelson (2009) examined the impact of growth in the healthcare sector and measured the degree to which urban hospitals constituted an export industry for struggling urban centers. She found that teaching hospitals and specialized care facilities accrued economic benefits to cities. However, growth in export-oriented medical services placed the availability of emergency services to local populations that were underinsured or indigent at risk. In addition to concerns about the inequitable distribution of benefits from anchor-led urban revitalization, there is evidence that disparities exist in local access to jobs and services provided by anchor institutions.

The Social Safety Net and Anchor-Based Urban Development

Adams (2003) offered another perspective on the relationship between anchor institutions and the social equity goals of public policy. Her research focuses on the nature and scope of partnership between local anchor institutions and the public sector. She concludes that despite the benefits investments by anchor institutions offered to cities, public officials entered into fewer direct partnerships focusing on urban revitalization with them during the 1990s. Instead, the public sector has focused on indirectly subsidizing anchor institutions. These indirect subsidies have come in the form of public subsidies for constituent groups that patronize anchor institutions. For instance, expanded public policy related to health insurance and student loans have focused on stabilizing revenue streams that anchor institutions depend upon. Although anchor institutions appear to be leading local economic development initiatives, these efforts are heavily dependent on the provision of public subsidies to groups that constitute their customer bases.

Hobor (2012) reached a similar conclusion in his analysis of economic revitalization in urban rust belt cities. He argued that many rust belt cities in the US have become healthcare-based economies. However, he points out that the transformation to a healthcare-based economy has been facilitated by concentrations of retired manufacturing workers with generous pension plans and other forms of insurance that make up the social safety net. This is an important insight, since it links anchor institutions to the broader social welfare system and creates space for expanding the dialogue about linking social equity goals to anchor-based development.

Enhanced Grassroots Engagement and Public Accountability

Other scholars have examined forms of inequality that have emerged with the ascent of anchor institutions in the contemporary city from a theoretical perspective. Marcuse's (2009) discussion of the *right to the city* tapped into the growing tension between divergent groups that share urban space. In essence, the concept of the right to the city highlights how the poor, minorities, and other disenfranchised groups have been left out of urban revitalization processes. As a result, new development has displaced and alienated these groups. Marcuse and others advocate for these groups to reclaim their right to inhabit the city and engage in processes that affect its development. The concept of the right to the city is grounded in a similar rationale to other arguments that link social equity goals to anchor-based development strategies. Anchor institutions are heavily subsidized by the public. In part, their embeddedness in the social welfare system entails an obligation to address the needs of the indigent. Moreover, many anchor institutions are nonprofit organizations and benefit from tax exempt status. This status compels them to be accountable and responsive to constituencies in the communities they serve.

New Urban Regimes and Inner-City Revitalization

The issues of accountability, responsiveness, and the need for broader engagement in urban revitalization processes are also discussed by scholars who critique the effects of new urban regimes on inner-city revitalization. Rae (2006) argued that deindustrialization led to the decline of older cities in the US and abroad. An outcome of this change was that new urban regimes emerged to replace older growth regimes composed of private industry, commercial interests, and public service unions. Rae's new urban regimes were comprised of nonprofit anchor institutions and their partners in the public and private sectors. This represented a shift away from urban policies that dispersed development across the urban landscape to policies focused on channeling investment into dense nodes surrounding anchor institutions. Silverman, Yin, and Patterson (2013) examined the implications of new urban regimes on patterns of neighborhood revitalization and abandonment. They argued that the emergence of anchor institutions as central actors in urban revitalization processes has contributed to inequality across the urban landscape. Consequently, they suggest that there is a need for enhancing the degree to which disenfranchised groups are incorporated into decision-making processes that determine inner-city revitalization policies. It is argued that this would curb some of the detrimental effects of redevelopment, such as gentrification and the displacement of the poor, and promote the redistribution of resources and power.

The Elevated Role of Anchors in Education and Community Development Policy

In the same settings where anchor institutions are actively transforming the urban landscape, new federal initiatives have been introduced to reform education and community development policies. Two of these initiatives have been pivotal in elevating the role of anchor institutions. The first of these initiatives is the Promise Neighborhoods demonstration program (PN) administered through the United States Department of Education (DOE). This program was introduced in 2010. It awarded over $40 million in grants during the first two years of its existence, was authorized to award an additional $60 million in 2012, and requested an additional $100 million for grants in 2013. PN was modeled after the Harlem Children's Zone (HCZ), a nonprofit run by Geoffrey Canada that offers comprehensive educational and social service programs to inner-city students. The HCZ model is based on leveraging philanthropic dollars and partnering with anchor institutions and other nonprofit social service providers to support charter schools. Based on the HCZ model, PN was designed to use federal funds to leverage comprehensive neighborhood-based educational and social service programing for disadvantaged youth. Grants funded under the PN program are designed to bring local foundations, and other nonprofit, private, and public sector partners together to implement comprehensive place-based education and community development reforms in inner-city neighborhoods adjacent to anchor institutions.

In addition to PN, the Obama Administration introduced the Choice Neighborhoods demonstration program (CN) in 2010. This program is administered through the US Department of Housing and Urban Development (HUD). CN awarded over $300 million in grants during the first three years of its existence, and requested an additional $150 million for the 2013 funding cycle. It is designed to link revitalization of public housing (particularly mixed-income development following the HOPE VI model) with comprehensive social services and educational programing. Like the PN program, grants funded under the CN program are designed to bring local foundations, and other nonprofit, private, and public sector partners together to implement housing and community revitalization programs in inner-city neighborhoods adjacent to anchor institutions. CN grants focus on linking housing revitalization to public education, social services, and workforce development programs. In a recent essay, HUD's assistant secretary for policy development and research described the CN approach as "one that emphasizes creating essential building blocks of healthy and strong communities – housing, offices and retail, schools, parks, and anchor institutions like universities and hospitals – to fuel revitalization with a focus on expanding access to opportunities and ending concentrated poverty" (Bostic & Tate, 2011).

Together, PN and CN make up a core component of the Obama Administration's inner-city revitalization policy. In many respects, the focus of this policy conforms to past efforts to revitalize urban neighborhoods which encompassed reducing public housing density, developing mixed-income neighborhoods, and poverty de-concentration. However, this policy goes a step further by strengthening the link between schools and neighborhoods. It also places greater emphasis on delivering comprehensive social services to poor communities through increased collaboration between the public, private, and nonprofit sectors. Both PN and CN pay specific attention to the role of anchor institutions in the neighborhood revitalization process.

It is noteworthy that the overarching emphasis of current policy has been on shifting the implementation of educational and housing programs from the public sector to the private and nonprofit sectors. For instance, PN's efforts to replicate the HCZ model have placed anchor institutions, philanthropic organizations, and other nonprofits at the center of the dialogue about education reform and neighborhood revitalization. Likewise, CN represents a continuation of HUD's use of mixed financing for public housing. This model allows HUD to mix public, private, and nonprofit funds to build and manage affordable housing developments. CN also identified partnerships with anchor institutions as central to the transformation of inner-city communities.

This emphasis is in stark contrast to earlier urban revitalization programs rooted in calls by scholars and practitioners to empower inner-city residents and enhance their control of public institutions (Blauner, 1972; Needleman & Needleman, 1974; Worthy, 1977; Kotler, 2005). These programs emerged in response to residential displacement caused by urban renewal and the expansion of anchor institutions in inner-city neighborhoods. Ironically, some of the same anchor institutions that contributed to the demise of inner-city communities half a century ago are now identified in federal policy as critical partners for neighborhood revitalization. To some extent, contemporary public policy has been informed by historical experiences with forms of institutional rape identified by Worthy (1977). For instance, PN and CN programs require substantial community engagement in the planning and implementation of educational and housing programs. However, the centrality of anchor institutions in the neighborhood transformation process is a cause for concern. The true test of anchor-based development strategies and programs like PN and CN will be the degree to which inner-city residents are empowered and gain access to the decision-making processes of anchor institutions and other urban social institutions.

Schools as Neighborhood-Based Anchors

Inner-city schools are emerging as critical institutions for community empowerment. In part, this is a byproduct of programs like PN and CN which focus on schools as stabilizing institutions and centers for community life in urban neighborhoods. Inner-city schools are also important due to their juxtaposition to larger anchor institutions engaged in neighborhood revitalization efforts and debates over public policy. Inner-city schools are often the focus of anchor-led initiatives while simultaneously serving as the most accessible neighborhood-based urban social institutions to residents who have been historically disenfranchised in society. In addition, schools have comprised a tangible link between inner-city neighborhoods and societal resources and opportunity structures. These characteristics make schools critical neighborhood-based anchors with the potential to offset the hegemonic influence of larger anchor institutions in inner-cities. These characteristics also give schools the potential to serve as centers for grassroots organizing and leadership development in inner-city neighborhoods.

In order to reach this potential, the scope of resident engagement and control within schools must expand. A promising approach to achieving this goal is found in the *education organizing movement*. This movement links urban education and community development by organizing residents through public schools. The education organizing framework enhances the level of community engagement in schools around issues of curriculum, student outcomes, school policies, and the coordination of social and community services through school buildings located in neighborhoods. Education organizing focuses on empowering inner-city residents, and it has the dual goal of enhancing public accountability in relation to both public schools and linked neighborhood development policies. This goal expands the scope of participation in school decision-making processes. School constituencies are conceived broadly, to include teachers, students and parents, as well as community residents and neighborhood-based organizations.

Scholars have identified several benefits to inner-city neighborhoods emanating from education organizing (Fruchter, 2007; Glickman & Scally, 2008; Warren & Mapp, 2011). Neighborhoods with active education organizing movements have generated sustained partnerships between school officials and neighborhood organizations that focus on enhancing internal school policies and neighborhood revitalization efforts. Education organizing has helped to build social capital in poor communities as a result of regular and purposive interactions across a spectrum of neighborhood residents. Experience participating in initiatives and projects that grow out of education organizing has cultivated leadership skills at the grassroots level. Partnerships, social capital, and new leadership at the neighborhood level have translated into the attraction of new resources for local community development and increased leverage in the neighborhood revitalization process.

Enhancing the voice of inner-city residents is a critical component of empowering grassroots groups to participate in the urban revitalization process. Education organizing is a particularly effective vehicle to achieve this goal, since inner-city schools have already caught the attention of private, nonprofit, and public sector actors engaged in community development work. Expanding the focus on education organizing would strengthen federal programs like PN and CN. These programs already identify a role for anchor institutions in school reform and neighborhood revitalization. Linking education organizing to the work of anchor institutions in inner-city neighborhoods would further efforts to institutionalize the role of grassroots decision-making in anchor-based development.

An expansion of education organizing would also change national, state and local school reform debates involving philanthropic organizations like the Bill & Melinda Gates Foundation, the Eli and Edythe Broad Foundation, and the Walton Family Foundation. These debates have shaped federal and state education policies. However, they have been relatively dominated by large institutions and a network of philanthropic organizations. The scope of direct grassroots input from inner-city residents who are served by urban schools has been comparatively absent from the debate concerning education reform. One strategy that could be applied to address this imbalance would be the adoption of mandates for community control and grassroots participation in schools receiving federal and state aid.

For instance, the federal Race to the Top grant program (RTTT) has served as a mechanism to institute reforms in underperforming inner-city schools. However, reforms adopted under RTTT are weighted toward evaluating teacher and school performance, rather than empowering teachers, students and parents in the decision-making processes of schools. Reforms under RTTT stress the adoption of teacher and student performance standards advocated for by the philanthropic community as well as mechanisms to facilitate the reorganization of traditional public schools into charter schools (Fabricant & Fine, 2012; Silverman, 2012). Less pronounced in RTTT are strategies designed to empower communities and neighborhoods and enhance the scope of grassroots governance in local schools. Programs like RTTT should be modified, adding more resources to support education organizing efforts in inner-city neighborhoods. Complementary changes to PN, CN, and other federal programs could serve as a foundation for the provision of technical assistance to inner-city residents and grassroots leadership development. The immediate goal of such policy changes would be to enhance resident engagement in school reform. The broader goal of these policy changes would be to develop a foundation for expanding the scope of community engagement in anchor-based neighborhood revitalization initiatives.

From Institutional Rape to Grassroots Control

There has been growing pressure for school reform from anchor institutions, national education reformers, philanthropic organizations, and state and federal education agencies. In many instances, inner-city school reforms have become integrated into broader neighborhood revitalization policies led by anchor institutions. The PN and CN programs are examples of neighborhood revitalization policies linked to public school reforms. In both cases, federal policy views local anchor institutions as integral to the neighborhood revitalization process. Other federal education reforms, like RTTT, have been shaped by advocacy groups in the private and nonprofit sectors with views about urban revitalization that are compatible with anchor-based strategies. The scope of reforms related to urban school and inner-city neighborhood revitalization policies have been shaped by a worldview that favors nonprofit leadership over public sector initiatives, school choice over traditional public education, and gentrification over the preservation of affordable housing.

At the neighborhood level, the transformation of public schools and affordable housing often occurs against the backdrop of anchor institutions pursuing projects to expand their campuses and physical plants. Inner-city residents are often left out of critical decision-making processes that affect the future of their homes, schools, and neighborhoods. As a result, schemes for education reform and community development are imposed on inner-city neighborhoods while their social fabric is permanently disrupted. Anchor-based revitalization projects are sold to inner-city residents as remedies for neighborhood decline, and residents are often encouraged to endure hardship or offered incentives to relocate to other communities in order to make way for progress. Residents who voice concerns about proposed anchor-based development strategies and resist them are sometimes characterized as obstructionists and impediments to change. In the absence of this type of backlash, resident input is often diluted in citizen participation processes designed to placate dissenters or their input is subsumed in consensus-based planning processes that are heavily influenced by stakeholders from anchor institutions and public agencies.

Too often the present-day environment surrounding agenda setting, policy development, and anchor-based neighborhood revitalization parallels the conditions that fostered institutional rape over three and a half decades ago (Worthy, 1977). Some would argue that anchor institutions should have greater control over the neighborhood revitalization process, since they have a substantial vested interest in the success or failure of neighborhood development initiatives. From this perspective, it is argued that anchor institutions have sizable capital investments in inner-city neighborhoods and their investments are at risk due to deteriorating conditions in the built environment surrounding their campuses and fiscal plants. However, this perspective ignores the underlying economic conditions that sustain large anchor institutions. These institutions are heavily subsidized by public expenditures and other government resources that form the social safety net in inner-city neighborhoods. For instance, one of the primary sources of revenue for colleges and universities is tuition, with the bulk of that revenue generated by federal student loans and other forms of public funding for education. Similarly, a substantial portion of the health care industry is financed with public dollars through Medicare and Medicaid, as well as public and private insurance programs. Anchor institutions in the arts and cultural sector also rely on subsidies from federal, state and local government. One of the largest public subsidies that educational, healthcare, cultural and other anchor institutions enjoy comes in the form of their nonprofit, tax-exempt status with the Internal Revenue Service (IRS).

There are solid arguments for increasing the scope of community control in anchor institutions, given the extent to which anchors thrive as a result of public subsidies. These arguments become even stronger when the scope of public investment in schools and affordable housing in inner-city neighborhoods surrounding anchor institutions is factored into the equation. One reason philanthropic groups and anchor institutions have become engaged in school reform and neighborhood revitalization is because growing public resources have been committed to programs in these areas. The PN and CN programs are prime examples of the mutually reinforcing relationship between anchor institutions' engagement in inner-city neighborhoods and public subsidies for education and housing. Anchor institutions have seized the moment and attempted to leverage these public resources to expand their influence in inner-city neighborhoods. In response to increased engagement by anchor institutions and the coupling of public and philanthropic agendas, there have been growing calls for public accountability and community empowerment.

This shift is visible with respect to urban education. The pace of contemporary education reform has overwhelmed some inner-city communities, and there has been a backlash from teachers, parents, and grassroots interests affected by it. This is reflected in the growth of education organizing as a tool for residents to regain control of the decision-making process in local schools. Increasingly, anchor institutions have been called upon to give grassroots interests a seat at the table when school reform and neighborhood revitalization are discussed. Anchor institutions and other nonprofits have also been encouraged to provide technical assistance and capacity building to grassroots groups engaged in education organizing (Shatkin & Gershberg, 2007). Quintessentially, growing calls for grassroots empowerment in the neighborhood revitalization process is a response to the institutional rape of inner-city neighborhoods.

Historically and contemporaneously, inner-city revitalization has been driven by large public, private, and nonprofit institutions. Today, this process is increasingly influenced by anchor institutions that form the core of new urban regimes. Many older core cities have adopted economic development strategies based on hospital and university expansion, under the banner of *Eds & Meds*. The scope of anchor institution engagement in inner-city neighborhoods has expanded with the advent of new federal policies focusing on school reform and neighborhood revitalization. To date, this engagement has been dominated by larger institutions and philanthropic organizations that advocate for policy reforms at the national level. However, calls for grassroots empowerment are increasing. This is reflected in the education organizing movement, as well as in pockets of resistance to neighborhood disruption caused by anchor institution expansion in inner-city neighborhoods. A new inner-city social compact is emerging which is built upon the obligation of anchor institutions to provide society with dividends for the public investment in their success and growth. The initial step in the process of redistributing these benefits in society is to enfranchise inner-city residents into the governance structure of the anchor institutions that occupy their communities.

References

Adams, C. (2003). The meds and eds in urban economic development. *Journal of Urban Affairs*, 25(5): 571–588.

Bartik, T.J. and Erickcek, G. (2008). *The local economic impact of "eds & meds": How policies to expand universities and hospitals affect metropolitan economies*. Washington, DC: The Brookings Institution.

Birch, E.L. (2009). Downtown in the new American city. *ANNALS of the American Academy of Political and Social Science*, 624: 134–153.

Birch, E. (2010). *Anchor institutions and their role in metropolitan change: White paper on PennIUR initiatives on anchor institutions*. Philadelphia: Penn Institute for Urban Research.

Blauner, R. (1972). *Racial oppression in America*. New York: Harper and Row.

Bostic, R. and Tate, L. (2011). Fighting poverty and creating opportunity: The choice neighborhood initiative. *PD&R Edge*, October 21, 2011. Retrieved October 30, 2012 from http://www.huduser.org/portal/pdr_edge_frm_asst_sec_101911.html .

Daniel, M. and Schons, S. (2010). *Measuring, attributing, and quantifying the return to anchor institutions making responsible community investments: Yale University and New Haven, CT*. New Haven: Yale School of Management.

Fabricant, M. and Fine, M. (2012). *Charter schools and the corporate makeover of public education: What's at stake*. New York: Teacher's College Press.

Fruchter, N. (2007). Education organizing and school reform. *Social Policy*, Spring/Summer: 38–40.

Gaffikin, F. and Perry, D.C. (2012). The Contemporary Urban Condition: Understanding the Globalizing City as Informal, Contested, and Anchored. *Urban Affairs Review*, 48(5): 701–730.

Glickman, N.J. and Scally, C.P. (2008). Can community and education organizing improve inner-city schools? *Journal of Urban Affairs*, 30(5): 557–577.

Harkavy, I. and Zuckerman, H. (1999). *Eds and meds: Cities' hidden assets*. Washington, DC: The Brookings Institution.

Hobor, G. (2012). Surviving the era of deindustrialization: The new economic geography of the urban rust belt. *Journal of Urban Affairs*, Online First: 1–18.

ICIC. (2011). Anchor institutions and urban economic development: From community benefit to shared value. *Inner City Insights*, 1(2): 1–9.

Kotler, M. (2005). *Neighborhood government: The local foundations of political life*. Lanham: Lexington Books.

Marcuse, P. (2009). From critical urban theory to the right to the city. *City*, 13(2/3): 185–197.

Murphy, T. (2011). Building on innovation: The significance of anchor institutions in a new era of city building. Washington, DC: Urban Land Institute.

Needleman, M.L. and Needleman, C.E. (1974). *Guerrillas in the bureaucracy: The community planning experiment in the United States*. New York: John Wiley & Sons.

Nelson, M. (2009). Are hospitals an export industry?: Empirical evidence from five lagging regions. *Economic Development Quarterly*, 23(2): 242–253.

Netter Center for Community Partnership. (2008). *Anchor institutions toolkit: A guide to neighborhood revitalization*. Philadelphia: Netter Center for Community Partnership.

Penn IUR. (2009). *Retooling HUD for a catalytic federal government: A report to secretary Shaun Donovan*. Philadelphia: Penn Institute for Urban Research.

Perry, D.C., Wiewel, W. and Menendez, C. (2009). The university's role in urban development: From enclave to anchor institution. *Land Lines*, July: 2–7.

Porter, M.E. (1995). The competitive advantage if the inner city. *Harvard Business Review*, May/June: 55–71.

Rae, D.W. (2006). Making life work in crowded places. *Urban Affairs Review* 41(3): 271–291.

Shatkin, G. and Gershberg, A.I. (2007). Empowering parents and building communities: The role of school-based councils in educational governance and accountability. *Urban Education*, 42(6): 582–615.

Silverman, R.M. (2012). The nonprofitization of public education: Implications of requiring charter schools to be nonprofits in New York. *Nonprofit Policy Forum*, 3(1), 1–22.

Silverman, R.M., Yin, L. and Patterson, K.L. (2013). Dawn of the dead city: An exploratory analysis of vacant addresses in Buffalo, NY 2008–2010. *Journal of Urban Affairs*, 35(2): 131–152.

Warren, M.R. and Mapp, K.L. (2011). *A match on dry grass: Community organizing as a catalyst for school reform*. Cambridge: Oxford University Press.

Webber, H.S. and Karlström, M. (2009). *Why community investment is good for anchor institutions: Understanding costs, benefits, and the range of strategic options*. Chicago: Chapin Hall at the University of Chicago.

Worthy, W. (1977). *The rape of our neighborhoods: And how communities are resisting takeovers by colleges, hospitals, churches, businesses, and public agencies*. New York: William Morrow.

3

SHRINKING CITIES, GROWING ADVERSARIES

The Politics of Territory for Community Nonprofits in 'Shrinking City' Planning Processes

Janice Bockmeyer, City University of New York

Introduction

It is hardly breaking news that much of the nonprofit sector in the United States is politically engaged. Community nonprofit organizations (CNPOs) – the focus of this chapter – have long been agents of neighborhood revitalization and advocates for neighborhood residents' needs. Decades of neoliberalism, privatization and marketization of urban service delivery transformed many into essential district-level service providers. As a result, CNPOs now have stakes in city elections, budgetary and other policies and the devices through which policies are forged, whether they are governmental, quasi-public or private mechanisms. The evolving governance structures for decision making, however, present a participatory challenge for urban community residents who must retool strategies as institutions change. Urban scholars widely recognize local political decision making as fractured beyond legislatures, executives and constitutionally or statute-bound formal governmental structures to more diffuse and opaque governance networks (Davies, 2012; John, 2001; Lowndes, 2001; Stone, 1989). 'New institutionalism,' the approach applied throughout the discussion below, acknowledges that urban decision making resides in both the public and private realms, with public-private partnerships and governance networks added to the discourse surrounding urban politics. Even as special purpose public authorities, contractors, for-profit 'partners' and others are addressed by scholars as part of the urban politics equation (Judd & Smith, 2007; Lowndes, 2001), divergence remains over whether more diffuse governance broadens the scope of political participation or coopts, constrains and controls weaker players (Davies, 2011; Denters & Klok, 2010; Denters & Rose, 2005;

Erie, Kogan & MacKenzie, 2010). This chapter addresses the impact of new institutional arrangements on the political roles of CNPOs, which continue to be underestimated and understudied.

Specifically, the chapter will highlight the changing relationship between CNPOs and urban political institutions with applications for deindustrialized urban areas and the so-called 'shrinking-cities' planning processes currently underway in many. The argument, stated simply, is that new institutions crafted in most shrinking cities processes threaten to diminish the political roles of CNPOs. Rapid shrinkage of population and local markets is inspiring new urban planning to include political reconfiguration and spatial recalibration of city infrastructure and services. In some cases, such plans also threaten the territorial basis of community nonprofits servicing distinct areas. Planning task forces, advisory councils or other mechanisms activated to 'right-size' cities suggest alterations in political institutions that establish 'rules-of-game,' including those served by CNPOs as they see their 'turf' threatened with service reductions, shrinkage or even abandonment. The discussion below first outlines the role of political institutions in setting the parameters for urban politics. It then examines the evolving relationship between CNPOs and institutions and analyzes the fragmented nature of the nonprofit sector in urban decision making. Similar to the fractured field of governmental and business sectors, the nonprofit sector contains diverse interests competing for scarce resources, struggling to maintain and expand territorial claims, and strategizing to preserve and extend influence. The chapter explores impacts that political institutions, such as at-large city council elections, mayors and city managers, and institutionalized actors, including foundations, funding intermediaries and anchor institutions, may have on the political behaviors of CNPOs. These behaviors are analyzed as CNPOs strategize within changing institutional conditions to produce desired benefits for their organizational and financial stability, serve their missions and communities. Finally, the chapter assesses what we know thus far about the changing institutions used in 'shrinking cities' processes, the role CNPOs are playing and the effects new planning processes have on their political behaviors.

New Institutionalism, Cities and Changing Rules-of-Game

As Lowndes (2009) observed, "institutional change is never a purely technical matter" (p. 95). So-called 'old institutionalism' scholars viewed institutions as political rules-of-game set exclusively by formal devices such as constitutions, statutes, administrative regulations and policies of public sector actors. 'New institutionalism' expanded the framework to acknowledge additionally "informal norms, roles, relationships and operating practices that are so stable, structured and accepted that they can be said to be 'institutionalized'" (Wolman, 1995, p. 135).[1] For present purposes, urban political institutions are simply the rules-of-game for collective endeavors within the local state. Relevant to the American federalist context are also institutions encompassed by the supra-local framework – including national, state, regional, county or other rules-setting dimensions.[2] The meaning of political institutions was significantly expanded as local governments downsized and privatized throughout the 1980s and 1990s. Attention to the institutional framework shifted from 'government,' meant as formal governmental structures, to *governance*, where governmental agencies and actors, rather than merely providing services, took on the role of 'producing' services by providing, contracting and vouchering them (V. Ostrom, Bish & E. Ostrom, 1988). New actors such as nonprofit organizations, foundations and funding intermediaries, became 'co-producers' of public 'products' (Ostrom, 1996) and, as such, entered into a synergistic relationship creating opportunities to impact the rules-of-game. Applying a neo-institutionalism approach, Smith and Grønbjerg (2006) suggest that public and nonprofit sectors become "interdependent and mutually reinforcing" (p. 236) as nonprofits provide expertise and policy input not already absorbed through existing governmental structures, and services that would encounter tough political resistance were they offered through governmental agencies. Public policies, meanwhile, continue to supply incentives for nonprofits to incorporate, support for organizations, and the legal framework for their operation. In some cases this 'complementarity' may open opportunities for NPOs to enter political processes.

The critical elements for understanding changes in political institutions are, first, their lack of neutrality (Lowndes, 2009; Ostrom, 1999) and, second, the difficulty in changing institutions. On the former, extant rules-of-game shaping 'who gets what,' if changed, can shift benefits to new 'winners,' creating "asymmetrical relations of power play" (Hall & Taylor, 1996, p. 940). Similarly, governance mechanisms intended to enable community input, such as neighborhood planning committees, may amplify some community voices while diminishing others (Bockmeyer, 2007). Just as shuffling cargo on and off a ship requires adjustments to maintain buoyancy, altering decision making instruments that give more weight to some political actors may lead to reductions in weight for others, resetting the *political metacenter*. As it will be taken here, the *political metacenter* is the institutionalized center of political buoyancy, the point of dynamism through which mayors, district representatives and party leaders, foundations, community nonprofits, activists and advocates for various sectors compete and cooperate in joint endeavors.[3] Once rules-of-game establish the *metacenter* – what Pierson calls 'equilibrium' – it becomes more difficult for the 'losers' to change them, creating 'path-dependency' (Pierson, 2004).

Two areas of concern to the present chapter where urban reforms have substantive impact on altering rules-of-game are in fundamental changes to formal and informal governance structures, and territorial boundaries. Either may evoke 'critical junctures,' or disturbances in the institutional equilibrium that sets a new trajectory that can be change-resistant (Pierson, 2004, p. 135). Territorial changes can alter political rules-of-game and redistribute benefits. Annexation, the creation of special districts, and other spatial mechanisms have been used to institutionalize development, manufacturing, business and other interests while dodging compromise with other local concerns (Burns, 1994; Trounstine, 2009). Governments too can become actors in the competition over boundary changes. Alterations to core cities' boundaries are likely to impact surrounding suburban interests; subsequently, suburban municipalities will attempt to impact that decision making. Similarly, state and county governments can become vital players. As Sbragia adeptly observed, "so much of what a government does and will be able to do in the future is shaped by other governments rather than by citizens" (Sbragia, 1996, p. 221).

Critically, alterations in rules can also be achieved through reforming governance structures, including changes to selection of decision makers and the scope of decision making given to particular officials or participants. Bridges (1997) demonstrated that, for example, in the case of southwestern US cities, urban reformers historically sought formal governmental structural changes to strengthen native-born residents' dominance at the expense of immigrant populations. Reforms that embraced at-large and nonpartisan elections, city-manager and commission forms of government institutionalized the dominance of a shrinking minority, non-Hispanic business elite from 1900 onward. Urban political institutions enshrined reform preferences for business sector participation by narrowing access to voting and reinforcing the place of reform office-holders in local governmental affairs in a second wave of reform from the 1940s through the 1960s (Bridges, 1997; see also Trounstine, 2009; Weir, 1999). As Trounstine demonstrates, mechanisms can be used effectively by reform, machine and other coalitions to achieve governance with preferred beneficiaries.

Once institutions are created to favor a coalition, the "processes of path dependence" suggest limited opportunities to broaden participation (Trounstine, 2009, p. 78). For example, during the 1960s new community-level advisory councils and similar devices were created to address urban unrest and demands for substantive decision making participation in underrepresented districts. These often temporary devices were viewed by many urban community advocates as instruments for manipulation or cooptation by city officials, rather than means for substantive political participation (Arnstein, 1969). The more recent 1999 Los Angeles experience with advisory Neighborhood Councils demonstrates that while the devices could potentially widen social networks and collective political engagement, where councils were embedded in extant networks of political influence, they were more likely to reinforce old patterns than generate new opportunities for previously underrepresented groups (Musso, Weare, Oztas & Loges, 2006). Musso and her colleagues conclude, "Institutions create patterns of behavior, and institutional change is slow, difficult, incremental, and costly" (p. 93). Mahoney and Thelen (2010) argue convincingly that most institutional reform evolves gradually and may result from multiple processes rather than a single 'critical juncture.' We will next examine key changes in political institutions, primarily those forged at the federal level, for impacts on the nonprofit sector and urban CNPOs.

Political Institutions, the Nonprofit Sector and CNPOs

During the 1970s and after, coinciding changes in the interrelationship between governmental policies, foundation and nonprofit sector practices contributed to the explosion of nonprofit organizations, their marketization and institutionalization in local service delivery (Smith & Grønbjerg, 2006). And as Mahoney and Thelen (2010) observe, institutional changes together with new rules interpretation and enforcement can "open up space for actors to implement existing rules in new ways" (p. 4). Institutional developments impacting community nonprofit organizations (CNPOs) are critical to four areas: organizational mission, size, levels of inter-group competition or cooperation, and types of political activities. The term community nonprofit organization is used here broadly as a tax-exempt community organization whose mission is to serve a geographically discrete area in ways determined by residents and a majority of board members based in the area through residence or other ties. Of institutional impacts perhaps most widely studied is that on the organizational missions of community nonprofits. Early CNPO organizing began as a 'backyard revolution' to activate underserved urban communities in the 1960s; along with movement activists, unions, religious institutions and foundations, they were able to maintain a focus on "citizen advocacy" (Boyte, 1980). Foundations have a long history of working with urban community organizations. Indeed the Ford Foundation is credited with launching the community development corporation model in the early 1960s with its Gray Areas and other programs in order to institutionalize its paradigmatic anti-poverty strategy (O'Connor, 1996; Ferguson, 2007). The effort was supported by the federal War on Poverty initiative, Community Action Program (CAP), with its requirement for "maximum feasible participation" of communities in establishing local Community Action Agencies (CAAs) through CAP. Mandating that neighborhood residents design the programs insured that policy formation remained in community hands (Nemon, 2007). Additionally, as Naples (1998) found, resident participation in CAAs provided leadership skills and developed the framework for becoming full citizens in political processes.

By the mid-1970s, the confluence of community organizing supported by foundation, civil rights and other efforts, with shifting federal policy devolving administrative responsibilities to cities and communities, created a conjuncture that would set CNPOs on a new direction. Institutional reforms created mission shift and an organizational metamorphosis from community advocacy to neighborhood social service delivery that is well documented (Bockmeyer, 2003; DeFilippis, 2004, 2009; Nemon, 2007; Silverman, 2008; Stoecker, 1997). In 1974 federal urban categorical grant programs were folded into the Community Development Block Grant (CDBG), giving state and city executives increased control over program development and funding decisions (Vidal, 2012). Shifting influence to city mayors generated pressure on CNPOs in urban lower income districts to focus concretely on economic revitalization, resulting in the transition of many nonprofits into Community Development Corporations (CDCs). CDCs as defined by Vidal and Keating (2004) are CNPOs with a 501(c)(3) tax exempt status, primarily serving economically distressed districts with a mission of "fostering physical and economic assets in their communities" (p. 127). By 2005, there were more than 5,500 CDCs found nationally (Vidal, 2012, p. 272).

The Role of Formal City Structures

CDCs' behaviors are also shaped by the juncture of formal local governmental structures and incremental federal policy changes. As Mahoney and Thelen (2010) observe, such shifts may be subtle and gradual as "actors are embedded in a multiplicity of institutions, and interactions among them may allow unforeseen changes in the ongoing distribution of resources" (p. 9). This is evidenced by the sometimes delicate, sometimes heavy-handed, political manipulation of CDCs as federal budgets tightened in the 1980s and mayors' grip on CDBG funding increased. Where at-large council structures keep funding negotiations at the city – rather than district – level, the opportunities for strong mayoral impact on CDCs may be greater. Taking Detroit with its at-large city council structure as an example, without council members to represent district CDCs' interests, bargaining for CDBGs played out directly with the mayor. CDCs found it strategically necessary to form a network and bargain collectively, thereby strengthening their position and thwarting the use of CDBG funding as punishment or reward for support of mayoral policies (Bockmeyer, 2000).

In the case of single-member district election structures for city legislatures, CDCs and other community nonprofits scramble to recruit the support of district council members for grant applications. In some cities this enables district-level *quid pro quo* bargaining as district politicians attempt to use organizations to mobilize voters, recruit campaign workers and solidify support within the community. As Marwell (2004) characterizes the impact in her study of New York City, cooperating organizations in some districts became "machine politics" community based organizations (CBOs) in order to undergird their service delivery function with a steady stream of government contracts secured through the political exchange with political party leaders and district representatives. As district CBOs compete for limited public contracts, machine politics CBOs enjoy a superior bargaining position. The potential for contracting out services to feed traditional machine-style politics may, at least partially, explain the findings of Feiock and Jang (2009) that cities with a council-manager form of government are more likely to produce joint public–nonprofit service delivery of elder services than are cities with more "politicized" mayor–council structures where services are more likely to be exclusively contracted out. In each circumstance, changes in federal institutions intersect uniquely with local institutions to produce new strategies by local and community actors to affect resource distribution.

The Role of Foundations and Funding Intermediaries

Mahoney and Thelen (2010) observe that even major institutional shifts can occur gradually. One such shift is the "displacement" of one set of political actors with another (p. 16). The diminished federal role in anti-poverty and community development programs in the urban arena during the early 1980s, together with the retreat of business investment in many increasingly economically distressed communities, contributed to the rise of powerful new actors on deck: the nation's largest nonprofit funding intermediaries, Local Initiatives Support Corporation (LISC) and Enterprise Community Partners (originally Enterprise Foundation). Intermediaries entered the urban community arena uniquely equipped to employ new funding devices in the service of communities with weak economies. Defined, intermediaries are foundations committed to community revitalization and that, most notably, create community development opportunities by bundling public and private resources for targeted community revitalization through nonprofits on the ground. The creation in 1986 of the federal low income tax credit (LITC) catalyzed the intermediaries as new institutional actors (Vidal, 2012), endowing them with substantial influence over CNPO priorities and practices. Although LITCs are difficult to navigate and apply on the ground, intermediaries maneuver through the process for private investors and assist CDCs in assembling various project funding sources; they also enable depository institutions to meet federal 1977 Community Reinvestment Act requirements to invest in low and moderate income communities (Anglin & Montezemolo, 2004; Walker, 2002). The number of funding intermediaries has grown to include those at the city and regional level, known as community development partnerships (CDPs), many of which also work directly with national intermediaries (Anglin & Montezemolo, 2004). By 2011, the two largest national intermediaries, LISC and Enterprise, funneled over $23 billion into revitalization efforts in distressed communities throughout the United States.[4] With diminished public support for community-designed programs, most CDCs focused attention on fundable activities, areas that a combination of sources – foundations, intermediaries and the public sector – would support. Resultingly, by the end of the 1990s CDCs concentrated primarily on housing development and management; they also transitioned to providing social services through intermediary support (Walker, 2002). Rohe, Bratt and Biswas (2003), in their careful study of CDCs that failed, downsized or merged with other CDCs, discovered that failed CDCs tended to have narrowly focused missions or concentrated efforts on low income populations exclusively. The lesson strongly impressed on CDCs is that fundable organizations diversify their missions, agree to growth and broaden services beyond those for highest need neighborhood residents. As CDCs interact with both governmental and foundation decision makers, in other words, one of the costs of the exchange of support for NPO services is that groups are gradually pushed to market services for 'subsidy bearing clients,' rather than focusing on their commitment to program quality (Smith & Grønbjerg, 2006).

As CNPOs adjusted to new rules-of-game and the shift in funding sources, many strategized by transitioning into CDCs primarily committed to broader housing and social welfare service provision; the struggle to continue community organizing and activism became yet more challenging throughout the 1980s and 1990s (DeFilippis, 2009; Silverman, 2005). In New York City alone by 2000 there were 27,474 nonprofit organizations, of which 9,078 were engaged in providing human service programs or supporting NPOs that did, servicing 2.2 million city residents (NYCnonprofits.org, 2003). Placing emphasis on administering community services, however, casts CNPOs in the role of policy implementation rather than formation (Silverman, 2001, 2003) and focuses nonprofits generally on being "more attentive to the bottom line" of organizational maintenance and survival (Lipsky & Smith, 1989, p. 647).

Across urban communities, inter-group competition and adversarial behavior also accelerated as a result of new institutional mechanisms, including those shifting governmental subsidies from producer to consumer side (Smith & Grønbjerg, 2006). Changes in federal administrative policies, especially those generated in 1983 and in the 1996 welfare reform policies, further enshrined a market-place preference for competing private sector organizations delivering government services (Salamon, 2012). The Bush Administration's Faith-Based and Community Initiatives was created in 2001 to encourage and fund non-profit, faith-based social service providing organizations. It had the effect of increasing the field of competing CDCs as faith-based institutions embraced the reforms to attract government contracts and collaborate on publicly-funded projects. Emphasis moved to market-place mechanisms where citizens became 'consumers' with choices across a spectrum of providers (Grønbjerg & Salamon, 2012; Vidal, 2012). The policy underscored a gradual differentiation of nonprofit interests in the community arena. As Owens (2007) finds, faith-based institutions are not necessarily community-based; their mission is to serve the larger congregation which may extend beyond neighborhood boundaries. Faith-based CDCs largely have spatially targeted missions, but may have board members more closely aligned with the mission of the religious institution than with neighborhood-specific needs.

The diminution of public funding creates resource scarcity and adds incentives for competing CNPOs to diversify funding; strengthening ties to foundations and other sources has become a necessity. While not a 'critical juncture' causing a sudden change, the shift 'on deck' causes gradual "displacement" (Mahoney & Thelen, 2010) as one set of rules – those largely public in origin – is gradually supplanted by those of the independent sector. Foundations and intermediaries, with their greater emphasis on organizational capacity-building, encourage CNPOs to further professionalize, merge with foundering smaller community groups and cut aspects of their missions that threaten enhanced capacity (Bratt & Rohe, 2004, Vidal, 2012). Rohe, Bratt and Biswas (2003) found that larger organizations resulting from mergers are more likely to reap greater organizational capacity and more success in fundraising. Nonprofits are heavily impacted by the "metric mania" of foundations that provide crucial funding but are committed to providing the benchmarks and measures they view as insuring the efficacy of their strategic investment (Bernstein, 2011). As Bratt and Rohe (2004) found, in some cases smaller CDCs have little option but to merge with other organizations to meet new standards when public authorities and foundations together generate pressure for CDCs to grow, despite the consequences for CDCs' self-determined missions.

Foundations have an amplified role in community governance, resulting not only from shrinking public resources, but also as they address the for-profit business investment vacuum in economically distressed communities, leaving CNPOs yet more dependent on their financing. Martin's (2004) portrait of foundation impact in St. Paul, Minnesota found city planning, housing and development officials expecting foundations to force community actions such as consolidating efforts and strengthening organizations. In one example, LISC provided adequate pressure on CNPOs to combine assets and create a new CDC to serve the neighborhood despite outstanding community division. Silverman (2009) similarly found in Buffalo that local officials and foundations formed close cross-sector ties to shape housing policy. The mayor and other officials directly lobbied NeighborWorks America – a national public-private, community development and housing intermediary – to acquire additional NeighborWorks-affiliated community-serving organizations and specify their service territories. In some cases, more aggressive involvement of foundations and intermediaries can aggravate extant tensions between CDCs over 'turf' when funding multi-organization projects that take some groups outside their service areas into the territories of others (Bockmeyer, 2003; Bratt & Rohe, 2004). A critical issue raised by these dynamics is the burgeoning role played by cooperating external actors – foundations, intermediaries and their boards – fundamentally shifting decision making over vital community concerns away from community-based actors.

Anchor Institutions and Community Governance

Anchor institutions take on an institutional governing role when their expanse is substantial enough to the local economy, or service provision is so critical to the survival of the community, that they have a sizable impact on rule-setting in local decisions. The term, 'anchor institution,' is meant here as a cultural, education, medical or other geographically-based, relatively immobile, and largely nonprofit, organization. Major hospitals and universities – so-called 'eds and meds' – often play this role. Important museums, a city philharmonic orchestra or other arts organization, if of substantial enough importance to a community, may also fit the definition. Their interests can be simultaneously local and regional, at times putting them in a discordant relation to CNPOs. On one hand, their significant 'sunk investment' ties their interests to the neighborhood. They may have stronger connections, however, to the regional economy when seeking collaborators for new investment (Gaffikin & Perry, 2012). The nature of their 'sticky capital' also gives them a stronger voice in local planning processes where CNPOs may be junior governance 'partners,' or, in some circumstances, potent adversaries (Gaffikin & Perry, 2012).

Cleveland is one example where informal urban governance over economic revitalization is dominated by anchor institutions including hospitals, local foundations, the city's universities and a community development authority, together with an association of nonprofits. With a combined purchasing power of over $3 billion, the city's three largest anchors have the potential to revitalize a shrinking city (Dubb & Howard, 2012, p. 24). The extent of their influence, however, together with the institutionalization of their role in governance also threatens to diminish residents' role in neighborhood revitalization decision making. The local Cleveland Foundation worked with local public officials, university, medical and cultural anchors and smaller NPOs to design a revitalization strategy for Cleveland's Greater University Circle. Planning covers transportation projects, commercial, residential, education initiatives and an ambitious project to create for-profit worker-owned cooperatives for new job creation. The response by University Hospitals in their five-year growth plan was impressive, including a commitment to build five new facilities and outpatient centers costing $1.2 billion and claiming to adhere to community resident hiring, contracting and local procurement goals (Dubb & Howard, 2012). In addition to the economic development boost for Cleveland, however, by shifting decisions away from public processes and without a formal role for CNPOs, the 'partnership governance' model is unlikely to produce a leadership role for CNPOs. In partnerships institutionalized by use of advisory committees, community representatives with a seat at the decision making table may forward proposals, but lack mechanisms to enforce them. Where 'true partnership' is achieved, including a formal structure and a Memorandum of Understanding for accountability, goals might find success and longer term joint action. The ongoing unequal relationship in organizational resources, commitment to outcomes benefitting communities and sustaining the partnership, however, points to challenges inherent to such arrangements (Fulbright-Anderson, Auspos & Anderson, 2001).

The discussion above highlights the fragmented nature of the nonprofit sector. Endogenous factors, such as organizational capacity and financial durability, place nonprofit anchors, foundations and intermediaries in a vastly stronger decision making position than CNPOs. As is often the case with well-resourced actors, they are better equipped to initiate rules-making and set into play the basis for policies that will establish opportunities or barriers for other actors to enter the 'game' (Pierson, 2004). When CNPOs win a 'seat at the table,' they are unlikely to enjoy equity in deliberations. On the community level, the increasing diversity of CNPOs, including faith-based CNPOs tied to religious institutions with interests extending beyond the community, larger comprehensive CNPOs that may result from mergers, and CNPOs with significant support from intermediaries, may all differ in their missions, concerns, interest and readiness to work jointly. The fragmentation in the field suggests potential for competition, discord and adversarial behavior. We next examine participatory patterns of CNPOs in various institutional arrangements to understand how they may affect shrinking cities decision making.

Institutions and the Political Participation of CNPOs

Given the significant change in the institutional framework within which CNPOs function, the question to be addressed next is how they respond to new institutional arrangements and new governance 'partners.' Scholars are currently focused on the political opportunities opened to nonprofits and constraints posed by changing rules-of-game, to be understood as crafted by a wide spectrum of governance structures through which public, private and nonprofit actors engage (Schmidt, 2006). As Lowndes (2001) writes, the critical concern is with "not just the impact of institutions upon behavior, but the interaction between individuals and institutions" (p. 1953). In the case of CNPOs, their political behaviors result from the unique juncture of endogenous elements – mission and history, organizational capacity, level of community support and other factors – and exogenous influences, including institutional context. Many of the participatory strategies employed by CNPOs can be characterized as residing in two broad categories, either as *insider engagement* or *oppositional activism*. Using very broad strokes, we might describe institutional environments that are most malleable to rules-changing and flexible in offering discretion over extant rules enforcement as most likely to generate *insider engagement*. Those institutional settings most rigid to challenges are generally more likely to evoke strongest oppositional behavior from community organizations, particularly where groups have the most to lose under existing rules.[5]

Insider engagement encompasses those activities which may be viewed as strengthening a CNPO's position to gain or maintain service delivery contracts, or to influence policies in service areas that affect group clientele. Through *insider engagement*, community nonprofits act individually and through networks to impact policies. Chiefly larger institutionalized human services nonprofits have been found to use direct, 'insider' policy advocacy by testifying on policy changes, joining governmental commissions and lobbying policy makers on issues that affect their funding and services to their constituencies (Majic, 2011; Mosley, 2011). Many of the African-American, church-founded CDCs grew to take on activist missions to impact public policies toward the service of their neighborhoods and to engage community residents in that endeavor (Owens, 2007). Rather than institutionalization proscribing political activism, the larger size of the organizations and greater dependence on governmental funding may create more political opportunity through additional contacts with and access to elected and administrative officials. As Mosley (2011) concluded from her large survey of human service nonprofits, they "are not marginalized outsiders, they are active players in the policy-making process" (p. 450). Groups using such an approach might be viewed as "subversives," who are dependent on the system for maintenance and cannot disobey the rules, but seek reforms of rules to forward their mission (Mahoney & Thelen, 2010). Consistent with this model, recent research indicates that public funding predicts advocacy behavior as nonprofits seek to shape those policies prone to impact their activities, even while funding from foundations appears to dampen such activism (Salamon, 2012).[6] The type of strategies CNPOs use, however, is also shaped by their institutionalization as they pursue organizational maintenance and policy reform that is more likely to yield increases in public funding and flexibility, rather than social change (Mosley, 2011).

Oppositional activism, or what Steil and Connolly (2009) frame as *counter-institutional* CNPO behavior,[7] is adversarial behavior most critically intertwined with CNPOs' unique relationship to geographically-bounded place. Such behavior increases in likelihood when groups are 'losers' under current rules-of-game and are "disadvantaged by multiple institutions that reinforce one another" leading to stronger group identity and collective action (Mahoney & Thelen, 2010, pp. 23–4). The surge in numbers of new urban CNPOs in the late 1970s was predominantly in reaction to neighborhood abandonment by private investors and higher income populations during economic downturns.

After decades of commitment to community revitalization, CNPOs became crucial political representatives for underserved areas (Boyte, 1980). Urban communities offer a scale at which disenfranchised or underrepresented residents who have not previously engaged in formal political institutions like party politics and elections may experience the pull of activism to battle urban renewal plans, a neighborhood school closing, policing practices that arouse community anger or environmental dangers that threaten families' health and homes. Community organizing was the focus of attention when community-based organizations heeded the call to resist urban renewal efforts in the 1950s. And despite the well-worn path of many community organizations toward institutionalized service-providing nonprofits, community organizing continues to provide a "mechanism for planning and empowerment" (Steil & Connolly, 2009, p. 183), especially in cases where governance networks, including foundations and economic anchor institutions, deem urban spaces unredeemable in areas that appear as 'ungoverned spaces' (Davies & Pill, 2012). As Steil and Connolly outline in the case of communities with significant brownfield sites, the issue of who decides what purpose claimed land will serve pits the economic development interests of, for instance, big box stores, against area residents with desires for residential and recreational land use. In this sense, grassroots organizations may use oppositional activism with goals directed at community control. In some cases, strategies may include alternative institutions like community land trusts, mutual housing associations and neighborhood-based financial institutions (DeFilippis, 2004). Importantly, community political behavior is more likely to include adversarial tactics to alter extant rules-of-game to achieve a more inclusive and "just urban environment" and decision making structure (Steil & Connolly, 2009, p. 184).

CNPOs and the Case of 'Shrinking Cities' Planning Processes

The case of shrinking cities planning in the current era represents a juncture producing new governing institutions that circumvent public processes, with the potential to move beyond public-private hybrid institutions and to be dominated by the independent sector. This section will address the emergence of these new rules-of-game and the impact we might expect on CNPOs and their active participation in decision making that impacts their communities. It should be noted that shrinking cities planning is currently unfolding. While processes are largely too fluid to allow extensive analysis, early research is helpful for building some expectations and pointing to areas where additional research is needed.

Shrinking cities are intrinsically places where community lines fade and shift, and where disappearing population undermines the foundation of community. Schilling and Logan (2008) define shrinking cities as older, deindustrialized cities that are sustaining population loss of 25 percent or greater over the previous forty years, with "increasing levels of vacant and abandoned properties, including blighted residential, commercial, and industrial building" (p. 452). In some instances urban shrinkage may occur outside the core city, within the larger urban region, as is more common in Europe. Shrinkage may also plague non-industrial areas, as is the case in New Orleans and San Francisco (Pallagst, 2009). Most American shrinking cities, however, are deindustrialized Midwestern cities and are suffering population loss to the urban core. Those with greatest losses between the 2000 and 2010 Census, for example, are Detroit, Cleveland, Buffalo, Cincinnati, Pittsburgh, Toledo, St. Louis and Chicago (Fee & Hartley, 2011). Planning approaches generally seek to address either all comprehensively or individual elements of the economic, safety and health, and community stability challenges that rapid population loss and disinvestment generate. Generally, the approaches might most accurately be called "right sizing," to reflect the more prevalent concerns with adjusting various elements of the city's infrastructure and long term land use plans. Schilling and Logan (2008) define "right sizing" as "stabilizing dysfunctional markets and distressed neighborhoods by more closely aligning a city's built environment with the needs of existing and foreseeable future populations by adjusting the amount of land available for development" (p. 453).

The questions of who decides a community's fate and how the decisions are reached are critical. Processes for 'shrinking' or 'right-sizing' cities are widely varying in type, from shrinking geographical territory to adjusting around smaller city population, to redeploying resources within extant boundaries as a targeted strategy to maintain or grow areas of remaining economic, cultural or other sources of vitality. The instances of the former are few, leading to some fundamental objections to the term 'shrinking.' Targeted investment, however, similarly 'shrinks' a city by retrenching resources overall; it seeks to generate new strategies for land use and fund those most likely to succeed. What Thomson (2013) refers to as "strategic geographical targeting" is neither particularly new nor indicative of purely public policy. The trend in nonprofit grants-making for over a decade has demonstrated general disfavor of needs-based funding and shift to targeting grants and programs for urban districts most likely to generate multiplier effects and enhance the market efficiency of the investment (Thomson, 2013). The strategy emphasizes investing where other 'partners' are already engaged, leveraging the presence of anchor institutions and surviving businesses. The strategy, as one foundation described it recently, means "looking for the points of leverage, the possibilities for collaboration, the potential that one action will yield a series of desirable reactions" (Kresge Foundation, 2012, p. 5). As a 'right-sizing' approach targeting, as presently practiced in US cities, also indicates decision making dominated by foundations and funding intermediaries, with support or mirroring by public officials. Once areas are targeted multiple funders, including city officials, are also likely to steer resources to those areas, as observed above in the case of Buffalo. The impact of such an institutional shift to independent sector decision making on CNPOs is a diminution of their voice as CNPOs are less likely to share in deliberations or have opportunities to respond openly.

Institutions in the most basic sense shape the rules-of-game; any alteration of those rules affects both the actors on the deck and their relative weight, and thus threatens to affect outcomes. Ostrom (1990) emphasized simply that, "Participants prefer a set of rules that will give them the most advantageous outcome" (p. 42). Once the metacenter is set, participants may have reason to fear new institutional arrangements, particularly where trust between actors is low (Ostrom, 1990). For example, communities that either benefitted from standing configurations or that fear negative impacts from a reconfigured city can be expected to react negatively, with a failure to cooperate, counterplans or protesting and various forms of resistance. As cities shrink, municipal executives seek to reduce the costs of delivering services to areas with high vacancy levels and target resources to those with potential to attract new residents and business investment. Legislators have electoral concerns and will fight against disinvestment in their particular districts. At-large councils may oppose shrinking services generally to protect their constituents and reelection chances citywide. The relevant questions suggested by new institutionalism are: who sets the rules-of-game for shrinkage planning and in what roles are community nonprofits cast?

It is not the intention of this chapter to identify the full breadth of shrinking cities planning types, but for present purposes we might categorize them broadly for how their institutional mechanisms incorporate various interests and actors. The three broad categories are: *public sector driven processes, public–private hybrid processes*, and private-nonprofit driven processes, or what we will refer to here as *governance without government*. Each type represents particular institutional arrangements with the capacity to favor some actors and disadvantage others. Public, governmental processes are most accessible to community residents and CNPOs as they work through and with district representatives and elected officials who are vulnerable through the ballot box, in styles most typical of insider advocacy. The very processes, such as lost tax revenues, reduced population density to support infrastructure costs, and loss of commercial and other investment that contribute to urban shrinkage, also diminish public capacity to act independently in response (Martinez-Fernandez, Audirac, Fol & Cunningham-Sabot, 2012). Even in historically 'statist' European cities with similar 'shrinking cities' profiles, local governments are increasingly compelled to 'partner' with private housing and development actors in hybrid governance arrangements in order to secure national and European grants for demolition of vacant buildings and restoration of housing market stability (Bernt, 2009).

Every city approaches right-sizing in ways shaped by unique local circumstances and institutions. In the United States, however, where national policies to support local planning are already especially weak and where local resources are severely diminished through decades of disinvestment, entirely public sector driven processes are largely absent. The Youngstown 2010 Plan is an example of a public-private hybrid process with a sizable public role in the formation stage. There the mayor, Jay Williams, played a leading role. A former community development director, he is credited with engaging community concerns after encountering strong opposition in the initial pilot projects (Shilling & Logan, 2008). City Council and other city officials also helped drive the process, working with the local anchor, Youngstown State University, a nonprofit consulting group, CNPOs and residents. But the implementation stage was left largely to residents and the nonprofit sector, begging the question of whether the public sector risks overburdening community residents (Schatz, 2013).

Detroit is an example of urban governance structures at a critical juncture, resulting in substantive impacts on nonprofit actors, including CNPOs. In what is best characterized as *governance without government,* Detroit's shrinking city planning processes are most notable for the smaller role public actors have played in comparison with those from the nonprofit sector. Detroit, with its extraordinary pace and extent of shrinkage and severe loss of governmental capacity, has seen the rise of activism from foundations, intermediaries, CNPOs, hybrid public-private authorities, and business-nonprofit development collaborations.

With a weakened public capacity, planning preferences are developed in pockets of collaboration and reflect broadly different interests. In an early exploratory report for a regional foundation in Detroit on 'revitalization prospects,' a consultant group observed that the various stakeholder groups differed widely on preferred investment. Community-based interests preferred "immediate and concrete projects" such as a new grocery or improved schools, while large nonprofit, civic, business or downtown stakeholders had strategic notions of revitalization investment that would reinforce ongoing downtown projects or attract new residents and investment (Urban Ventures Group Inc., 2007, p. 44). With such divergent stakeholder interests, the process through which 'right-sizing' planning takes place and the weight given to each set of actors in decision making are likely to affect the priorities set and the type of political response by communities and CNPOs.

Detroit's fast decline explains much of the public sector's limited capacity. Down to a population of 717,000 in the 2010 Census from a peak of 1.8 million in 1950, the city's decline is sharp and still falling, with a projected drop to 610,000 by 2030 (Detroit Works Project, 2012, p. 11). School enrollments declined by 32.1 percent just during the period between 2005–6 and 2009–10

(*New York Times*, 2012). The result of this unprecedented depopulation is approximately 150,000 vacant lots scattered unevenly across the city and a mix of neighborhood densities from relatively stable to sparsely populated (Detroit Works Project, 2012, p. 11). Financially, the City of Detroit has plummeted into red ink as its lost income, property tax and other revenues decline even as its costs increase to pay for escalating needs for areas from demolition to social services for a poorer population in a "capacity–needs mismatch" (Galster, 2012, p. 234). The city has struggled to service the geographical expanse within its emptying neighborhoods with insufficient revenues; negotiations over assistance from the State of Michigan, meanwhile, focused heavily on the protracted battle over the appointment of a state emergency financial manager.

CNPO approaches to the limited capacity of city government have been both collaborative and counter-institutional. Beginning in 2009, as a result of declining city services and concerns about the fate of districts with largest numbers of vacant parcels, a city-wide community development trade organization, called Community Development Advocates of Detroit (CDAD), developed a Neighborhood Revitalization Strategic Framework for use as a tool-kit for participatory planning processes. The Strategic Framework created a colorful spectrum of zoning types from 'traditional residential' for densely populated, stable neighborhoods, to innovative approaches for extensively vacant areas such as 'green thoroughfare' zones, 'spacious residential,' 'urban homesteads' where residents might remain in sparsely populated areas and provide for their own needs, and 'green venture,' with possibilities for urban agriculture. From this effort, a planning group, Lower Eastside Action Plan (LEAP) was founded in 2010 to pilot the typologies in Detroit's Lower Eastside – the community with highest concentration of vacant parcels. LEAP's ambitions were to enable self-determination for community residents through participation in planning, development of effective strategies for land use, and policy advocacy for changes to support locally generated preferences for vacant land adaptation (LEAP, 2012).[8] One of the CDAD members, Warren/Connor Development Coalition (W/CDC) housed LEAP and hired an urban planner to manage the project. LEAP then secured funding from two foundations to undertake the work, hired Data Driven Detroit, a nonprofit research organization to provide data and analysis of actual circumstances within districts, and worked with several university and nonprofit partners. Community resident activists were engaged in each part of the district to recruit other resident activists to join a Stakeholder Advisory Committee. The process of devising community plans was then undertaken over the course of approximately two years of meticulous community surveys, technical data collection, and the ongoing deliberation of residents. Through the process residents' dreams were tempered by the realities of the possible and a multi-faceted plan emerged including new ideas about most effective use of community land. The final product was both new expectations from residents about the strengths and potential of their community and a set of concrete recommendations to the city for zoning and other changes needed to realize the community plan.

The City launched its own shrinking city plan, the Detroit Works Project, in 2010 through a partnership with the Kresge Foundation. Although a public planning endeavor championed by Mayor Dave Bing, Detroit had few resources to support the ambitious undertaking. Kresge funded the hiring of the nationally-renowned urban planner, Toni Griffin, and external visioning consultants to advise on community engagement. Community outreach took the form of a 55-member Mayor's Advisory Task Force, including a number of key CNPOs from throughout the city who gathered monthly for presentations on progress, and an early round of town hall events. The latter were intended as small gatherings with a few hundred residents to present a shrinking city vision. Numbers exploded from the expected 100–300 to approximately 1,000, however, when residents heard the mayor's media comments regarding the need to strengthen viable communities and encourage residents to leave others. Enraged community residents stymied the planned presentations and demanded attention to the daily crises in their neighborhoods such as broken street lamps and lacking city services.

In the face of widespread criticism for mishandling community engagement, in July 2011, Mayor Bing and Kresge CEO Rip Rapson engaged in a media battle over whom to blame. Bing publicly took on Kresge to demonstrate that the City would make critical decisions important to residents, saying that "Everyone talks about Kresge, Kresge, Kresge … Kresge is not doing this in a vacuum by themselves" (in Dolan, 2011). The open squabble resulted in DWP's reorganization into Short Term Actions (STA) and Long Term Planning (LTP). The former was launched as a public responsibility, under the Mayor's Office, to focus on residents' daily needs and concerns such as street lights, safety and repairs. LTP, meanwhile, began to emerge fully as a nonprofit endeavor. LTP was chiefly funded by the Ford and Kresge Foundations. Daily administrative management was handled by the hybrid entity, Detroit Economic Growth Corporation (DEGC), which is enabled to receive funding from foundation and intermediaries through its 501(c)(3) arm, Detroit Economic Growth Association (DEGA). Kresge was also instrumental in bringing in and funding the University of Detroit Mercy – Detroit Collaborative Design Center (DCDC) team heading LTP's two parts, Civic Engagement and the Technical Team in mid-2011. After retooling to what many referred to as DWP 2.0, participants widely noted the greater outreach and more effective collaboration with community residents and other stakeholders. Throughout 2012 the Civic Engagement team ran community events, worked with CNPOs to host a road show of land use data and typologies to stimulate resident visioning of how they might address neighborhood conditions. Other outreach devices included a virtual game that both city residents and others could engage with, maintaining a Home Base where residents, CNPOs and other groups could meet with the DWP team to refine mapping and typologies and discuss impacts on local sites, and an energetic virtual and media presence to keep public discourse alive. CNPOs noted working with the Civic Engagement team in a number of ways, in part because of their longer-term relationship with DCDC collaborative planners and architects over earlier projects. But while they expressed satisfaction with Civic Engagement, CNPOs had no access to the Technical Team and the actual creation of the Detroit Future City Strategic Plan.

With the Detroit Future City Strategic Plan completed in January 2013, the city-wide, right-sizing endeavor is now in the DWP 3.0 implementation stages. DWP chose to guide the stage through a 'consortium' of members. Determining how members would be chosen, however, and what powers they would enjoy are outside the reach of Detroit community residents and CNPOs. New institutional governance structures are evolving in Detroit without substantive governmental elements. The Detroit Neighborhood Investment Forum – a collaboration of Detroit-area foundations – is an example of one independent sector element. It meets monthly to discuss common concerns and strategies for revitalization. When DWP 1.0 was in jeopardy, foundations searched for alternatives that they could support. The foundation's role in rescuing DWP and launching of DWP 2.0 resulted in the public–nonprofit splitting of decision making and largely excluded government from that policy arena with greatest potential to fundamentally mold the city's future direction. The independent sector is also determined to see the plan implemented. Acknowledging that DWP 3.0 or 'Detroit Future City' requires private commitment for realization, the Kresge Foundation CEO, Rip Rapson, dramatically announced at the Detroit Future City report's unveiling that Kresge intends to contribute $150 million in support of various projects within the plan over five years. Ford, Kellogg, Knight and Detroit's other foundations are expected to invest heavily as well (Gallagher, Reindl & Helms, 2013). With funding in the hands of the independent sector, foundations become the critical decision makers, able to focus on those projects they support, through processes inaccessible to other sectors. Despite employing participatory planning mechanisms, as Sirianni (2007) concluded of Seattle's neighborhood planning efforts, even "participatory planning offers no substitute for democratic politics" (p. 386).

Conclusions

This chapter has highlighted the political role of CNPOs in decision making that impacts their communities. First, the clear message urban scholars leave us with is that urban decision making is severely fractured across many sectors beyond formal public structures of city executives and legislatures. But the case of shrinking cities suggests that the spectrum of actors is broader than often considered. The nonprofit sector is a vital player in rebuilding and redesigning shrinking cities. Major national and regional foundations and intermediaries have taken a leading role and demonstrated the necessary financial capacity and commitment to urban centers that the federal government and significant for-profit actors have largely abandoned. At the same time, the review of research above indicates that the nonprofit sector is not monolithic. Community-based nonprofits, cultural anchor institutions, foundations and funding intermediaries, charitable organizations and others may exhibit conflicting interests, mandates and agendas. Additionally, in some cases foundations and other city-wide nonprofit actors may align with city-wide public actors more comfortably than community-based nonprofits and resident interests.

The discussion above also underscores the political nature of all stakeholders. Whether special-purpose public authorities and hybrid entities that appear far removed from electoral arena politics, or foundations, intermediaries and community nonprofits, all have constituents, sponsors, allies and sets of interests that can be expected to either coalesce or conflict with others' missions and mandates. What Gallagher (2010) refers to in Detroit as the "new decision-making matrix" (p. 146) is a "private or quasi-public governance model" (p. 145) including corporations, local and national foundations, quasi-public economic development special purpose authorities and others. And although less well understood by citizens and residents, the new governance model is replete with political conflict. "It's there, and it's real," as Gallagher writes (2010, p. 146): "… it's no surprise that unelected leaders squabble as much as elected ones" (p. 147).

Finally, new institutional structures in shrinking cities are evolving and CNPOs will again need to adjust to new rules-of-game. The structures characterized above as *governance without government* create a new challenge for urban CNPOs. They must now maneuver through new institutions that present limited points of access, and do so even as the new political metacenter is shifting. CNPOs will need to gain access and create a role for themselves before the processes of path dependence are established without their secure place at the decision making table in order to serve neighborhood residents and the territories they occupy. Although greater exploration of impacts of the new urban institutions on CNPOs is necessary, should CNPOs not succeed in gaining access, the resulting new political behaviors for the most vulnerable CNPOs in shrinking cities may well be oppositional activism as they attempt to serve areas that major independent sector actors choose not to fund through targeting strategies or right-sizing plans.

Acknowledgments

The author gratefully acknowledges support for this research from Professional Staff Congress of the City University of New York (PSC-CUNY) grant #64364-0042. The author thanks Samantha Majic, Robert Mark Silverman and Kelly L. Patterson for insights that much improved the chapter; responsibility for any shortcomings remains with the author.

8

8 Janice Bockmeyer

Notes

1 For an excellent account of the transition within social science from 'old' to 'new' institutionalism and greater elaboration of schools within the latter, see V. Schmidt (2006).
2 Definitions for 'institution' are many and wide-ranging. That used above is based on Lowndes' (2005) inclusive 'rules of the game' (p. 292). The most definitive to date, with which this approach is viewed as compatible, is found in McGinnis (2011): "*Institutions* are human-constructed constraints or opportunities within which individual choices take place and which shape the consequences of their choices" (p. 170). For many, these constraints also include norms and rules of behavior, or the "logic of appropriateness" (see B. Guy Peters, 2012, p. 31), as that seen in Hall and Taylor's (1996): "formal or informal procedures, routines, norms and conventions embedded in the organizational structure of the polity or political economy" (p. 938).
3 A portion of this discussion and use of the term, 'political metacenter,' are based on papers presented at the 104th Annual Meeting of the American Political Science Association, Boston, 28–31 August 2008, "The Politics of Supra-local Nonprofits: Do 'Good Practices' Reset the Community Metacenter?" and the 37th Annual Urban Affairs Association Meeting in Seattle, 25–28 April 2007, "Are Global 'Good Practices' Good? A Metacentric Analysis of German Community Governance."
4 LISC invested $12 billion between 1980 and 2011 (see: www.lisc.org/accomplishments/LISSC_By_Numbers_2011.pdf); Enterprise reported investing $11.3 billion between 1982 and 2010 (see Build Tomorrow's Communities Today: Annual Report 2010 accessed at: www.enterprisecommunity.org).
5 For the most detailed typology to date of institutional models and types of change agents evoked by each, see James Mahoney and Kathleen Thelen (2010).
6 Salamon (2012, p. 63) suggests there is a research gap in explaining this differential, but speculates that foundations may discourage activism by grantees due to restrictions imposed on foundations by the 1969 Tax Reform Act. See also Ferguson (2007) for discussion of Ford Foundation's role in Congress for Racial Equality (CORE), early community development and draw-back from funding activism after passage of the Act. Ferguson's research suggests the Act was partly in response to Ford's funding of the CORE's electoral activism.
7 Mahoney and Thelen (2010) refer to this behavior type as "insurrectionaries," or those seeking rapid displacement of extant rules (pp. 27–8).
8 The Detroit site analysis is based on document review and 17 personal, in-depth interviews conducted by the author with interviewees from all relevant sectors in December, 2012.

References

Anglin, R. & S.C. Montezemolo (2004). Supporting the community development movement: The achievements and challenges of intermediary organizations. In R. Anglin (Ed.), *Building the Organizations that Build Communities: Strengthening the Capacity of Faith and Community-Based Development Organizations* (pp. 55–72). Washington, DC: US Dept. of Housing and Urban Development. Retrieved from HUD website: http://www.huduser.org/portal/publications/pdf/BuildOrgComms/Section1_Paper4.pdf.
Arnstein, S. (1969). A ladder of citizen participation. *Journal of the American Institute of Planners, 35*, 216–224.
Bernstein, A.R. (2011). Metrics mania: The growing corporatization of U.S. philanthropy. *Thought and Action, 27(Fall)*, 33–41.

Bernt, M. (2009). Partnerships for demolition: The governance of urban renewal in East Germany's shrinking cities. *International Journal of Urban and Regional Research, 33.3,* 754–769.

Bockmeyer, J. (2000). A culture of distrust: The impact of local political culture on participation in the Detroit EZ. *Urban Studies, 37,* 2417–2440.

Bockmeyer, J. (2003). Devolution and the transformation of community housing activism. *Social Science Journal, 40,* 175–188.

Bockmeyer, J. (2007). Building the global city – The Immigrant experience of urban revitalization. In R. Hambleton & J.S. Gross (Eds.), *Governing cities in a global era: Urban innovation, competition, and democratic reform* (pp. 177–188). New York: Palgrave Macmillan.

Boyte, H.C. (1980). *The backyard revolution: Understanding the new citizen movement.* Philadelphia: Temple University Press.

Bratt, R.G. & W.M. Rohe. (2004). Organizational changes among CDCs: Assessing the impacts and navigating the challenges. *Journal of Urban Affairs, 26,* 97–220.

Bridges, A. (1997). *Morning glories: Municipal reform in the southwest.* Princeton, NJ: Princeton University Press.

Burns, N. (1994). *The formation of American local governments: Private values in public institutions.* New York: Oxford University Press.

Davies, J.S. (2011). *Challenging governance theory: From networks to hegemony.* Bristol, UK: The Policy Press.

Davies, J.S. (2012). Network governance theory: A Gramscian critique. *Environment and Planning A.* Available at SSRN: http://ssrn.com/abstract=2029022.

Davies, J.E. & M. Pill. (2012). Hollowing out neighbourhood governance? Rescaling revitalization in Baltimore and Bristol. *Urban Studies, 49,* 2199–2217.

DeFilippis, J. (2004). *Unmaking Goliath: Community control in the face of global capital.* New York: Routledge.

DeFilippis, J. (2009). Paradoxes of community-building: Community control in the global economy. *International Social Science Journal, 192,* 223–234.

Denters, B. & P. Klok. (2010). Rebuilding Roombeek: Patterns of citizen participation in urban governance. *Urban Affairs Review, 45,* 583–607.

Denters, B. & L.E. Rose. (2005). Towards local governance? In B. Denters & L.E. Rose (Eds.), *Comparing local governance: Trends and developments* (pp. 246–262). New York: Palgrave Macmillan.

Dolan, M. (2011). Revival bid pits Detroit vs. Donor. *The Wall Street Journal,* 2 July. Retrieved at: file:///F:/Mayor and Private Donor Clash over Detroit Revewal – WSJ.com.htm.

Dubb, S. & T. Howard. (2012). Leveraging anchor institutions for local job creation and wealth building. College Park, MD: The Democracy Collaborative at the University of Maryland. Retrieved at: http://community-wealth.com/_pdfs/news/recent-articles/04-12/paper-dubb-howard.pdf.

DWP/Detroit Works Project Long Term Planning. (2012). Detroit Future City: Detroit Strategic Framework Plan. Detroit: Author. Retrieved at: detroitworksproject.com/wp-content/uploads/2013/01/The-DFC-Plan.pdf.

Erie, S.P., V. Kogan & S.A. MacKenzie. (2010). Redevelopment, San Diego Style: The Limits of Public-Private Partnerships. *Urban Affairs Review, 45,* 644–678.

Fee, K. & D. Hartley. (2011). Economic trends: Growing cities, shrinking cities. 14 April. Cleveland: Federal Reserve Bank of Cleveland. Retrieved from www.clevelandfed.org/research/trends/2011/0411/01labmar.cfm.

Feiock, R. & H.S. Jang. (2009). Nonprofits as local government service contractors. *Public Administration Review, July/August,* 668–680.

Ferguson, K. (2007). Organizing the ghetto: The Ford Foundation, CORE, and White Power in the Black Power era, 1967–1969. *Journal of Urban History, 34,* 67–100.

Fulbright-Anderson, K., P. Auspos & N. Anderson. (2001). Community involvement in partnerships with educational institutions, medical centers, and utility companies. New York: Annie E. Casey Foundation.

Gaffikin, F. & D.C. Perry (2012). The contemporary urban condition: Understanding the globalizing city as informal, contested, and anchored. *Urban Affairs Review, 48,* 701–730.

Gallagher, J. (2010). *Reimaging Detroit: Opportunities for redefining an American city.* Detroit: Wayne State University Press.

Gallagher, J., J.C. Reindl & M. Helms. (2013). Kresge Foundation gives $150 million to help make a leaner, greener Detroit. *Detroit Free Press.* 10 January. Retrieved at: www.freep.com/article/20130110/BUSINESS06/301100246.

Galster. G. (2012). *Driving Detroit.* Philadelphia: University of Pennsylvania Press.

Grønbjerg, K. & L.M. Salamon. (2012). Devolution, marketization, and the changing shape of government-nonprofit relations. In L.M. Salamon (Ed.), *The state of nonprofit America* (2nd Edn) (pp. 549–586). Washington, DC: Brookings Institution Press.

Hall, P.A. & R.C.R. Taylor. (1996). Political science and the three new institutionalisms. *Political Studies, 44,* 936–957.

John, P. (2001). *Local governance in Western Europe.* London: Sage.

Judd, D.R. & J.M. Smith. (2007). The new ecology of urban governance: Special-purpose authorities and urban development. In R. Hambleton & J.S. Gross (Eds.), *Governing cities in a global era: Urban innovation, competition, and democratic reform* (pp. 151–160). New York: Palgrave Macmillan.

Kresge Foundation. (2012). Today and tomorrow: The Kresge Foundation 2010 and 2011 Annual Report. Troy, MI: Author.

LEAP. (2012, October). Reinventing Detroit's Lower Eastside. Phase II. Detroit: Author.

Lipsky, M. & S.R. Smith. (1989). Nonprofit organizations, government and the welfare state. *Political Science Quarterly, 104,* 625–648.

Lowndes, V. (2001).Rescuing Aunt Sally: Taking institutional theory seriously in urban politics. *Urban Studies, 38,* 1953–1971.

Lowndes, V. (2005). Something old, something new, something borrowed...How institutions change (and stay the same) in local governance. *Policy Studies, 26,* 291–309.

Lowndes, V. (2009). New institutionalism and urban politics. In J.S. Davies & D.L. Imbroscio (Eds.), *Theories of Urban Politics* (2nd edn)(pp. 91–105). London: Sage.

Mahoney, J. & K. Thelen. (2010). A theory of gradual institutional change. In J. Mahoney & K. Thelen (Eds.), *Explaining institutional change: Ambiguity, agency and power* (pp. 1–37). New York: Cambridge University Press.

Majic, S. (2011). Serving sex workers and promoting democratic engagement: Rethinking nonprofits' role in American civic and political life. *Perspectives on Politics, 9,* 821–839.

Martin, D.G. (2004). Nonprofit foundations and grassroots organizing: Reshaping urban governance. *The Professional Geographer, 56,* pp. 394–405.

Martinez-Fernandez, C., I. Audirac, S. Fol & E. Cunningham-Sabot. (2012). Shrinking cities: Urban challenges of globalization. *International Journal of Urban and Regional Research, 36.2,* 213–25.

Marwell, N.P. (2004). Privatizing the welfare state: Nonprofit community-based organizations as political actors. *American Sociological Review. 69,* 265–291.

McGinnis, M.D. (2011). An introduction to IAD and the language of the Ostrom workshop: A simple guide to a complex framework. *Policy Studies Journal, 39,* 169–183.

Mosley, J.E. (2011). Institutionalization, privatization, and political opportunity: What tactical choices reveal about the policy advocacy of human service nonprofits. *Nonprofit and Voluntary Sector Quarterly, 40,* 435–457.

Musso, J.A., C. Weare, N. Oztas & W.E. Loges. (2006). Neighborhood governance reform and networks of community power in Los Angeles. *American Review of Public Administration, 36,* 79–97.

Naples, N. (1998). From maximum feasible participation to disenfranchisement. *Social Justice, 25,* 47–66.

Nemon, H. (2007). Community action: Lessons from forty years of federal funding, anti-poverty strategies, and participation of the poor. *Journal of Poverty, 11* (1), 1–22.

New York Times. (2012). Greatest declines in enrollment. 24 July, A3.

New York City Nonprofits Project. (2003). *New York City's Nonprofit Sector.* New York: Author. Retrieved from: nycnonprofits.org.

O'Connor, A. (1996). Community action, urban reform, and the fight against poverty: The Ford Foundation's Gray Areas program. *Journal of Urban History, 22,* 586–625.

Ostrom, E. (1990). *Governing the commons: The evolution of institutions for collective action.* Cambridge: Cambridge University Press.

Ostrom, E. (1996). Crossing the great divide: Coproduction, synergy, and development. *World Development, 24,* 1073–1087.

Ostrom, E. (1999). Coping with tragedies of the commons. *Annual Review of Political Science, 2,* 493–535.

Ostrom, V., R. Bish & E. Ostrom. (1988). *Local government in the United States.* San Francisco, CA: Institute for Contemporary Studies.

Owens, M.L. (2007). *God and government in the ghetto: The politics of church-state collaboration in Black America.* Chicago: University of Chicago Press.

Pallagst, K. (2009). Shrinking cities in the United States of America: Three cases, three planning stories. In K. Pallagst, J. Aber, I. Audirac, E. Cunningham-Sabot, S. Fol, C. Martinez-Fernandez, S. Moraes, H. Mulligan, J. Vargas-Hernandez, T. Wiechmann & T. Wu (Eds.), *The Future of Shrinking Cities: Problems, Patterns and Strategies of Urban Transformation in a Global Context* (pp. 81–88). Berkeley, CA: IURD.

Peters, B.G. (2012). *Institutional theory in political science: The new institutionalism.* 3rd edn. New York: Continuum.

Pierson, P. (2004). *Politics in time: History, institutions, and social analysis.* Princeton, NJ: Princeton University Press.

Rohe, W.M., R.G. Bratt & P. Biswas. (2003). *Evolving challenges for community development corporations: The causes and impacts of failures, downsizings and mergers.* Chapel Hill, NC: Center for Urban and Regional Studies, University of North Carolina.

Salamon, L.M. (2012). The resilient sector: The future of nonprofit America. In L.M. Salamon (Ed.), *The state of nonprofit America* (2nd Edn) (pp. 3–86). Washington, DC: Brookings Institution Press.

Sbragia, A.M. (1996). *Debt wish: Entrepreneurial cities, U.S. federalism, and economic development.* Pittsburgh, PA: University of Pittsburgh Press.

Schatz, L. (2013). Decline-oriented urban governance in Youngstown, Ohio. In M. Dewar & J. Manning Thomas (Eds.), *The city after abandonment* (pp. 87–103). Philadelphia, PA: University of Pennsylvania Press.

Schilling, J. & J. Logan. (2008). Greening the rust belt: A green infrastructure model for right sizing American's shrinking cities. *Journal of the American Planning Association, 74,* 451–466.

Schmidt, V. (2006). Institutionalism. In C. Hay, M. Lister & D. Marsh (Eds.), *The state: Theories and issues* (pp. 98–117). New York: Palgrave Macmillan.

Silverman, R.M. (2001). Neighborhood characteristics, CDC emergence and the community development industry system: A case study of the American deep South. *Community Development Journal, 36,* 234–245.

Silverman, R.M. (2003). Progressive reform, gender and institutional structure: A critical analysis of citizen participation in Detroit's community development corporations (CDCs). *Urban Studies, 40,* 2731–2750.

Silverman, R.M. (2005). Caught in the middle: community development corporations and the conflict between grassroots and instrumental forms of citizen participation. *Community Development, 36,* 35–51.

Silverman, R.M. (2008). The influence of nonprofit networks on local affordable housing funding: Findings from a national survey of local public administrators. *Urban Affairs Review, 44,* 126–141.

Silverman, R.M. (2009). Sandwiched between patronage and bureaucracy: The plight of citizen participation in community-based housing organizations in the US. *Urban Studies, 46,* 3–25.

Sirianni, C. (2007). Neighborhood planning as collaborative democratic design: The case of Seattle. *Journal of the American Planning Association, 73,* 373–387.

Smith, S.R. & K.A. Grønbjerg. (2006). Scope and theory of government – nonprofit relations. In W. Powell & R. Steinberg (Eds.), *The non-profit sector: A research handbook* (pp. 221–242). New Haven, CT: Yale University Press.

Steil, J. & J. Connolly. (2009). Can the just city be built from below? In P. Marcuse, J. Connolly, J. Novy, I. Olivo, C. Potter & J. Steil (Eds.), *Searching for the just city: Debates in urban theory and practice* (pp. 173–193). New York: Routledge.

Stoecker, R. (1997). The CDC model of urban development: A critique and alternative. *Journal of Urban Affairs, 19,* 1–22.

Stone, C. (1989). *Regime politics: Governing Atlanta, 1946–1988.* Lawrence, KS: University Press of Kansas.

Thomson, D.E. (2013). Targeting neighborhoods, stimulating markets: The role of political, institutional, and technical factors in three cities. In M. Dewar & J. Manning Thomas (Eds.), *The city after abandonment* (pp. 104–132). Philadelphia, PA: University of Pennsylvania Press.

Trounstine, J. (2009). Challenging the machine-reform dichotomy. In R. Dilworth (Ed.), *The city in American political development* (pp. 77–97). New York: Routledge.

Urban Ventures Group Inc. (2007). Assets and opportunities of Detroit's near-East Side: A Community Profile. Retrieved from cfsem.org/sites/cfsem.org/files/DNF_Community_Profile.pdf.

Vidal, A. (2012). Housing and community development. In L.M. Salamon (Ed.), *The state of nonprofit America,* 2nd edn (pp. 266–293). Washington, DC: Brookings Institution Press.

Vidal, A. & W.D. Keating. (2004). Community development: Current issues and emerging challenges. *Journal of Urban Affairs, 26,* 125–137.

Walker, C. (2002). *Community development corporations and their changing support systems.* Washington, DC: The Urban Institute.

Weir, Margaret. (1999). Power, money, and politics in community development. In R.F. Ferguson & W.T. Dickens (Eds.), *Urban problems and community development* (pp. 139–192). Washington, DC: Brookings Institution Press.

Wolman, H. (1995). Local government institutions and democratic governance. In D. Judge, G. Stoker & H. Wolman (Eds.), *Theories of urban politics* (pp. 135–159). London: Sage.

4

ANCHOR-DRIVEN REDEVELOPMENT IN A VERY WEAK MARKET

The Case of Midtown, Detroit

Avis C. Vidal, Wayne State University

Introduction

Anchor institutions in distressed urban neighborhoods have become increasingly visible as agents of neighborhood improvement. The University of Pennsylvania is the best known example, but is by no means alone. As early as the 1950s, universities like the University of Chicago and Yale decided to make significant investments in their surroundings to keep them safe and attractive to mainly-white students as the neighborhoods around them became increasingly black and poor. More recently, anchors as varied as the University of Illinois at Chicago, Trinity College, the Cleveland Clinic, Case Western Reserve, and University of Southern California have committed to major neighborhood revitalization programs. These institutions are attracting partners – including city governments and major foundations – that see them as key entries in the "short list" of major employers that have growth potential, are committed to remaining in the city, and depend on improved neighborhood environments to compete successfully. The Ford Foundation, the Casey Foundation, the Cleveland Foundation, and CEOs for Cities are prominent among the supporters of what many have labeled the "eds and meds" urban revitalization strategy.

This approach has now found its way to Detroit at a critical time in the city's history; its current difficulties have been long in the making. The city has seen a steady exodus of population and jobs over the past six decades, losing more than 60 percent of its population and more than 80 percent of its manufacturing jobs during that period. Once an industrial powerhouse, Detroit has become an iconic "shrinking city." Decline was especially abrupt after the turn of the century: the 2010 census reported a record 25 percent 10-year population loss, and over a third of the remaining households live below the poverty line. The resulting massive abandonment has left Detroit with more than 40,000 vacant buildings in need of demolition and vast tracts of vacant land – totaling about 20 square miles (*Detroit Future City*, 2012) – that the City cannot afford to service. The City's dire straits, compounded by the threat of impending bankruptcy, have stimulated numerous efforts to address its problems. Three stand out, and have received national attention.

Mayor Dave Bing (with substantial financial support from the philanthropic community) launched the Detroit Works Project (DWP) in 2010 in an effort to (a) identify residential neighborhoods that can survive and thrive despite the wrenching economic restructuring facing the region; (b) develop promising strategies (e.g., targeted investments, improvements in selected services) to strengthen them in the near term; (c) craft modest incentives to consolidate housing and investment in those neighborhoods; and (d) devise cost-effective land management and service delivery strategies for other neighborhoods that have been rapidly emptying out. DWP's final report, issued early in 2013, provides a detailed portrait of the city, a vision of what each part of the city might become at different points in the future, and suggested strategies for moving forward (*Detroit Future City*, 2012). The newly-renamed Detroit Future City is charged with helping a wide variety of local stakeholders, both large and small, find effective ways to engage in implementation.

Downtown has gotten a major lift from the decision of Dan Gilbert, founder and Chairman of Quicken Loans, to purchase more than a dozen major downtown properties and move three of his companies there. Several other major employers, most notably Blue Cross Blue Shield, have followed his lead by moving to the Downtown area, and several additional large employers (e.g. Chrysler) are moving some of their employees Downtown as well. Gilbert and other investors have established a business incubator for high-tech start-up companies in Downtown office space that provides on-site access to their high-tech venture capital firm. Collectively, these moves have added an estimated 10,000 jobs to the central business district over several years, and considerably enhance the longstanding revitalization activities of the corporate-led Downtown Detroit Partnership.

Planning is underway for a light rail line on Woodward Avenue, the city's premier north–south arterial that connects Downtown to the city's northern suburbs. The long-term vision is for a line that runs from the riverfront to the State Fairgrounds at Eight Mile Road (the city's northern border). Current planning focuses on a more modest, three-mile connection between the riverfront and New Center (described below) that has drawn strong corporate and philanthropic support, including financial support for the planning process and some pledges to "sponsor" individual stations. A new regional transit authority, created by the State in late 2012, and a federal award of partial funding in early 2013 led sponsors to announce that construction will start in 2014.

In this context, a collaborative of local foundations, nonprofit organizations, and public entities launched the Woodward Corridor Initiative (WCI) in 2010 with significant national philanthropic support from Living Cities, Inc. WCI is a multi-pronged effort to "re-densify" the portion of the urban core that straddles Woodward Avenue immediately north of Downtown. This corridor is by far the largest employment center outside of Downtown, and the DWP final report identifies it as the center with the largest job growth potential. The Anchor Strategy is part of this initiative.

Despite these positive developments and the large number of prominent local stakeholders committed to them, the revitalization of the Corridor faces formidable challenges. Some of these are contextual. The neighborhood is embedded in, and inevitably affected by, a city with serious economic problems and a City government with acute fiscal problems and limited political and administrative capacity. Although foreclosure rates have fallen sharply state-wide, real estate markets for all types of property remain weak, especially in Detroit. Lenders formerly active in supporting real estate development remain risk averse, so credit is tight.

Other challenges are internal. The stretch of Woodward that bisects the WCI target area has some strong retail blocks, and some of the city's premier cultural institutions, most notably the Detroit Institute of the Arts, the Detroit Public Library, the Detroit Historical Museum, the Max M. Fisher Music Center (home of the Detroit Symphony Orchestra), and the Episcopal Cathedral Church of St. Paul, front attractively on the Avenue. Unfortunately, stretches of low-quality commercial structures and vacant lots are more common. The area's 2010 population of just over 22,000 was down 21 percent from its 2000 level, and one third of neighborhood households have annual incomes of less than $10,000. The 2010 census reported that 28 percent of the area's 15,483 housing units were vacant (Data Driven Detroit, n.d.a). In addition to that housing and the substantial institutional presence described earlier, the neighborhood also has considerable vacant land (including many surface parking lots) and pockets of vacant or underused industrial property.

This weak market context – notably weaker than the settings of many older and better-known anchor-driven initiatives – influences the Anchor Strategy, the broader WCI of which it is a part, and investments by the individual anchor institutions. This chapter discusses the start-up phase of this very challenging revitalization effort, focusing specifically on two elements with the potential to directly affect WCI residential communities: one element of the Anchor Strategy, called Live Midtown, and real estate investments by the anchors, particularly Henry Ford Health System (HFHS). It also explores some of the ways in which the weak market context may account for some differences between the Detroit experience and comparable interventions in less troubled places.

The Structure of the Revitalization Effort

WCI is a complex initiative. It has eight major programmatic thrusts, each with multiple elements (*Woodward Corridor Initiative Overview*, n.d.).[1] Some of these are focused on the revitalization of the Corridor target area. Others have important components that are citywide and seek to strengthen the city's economy and improve the way City government does business. Its design reflects the objective of bringing representatives of all sectors "to 'one table' to address and solve complex social problems that improve the quality of life of residents" (*Woodward Corridor Initiative Overview*, n.d.). Following the "one table" philosophy, it has a Governing Council that represents major stakeholders from all sectors. It is administered by Midtown Detroit Inc. (MDI), one of the lead nonprofit members of the collaborative.[2]

The Anchor Strategy seeks to align the resources of three major "eds and meds" institutions located in the Corridor – HFHS, Wayne State University (WSU), and the Detroit Medical Center (DMC). They are a significant presence in Midtown and in the region. Together, they employ almost 30,000 people and have annual operating expenses in excess of $1.5 billion. WSU enrolls about 30,000 each year. Although the Corridor includes many highly visible cultural institutions, such as those noted earlier, many of them are financially fragile. They are not in a position to make the kinds of investments needed to stimulate the Midtown real estate market.

The strategy has three components, only one of which targets the Corridor: Live Midtown provides financial incentives to induce more employees of the anchors to live in the neighborhood.[3] Its goal is to stimulate the local real estate market by increasing the demand for housing. Its potential to achieve this goal is contingent on both the success of other major WCI program strategies and major investments the anchors hope to make in the neighborhood that are not explicitly part of WCI.

WCI includes two strategies that directly complement Live Midtown. The first, New Housing and Real Estate Development, is a diverse set of activities traditionally undertaken by MDI in collaboration with many other local stakeholders to promote development in the area. These activities include detailed neighborhood planning, raising funds for strategic neighborhood improvements, working closely to support local commercial property owners and prospective developers, and helping developers gain access to capital for their projects. The second strategy, Finance, seeks both to leverage existing capital (including the Living Cities funds) and to develop an expanded pool of private capital to offset diminishing public subsidies for development. It also works closely with several local community development financial institutions. Taken together, these two strategy elements are positioned to enable the real estate market to respond to the increased housing demand

Live Midtown seeks to stimulate by facilitating development of new housing supply.

Not directly linked to WCI, but clearly relevant to its potential impact, is the fact that all three anchors have strategic plans that call for major investments in and around their respective campuses. Early in 2010, HFHS announced preliminary plans for approximately $1 billion of new development over twenty years and indicated that it had already begun land acquisition (Kavanaugh, 2010). The plan includes an expansion of its campus, directly across West Grand Boulevard from Henry Ford Hospital, that will add new medical treatment and research facilities. It also includes mixed use commercial space, new housing at a variety of prices, and some light industrial space, with an emphasis on health-care related support services. HFHS hopes to induce others to develop and own most of this non-medical space (Greene, 2012). Vanguard Health Systems committed to an $850 million package of improvements and new facilities at the DMC when it purchased the facility in 2010 (Koslowski & Aguilar, 2010).[4] WSU has been working for more than a decade to become a more residential campus, developing dormitories for between 2,000 and 2,500 students since 2000. During that same period it also built or expanded several academic buildings; acquired and renovated a major office building on Woodward; established and subsequently expanded Tech Town (a business incubator); broke ground for a major new bio-medical research facility on Woodward; and acquired considerable property in anticipation of further growth, assuming financing can be raised. If these investments can be brought to fruition, they have the potential to increase anchor economic activity and employment, attract more visitors (e.g., patients) to the neighborhood, and make it a more attractive place to live.

Live Midtown – Program Design

Launched in 2011, Live Midtown is an attractive and well-publicized package of incentives worth about $1.2 million annually to entice employees to live in the surrounding community.[5] Home purchasers receive a $20,000 loan at closing, forgiven over five years. If the owner becomes ineligible before the end of the five-year period, the un-forgiven portion of the incentive must be repaid. Existing owners receive up to $5,000 (no more than half of the total cost) toward external home improvements; if the owner becomes ineligible before the end of the five-year period, the match must be repaid in full. New renters receive $2,500 toward rental costs during their first year in Midtown if they sign a lease, and are eligible for an additional $1,000 if the lease is renewed. Existing Midtown renters receive $1,000 for renewing a lease.[6] All incentives are contingent on maintaining the home or apartment as a primary residence for the duration of the incentive and remaining in the employ of the anchor institution. At WSU and the DMC, employees must be benefits-eligible. At

HFHS, part-time employees, Residents and Fellows are also eligible. Students are not eligible. Finally, the incentives must be used for housing within the officially designated Live Midtown target area.

Although it is part of WCI, Live Midtown does not target exactly the same geographic area. Rather, its target area was strategically defined to maximize the likelihood that it would "jump start" the local real estate market, given its very weak market context. The WCI target area includes three historically recognized neighborhoods. The area between M-10 and I-75 from the northern edge of Downtown to I-94 is known as Midtown; it is bisected by Woodward Avenue (see Map 4.1). WSU, DMC, and the major cultural institutions are in Midtown. North of I-94, the area west of Woodward is New Center, dominated visually by the historic Fisher Building, Cadillac Place (formerly General Motors Headquarters, now a State office building), Henry Ford Hospital, and Tech Town. The area east of Woodward is the North End; it is primarily residential, but also includes both active and vacant industrial space, mostly concentrated on the fringes of the neighborhood near the freeways and railroad.

Live Midtown's target area excludes the southern part of Midtown and the northern part of the North End, the two portions of the WCI footprint that suffered the greatest population losses after 2000. The excluded southern area has a great deal of vacant land and is very low-income, containing considerable subsidized housing and numerous social service providers who assist homeless persons. At the same time, the target area adds a considerable area south of West Grand Boulevard and west of M-10. This area includes the western part of the WSU campus; the Woodbridge neighborhood, a relatively solid neighborhood with much attractive housing that began drawing WSU faculty and students in the 1990s; and the area south of Henry Ford Hospital, where HFHS plans to expand its medical treatment and research campus and hopes to foster the development of a walk-able mixed use area that includes a variety of new housing options. These boundary changes enable the initiative to target the smallest geography likely to be attractive to anchor employees, including the most solid existing residential areas.

These boundary changes create a target area that shows notable market potential. As noted earlier, the WCI target area lost more than 20 percent of its population between 2000 and 2010. Its census-reported residential vacancy rate more than doubled.[7] While the area did fare better than the city as a whole, the picture painted by the census figures is still a hard package to market to funders and real estate developers interested in a market with strong potential. In contrast, the Live Midtown target area registered a 4 percent population *gain* during the same period.

In addition to strategically defining the target area, the initiative adopted the practice long followed by MDI in planning and promoting the neighborhood. MDI maintains very close contacts with local developers and larger property owners, and based on information from them monitors rental vacancy rates that

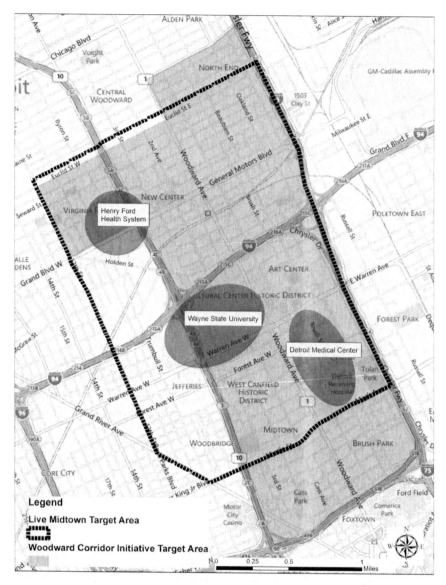

MAP 4.1   Live Midtown and Woodward Corridor Initiative Target Areas

are based not on the total number of non-occupied dwelling units, but on the number of non-occupied units that are move-in ready or near move-in ready and thus actually available to potential renters.[8] Framed this way, MDI reported that in 2010 the rental occupancy rate was 92 percent (Gregor, 2010). *That* is a profile that engenders stakeholder confidence.

Live Midtown – Early Program Results

Live Midtown is widely viewed as a successful program. During its first 18 months, 374 anchor employees received some type of incentive.[9] Thirty-seven employees received forgivable purchase loans, and seven owners got home improvement loans. Almost 90 percent of participants are renters, with renewals slightly more common than new leases. The predominance of renters is to be expected, since 86 percent of the housing units in the target area are rentals. About 40 percent of participants are WSU employees, with the balance almost equally distributed between DMC and HFHS.[10]

Buyers

The profile of the buyers holds few surprises. More than three quarters are one- or two-person households – what one would expect given the Gen-X "buzz" Midtown seeks to cultivate and the state of Detroit's public schools. Most purchased condominiums, with two-bedroom units being the most common choice. Indeed, even single person households showed a strong preference for units that had two bedrooms or more. The preponderance of condo purchases reflects the composition of the area's for-sale housing stock.

Purchase prices reflect the distressed state of the Detroit housing market. Sixty-two percent of buyers paid $45,000 or less for their units, and of these, three quarters paid $20,000 or less. These are all distressed sales of some sort, and it is likely all are cash transactions; the $20,000 incentive puts many buyers in a position to make a cash purchase at those prices, and obtaining mortgage financing for condominiums is quite difficult in the tight credit market. The remaining buyers paid $60,000 or more; note the complete absence of sales in the $45,000 to $60,000 range. These sales were more diverse. Some of these units clearly sold for market prices, with most buyers paying more than $50 per square foot, typically much more, but a few sold for per-square-foot prices that are similar to those at the low end of the market.

It will clearly be some time before the Live Midtown initiative can serve as a stimulus to the owner-occupied housing market. There are two key reasons for this. First, even at the upper end of the market, the highest per-square-foot prices are still considerably less than the per-square-foot cost of new residential construction. Second, when the financial crisis hit, a number of condominium developments were caught with units (sometimes a sizeable number of units) they could not to sell. Most developers converted the unsold units to rentals with the expectation of returning them to the for-sale market when conditions improved. These project owners can bring additional condo units to market more quickly, flexibly, and cheaply than developers starting new projects, and this seems likely to serve as a strong disincentive to new condominium development until the stock of units-in-waiting is reduced.

Renters

Like buyers, the majority of Live Midtown renters – 60 percent – are single person households, and there are few with more than two people. Renters occupy smaller units than buyers. More than half of renters chose one-bedroom or studio apartments (with studio rentals being few), and rented units have an average of 1.5 bedrooms, versus 2.6 for purchased units. In sharp contrast to single buyers, single renters were about twice as likely to choose one-bedroom or studio units rather than larger units. Three quarters of renters have apartments in multifamily buildings – exactly what one would expect given the local housing stock.

Renters new to Midtown and those renewing existing leases differ in some respects. Sixty-five percent of new renters are single person households, 10 percentage points higher than those remaining in place. New renters are more likely than those renewing leases to be in condominiums; this almost certainly reflects the decision of some condo owners who wanted to move to rent their units rather than sell in the depressed market and incur a large capital loss.

More significantly, new renters are paying higher rents: an average of $804 per month, versus only $664 for those who renewed leases. The difference in their average annual rents is $1,560, which is very close to the difference in the annual incentive they receive. This enabled them to move to somewhat larger units: 945 square feet for new renters, 850 square feet for those who renewed leases.[11] In addition, new renters are paying almost 10 percent more per square foot than those renters remaining in place; this could be quite important *if* they continue to be willing to pay those prices after the incentive period is over. However, only one quarter of new renters who chose one-bedroom apartments (and even fewer renters who renewed their leases) are paying a rent that is at or above the least expensive one-bedroom apartment ($920) in the only new rental property to be built in the neighborhood since the onset of the financial crisis.

These early results are encouraging. Demand for the Live Midtown program remains strong, and all the funds available in 2012 were used. It is difficult to know how many additional anchor employees might eventually be interested in moving to the neighborhood, but Midtown is one of the few areas of Detroit with a genuinely "urban" character, and the incentives are generous relative to current market rents. MDI reported that the rental vacancy rate has fallen below 4 percent and that about three quarters of Midtown apartment buildings raised rents during the first half of 2012 (Henkel & Aguilar, 2012). In response, several rental rehabilitation projects are "in the pipeline," either under construction or actively seeking financing.

These market changes cannot all be attributed to Live Midtown. The program simply has not yet had enough participants, specifically new renters, to make this large a change in the vacancy rate. The neighborhood is attractive to many renters not employed by the anchors, including students and office workers whose jobs have recently moved to Downtown and who want to live close to work, but prefer Midtown to Downtown because it has a wider range of retailing (especially grocery stores) and is somewhat more lively on weekends.

It is important to note that the one new rental project in the neighborhood required very complex financing, including tax credits, below-market rate loans, and patient equity investments (in addition to developer equity and market-rate financing). Since credit remains tight, it seems likely that projects in the pipeline will require similar types of incentives. These types of funds are available through the New Housing and Real Estate Development portion of WCI, and this creates local optimism that the pipeline will grow. However, even with the "creative" financial arrangements those funds make possible, pipeline projects will all likely come on line at the upper end of the market, and as noted above, not many Live Midtown renters are currently paying rents that high. The open question is whether demand is strong enough to support those rents over time.

Community Reactions to the Anchor Strategy

There has been relatively little community response to Live Midtown, or to the anchors' broader investment strategy. This is surely due, in part, to the fact that Live Midtown is still fairly new, and that media coverage of it has been strongly positive. Recent anchor investments have renovated under-used properties or built on vacant land in non-residential areas or on the WSU campus. However, other factors are also at work, and many are by-products of the weak market context, but they play out somewhat differently in different residential areas.

The area of Midtown immediately south of the WSU campus, where most students live and where the pipeline rental projects are located, has no resident-driven community organization. Students who report rent increases voice some concern that they may ultimately be priced out of the market, but they also see value in prospective new development that could eliminate blight, bring new amenities, create a more lively street life that would improve safety, and help the City's tax base. Cass Corridor Neighborhood Development Corporation, located at the southern border of the Live Midtown target area, has eight low-cost apartment buildings that it has developed or acquired over a 30-year period; they are concentrated near its offices, and some are federally subsidized. It also operates a community center that primarily serves the low-income population that predominates in the South Cass Corridor, much of which lies outside the target area. Few Live Midtown participants live in this part of the target area, and it will be unaffected by the investments planned by DMC and WSU.

Vanguard Community Development Corporation (CDC) is widely seen as benefiting from WCI. It was founded in 1994 to serve as the nonprofit development arm of Second Ebenezer Church in its North End neighborhood.

The Church is now located about a mile outside the neighborhood, a move necessitated by its growth to more than 5,000 members under the 35-year leadership of the dynamic Bishop Edgar L. Vann II, also the CDC's founder and President/CEO. The CDC's agenda emphasizes social service delivery (especially youth development); organizing and improvements in the industrial district along the neighborhood's southern edge, especially between I-94 and East Grand Boulevard, where it operates a business incubator; and housing development. The North End has a very high concentration of vacant residential parcels, and very few Live Midtown participants live there. Anchor expansion plans pose no threat, and some new investments will improve the stretch of Woodward immediately west of the North End, supporting the CDC's agenda. The CDC also sits on the WCI Governing Council, and received some of WIC's Living Cities funds to add staff members and expand its development activities.

Two of the residential areas in the WCI target area are served by Citizens' District Councils. Citizens' District Councils were created in the 1960s and 1970s to represent residents of neighborhoods targeted by the urban renewal program. The City was required to have the Councils review any proposed changes to the City Plan that would affect their districts. Council representatives are elected, and serve as volunteers with no support staff. Some of these Councils withered, but about 20 remain. They will lose their official status when the new City Charter adopted in 2011 is fully implemented, and it is unclear whether the financially-strapped City will continue to pay for Council elections.

Woodbridge Citizens' District Council (WCDC), which serves the area southwest of WSU, remains quite active. Woodbridge has a troubled history with the University. Residents still remember the hard-fought, but ultimately unsuccessful, effort in the 1960s to stop the University City urban renewal project, which ultimately cleared about 1,500 Woodbridge homes to make way for new University athletic facilities. Cleared land slated for new replacement housing and a new school remained vacant for many years (Thomas, 1997), and later efforts by residents to gain access privileges to the athletic facilities went nowhere. If the University's long-term expansion plans posed a threat to the neighborhood, residents would likely be wary, but Woodbridge is quite distant from the places where WSU hopes to grow. The history of the neighborhood on WCDC's web site credits moves to Woodbridge by WSU faculty and students during the 1990s with major investments in both rental and owner-occupied housing that reversed two decades of neighborhood decline (http://www.safeinwoodbridge.com/about_woodbridge.html). The foreclosure crisis and recession eroded these gains, so revived demand for the area's housing, much of which is quite attractive, would clearly benefit existing owners (who are the majority) even if they resent WSU as an institution.

Virginia Park Citizens' District Council (VPCDC) serves the area immediately west and north of Henry Ford Hospital. It has a mixed history with

HFHS. Some residents felt that the hospital was not a good neighbor in the years following the 1967 Detroit riots, "turning its back" on the community. In the late 1990s, the Council fought hard (with other community organizations and churches) to get the hospital to close its on-site incinerator, which raised air pollution levels in Virginia Park and other nearby areas with documented adverse effects on residents' health (Lott, 2000). Residents immediately adjacent to the hospital continue to have issues with traffic and litter generated by the hospital's many employees and visitors; they acknowledge that the hospital has taken steps to address them, but say they are inadequate. On the other hand, HFHS partnered with the Council in 1975 to create a CDC to address the neighborhood's affordable housing needs. Unfortunately, that CDC is currently dormant and its future is uncertain. Live Midtown's impact on Virginia Park has been modest to date, and the proposed campus expansion, which has gotten considerable visibility since the 2010 announcement of the preliminary plan, will occur south of West Grand Boulevard, outside Virginia Park.

That area has had no recognized community-based organization. Historically part of Northwest Goldberg and now in the southwest corner of the neighborhood officially designated as Rosa Parks, it is generally not referred to by any name. Formerly a mix of residential, light industrial, and warehouse uses, it is now among the most severely "emptied out" parts of the city. The majority of residential parcels are vacant and additional abandoned homes remain to be demolished (Data Driven Detroit, n.d.b); much of the industrial land is also vacant. It is completely unaffected by Live Midtown, but HFHS has gradually bought up land for the expanded campus, both at auction and from willing sellers, and has helped some resident sellers to relocate. This activity became more visible when HFHS announced a preliminary plan for the area and proposed an initial project, and the West Grand Boulevard Collaborative (WGBC) gradually assumed the role of speaking for the community.

WGBC formed in 2005 to counter deteriorating conditions on a 20-block segment of this once-vibrant commercial and residential street. Its members include both businesses and nonprofit organizations located on the Boulevard, including Henry Ford Hospital (one of two sustaining members), as well as Motown Historical Museum, Black United Fund of Michigan, a branch of the Detroit Public Library, and several prominent churches. The Collaborative has no staff, and relies on volunteers and contributions to execute its projects, which include creating an eco-friendly reading garden at the public library, supporting the installation of bio-swales to help manage storm water, and supporting a Main Street Overlay in the City zoning code for a segment of the Boulevard to promote walk-ability. WGBC board members and volunteers have been active participants in the public meetings held by HFHS to solicit community input into the planning process. Many in the community agree that the community desperately needs new housing and jobs, but there is a widespread feeling that

Henry Ford has not been as forthcoming with information as residents and others would like, and considerable suspicion that planning and development will inevitably put HFHS's interests before those of the community.

The first project proposed by HFHS is a warehouse for a medical supply firm that serves both Henry Ford Hospital and the DMC; the supplier has agreed to relocate its warehouse, which employs about 130 people, from a suburban location to Detroit. Public meetings about this project, both informational meetings for the community and public hearings by the Zoning Board and City Council, raised numerous concerns. Some were directly related to the proposed project, such as a desire to minimize the impact of truck traffic on remaining residents, and a wish to see Detroit residents employed in the new facility. Others were efforts by community members (some affiliated with WGBC, others not) to get financial commitments from HFHS for things that are unrelated to the project. Some, such as a neighborhood park, might become part of the neighborhood plan; others were completely unrelated, most notably a request that HFHS agree to maintain an existing park well outside the neighborhood. Over time, WGBC worked to pull the community together around a shared agenda, and broadened its base by fostering a new community coalition to represent residents, but was still unable to get firm commitments from HFHS, which noted that the finished project would be owned and operated by the medical supply firm and that HFHS would have no control over its employment practices. Frustrated, WGBC organized a letter-writing campaign asking City Council to press HFHS to negotiate a community benefits agreement with WGBC. City Council endorsed the idea and negotiations began. However, the delay created by the extended community process and other unexpected challenges in piecing together such a complex project resulted in the loss of some critical financing at the end of 2012. A new financial package appears to be coming together, but is not yet in place. Negotiations have reached an impasse; the parties are no longer meeting, although they have exchanged proposed drafts of an agreement, and the outcome remains unclear. How the relationship between HFHS and WGBC will develop over time remains to be seen. It is tempting to think that both might benefit if HFHS were to invest in enhancing the organizational capacity in the community, but as the relationship now stands it is hard to image what they could offer that would be well received.

Conclusion

The weak market context of the anchors' efforts to strengthen Midtown appears at this early stage to present a mix of advantages and challenges – at least so far. The housing market generally continues to be very weak, as is the Midtown for-sale market. Distressed-sale prices in Midtown are creeping up, but with many rentals in buildings originally built for the condominium market "in waiting," construction of new units in the foreseeable future is unlikely.

The rental market tells a different story, and it is the bulk of the neighborhood's housing stock. Live Midtown is well designed and well supported by other elements of WCI. It is very simple for employees to access, and the incentives are generous when compared with market rents. Rising commuting costs have made living near work more attractive, and the program has had no difficulty dispersing all the funds that are available with a modest amount of marketing. Additionally, the timing of the program is good. Midtown has long been one of the few "urban" neighborhoods in the city, albeit one with challenges, and is gradually becoming a more attractive place to live as the anchors have collaborated with local police to improve safety considerably and as retailing improves; several new restaurants opened in 2012 and early 2013, and a Whole Foods supermarket opened in 2013. The many new jobs recently relocated Downtown also stimulate demand, leading to a quicker market response than Live Midtown alone could produce. This is very encouraging.

Anchor institutions seeking to expand have the advantage that a great deal of well-located land is vacant or holds structures that everyone would like to see improved or replaced. Residential displacement will be minimal. Assembling large parcels is time-consuming and challenging (recall that HFHS spent several years acquiring property); City systems for selling publicly-held land are widely agreed to be poorly managed, and many such parcels lack clear title. However, acquisition prices are clearly lower than they would be in stronger markets, making projects somewhat more feasible financially. Raising capital in the current environment, both locally and nationally, is challenging, and financing packages typically have many components and are thus complex. Public funds are becoming harder to get given the City's fiscal problems and the State's announced intention to continue reducing, and to carefully target, its support for projects as State budget cuts become more painful. Gaining City approvals for building, always slow and unpredictable, becomes more so as layoffs leave departments short-staffed.

The weak market context also has implications for communities, and helps to account for the relatively modest response to the anchors' activities by community-based organizations. Significant population losses weaken community fabric and make effective community organizations more challenging to sustain. Many Detroit CDCs closed or reduced staff size during the financial crisis (as the CDC in Cass Corridor did), and operating support is scarce, making it hard to build up existing groups or establish new ones. HFHS representatives have made many statements about their desire to be sure that their planned activities benefit the community, and it is clear that this would be easier for them to do if they had a seasoned community partner, but they don't, and their capacity to foster increased capacity appears limited. On the other hand, three community organizations (Vanguard CDC, WGBC, and VPCDC) benefit directly from WCI and/or their relationships with the anchors, or have done so in the recent past. WGBC has strongly challenged HFHS despite the annual funding it receives from them.

Community residents, too, commonly see limited reason to engage. Some live in areas that are still unaffected by Live Midtown or anchor expansion. Students tend to move frequently, and other renters in the areas most affected may or may not see themselves as wanting to stay long term. Local property owners, both owner-occupants and owners of the area's many small rental properties, might, under other circumstances, be active in strong community organizations that would try to hold the anchors accountable if they saw the need. However, few are threatened directly by anchor expansion because most of it will occur on vacant or non-residential land. Owner-occupants are likely to benefit if Live Midtown succeeds. Housing values dropped dramatically in Detroit even though the region (and certainly the city) did not experience a pre-crisis housing price bubble, and many home owners have mortgages that are under water.[12] Rising prices, if they occur, would be good news for this group. Owners of rental properties clearly stand to benefit if their properties are in places where anchor employees (current or prospective) want to live. Finally, and perhaps most fundamentally, the collapse of Detroit's economic base, widespread housing abandonment and vacant land, the City's financial crisis, and cutbacks in City services are painful, common knowledge in the city's communities. Investments that hold the promise of countering the downward spiral are signs of hope. Even those who are committed to mitigating any negative impacts of new development on existing residents understand that this kind of new development is critical to Detroit's future.

Notes

1 The eight major thrusts are the anchor strategy, new housing and real estate development, land use policies and practices, business, education, finance, capacity and leadership, and data driven decision-making.

2 Midtown Detroit Inc. is a very well-regarded, high capacity organization that has a long history of working to improve Midtown. It continues its traditional activities, many of which have become part of WCI, and also administers the entire WCI; however, the MDI Board of Directors and the WCI Governing Council are very different.

3 The other two strategic components seek to increase the number of Detroit residents who work for the anchors and the share of anchor expenditures that flow to Detroit-based firms. Since they target the city as a whole rather than the neighborhood, they are not treated here.

4 These commitments are part of a package that includes a 15-year tax abatement, viewed as necessary to enable the new for-profit owner to operate the debt-laden, formerly-nonprofit medical facility successfully; DMC is a major health care provider for Detroiters, including many who are uninsured.

5 Each of the anchors contributes $200,000 annually to fund the program; these funds are matched by local foundations. The Hudson-Webber Foundation supported Live Midtown in its pilot year. The Kresge Foundation joined the partnership for years two through five.

6 These incentives are a bit different from those offered in the program's first year. Those guidelines indicated that purchasers could receive $20,000 – $25,000, although it appears that they actually received $20,000. New renters were initially offered $2,000; this was increased starting in year two, presumably because one goal of the program is to stimulate the development of additional housing stock, but lease renewals were more numerous than new rentals in the first round. Finally, the initial round included a modest commitment from the state housing finance agency to provide additional help to low- and moderate-income buyers; this funding was not well publicized and does not appear to have been used.

7 The census vacancy rate of 28 percent is the number of unoccupied housing units divided by the total number of housing units.

8 This excludes several types of dwellings that are not actively in the market, including those that are abandoned; foreclosed and held by banks, mortgage insurers, or the City; or in need of substantial rehabilitation.

9 The findings reported here use data taken from approved employee applications. The application includes limited information about the characteristics of the housing program recipients chose, but no demographic information other than household size.

10 While no information is available about the number of program-eligible staff at each of the anchors, this distribution of participants appears to roughly mirror the size of the institutions themselves.

11 Almost half of renters did not report the square footage of the unit they rented, so estimates based on this data element may be less reliable than the other estimates presented here.

12 This situation occurs when the mortgage amount owed to the lender exceeds the market value of the property.

References

Data Driven Detroit. (n.d.a) Available from http://www.cridata.org/GeoProfile.aspx?tmplt=D3&type=105&loc=2622000105001

Data Driven Detroit. (n.d.b). Available from http://datadrivendetroit.org/data-mapping/

Detroit Future City. (2012). Available from http://detroitworksproject.com/the-framework/

Greene, J. (2012, June 3). Henry Ford lands first tenant for health park in Midtown. *Crain's Detroit Business.* Available from http://www.crainsdetroit.com/article/20120603/SUB01/306039941/henry-ford-lands-first-tenant-for-health-park-in-midtown

Gregor, A. (2010, August 31). A Detroit district thrives by building on the past. *The New York Times.* Available at http://www.nytimes.com/2010/09/01/realestate/01detroit.html?_r=0

Henkel, K. & Aguilar, L. (2012, June 5). Rental unit demand grows near downtown. *The Detroit News.* Available at http://friedmannews.com/2012/06/05/rental-unit-demand-grows-near-downtown/

Kavanaugh, K. (2010, April 13). Henry Ford eyes neighborhood south for expansion, mixed-use redevelopment. *Model D.* Available at http://www.modeldmedia.com/devnews/hfhs041310.aspx

Koslowski, K. & Aguilar, L. (2010, March 20). It struggled to raise money to modernize its Detroit hospitals. *The Detroit News.* pp. A1, A10.

Lott, L. (2000). A study of the initiative to shut down Henry Ford Hospital's medical waste incinerator in Detroit, Michigan. Available from http://www.umich.edu/~snre492/Jones/henryford.htm

Thomas, J.M. (1997). *Redevelopment and race: Planning a finer city in postwar Detroit*. Baltimore: Johns Hopkins University Press.

Woodward Corridor Initiative Overview. (n.d.). Available from http://woodwardcorridorinitiative.org/index.php/woodward-corridor-initiative/

5

A DUAL NATURE

The Archdiocesan Community Development Corporation[1]

Bethany J. Welch, Aquinas Center

Introduction

New models for urban revitalization continue to emerge as the community development movement evolves. This chapter discusses a qualitative study that explored the formation and activities of a community development corporation (CDC) that is situated within the Archdiocese of Philadelphia, a part of the Roman Catholic Church in America. It begins with a look at how churches have historically served both anchoring and mediating functions in cities. The discussion then turns to the structure and nature of the archdiocesan CDC, particularly examining the challenge of applying a traditionally place-based model within an institutional setting that encompasses a five-county region. The viability and legitimacy of that model and its impact, or lack of impact, on the city's blighted neighborhoods are addressed. The chapter concludes with recommendations for engaging deeper citizen participation with the CDC and the codification and adoption of a formal process to secure and then adaptively reuse vacant church properties to advance urban revitalization.

Anchoring and Mediating Functions

The concept of the church as an "anchor" or serving in an "anchoring" function in the city is discussed in a wide array of past and present literature (Gamm, 1999; Kotkin & Speicher, 2003; Livezey, 2000; McGreevy, 1996; McKinney, 1971; Moberg, 1962; Price, 2000; Ramsay, 1998). There are two parts to this function. One is the description of a physical characteristic where the property, home to the operation of the institution, becomes central to community life.

Dolan (1985) depicts the Catholic parish as a space in which members both express their faith and find outlets for civic participation. Most recently, research during the post-welfare reform era has characterized the urban church as a vital stakeholder in distressed communities, chiefly due to church provision of community-based social services (Bane, Coffin & Thiemann, 2000; Dionne & Chen, 2001; Gornik, 2002; Owens & Smith, 2005; Smith, 2001; Wuthnow, 1998). This role of anchoring is a departure from the second category, which is a theoretical anchoring whereby the religious institution acts as a guardian of society. Moberg (1962) remarks, "By preserving and transmitting such values the church provides an anchorage for the social order, acting as a primary agency of stability and continuity" (p. 51).

The mediating quality of religious institutions is a foundational concept in research on civil society and religion (Wuthnow, 2006). Sociologists Peter Berger and Richard John Neuhaus (1977) defined the latent potential of alternative mediating structures in the 1970s against the backdrop of flawed government attempts to renew the urban core and the social unrest of cities facing discrimination and oppression. Berger and Neuhaus argued that families, churches, neighborhoods, and voluntary associations (nonprofit organizations) provided both a forum and a means to engage citizens while collectively buffering them from hardship.

During the height of industrialization and immigration, the Catholic Church in America was a major provider of education and social services to urban residents. Over time, it also became known for its national advocacy campaigns seeking to break the cycle of poverty in the United States. Like its secular or Protestant counterparts, Catholic-sponsored community development eventually emerged in the 1960s as a viable strategy to respond to declining inner city neighborhoods, shifting demographics and devolution in the public sector. For example, New Community Corporation in Newark, NJ, one of the largest CDCs in the country, was founded in 1967 by a parish priest desperate to assist the fragile local community that was devastated by race riots (Gittell & Wilder, 1999).

In urban studies literature, Brodie (2000) argues that it is the very place-oriented structures and identity of cities that makes them ideal agents to foster citizenship and democracy in an ever-globalized world. The neighborhood church engaged in community development furthers this aim. Many Catholic-sponsored community development corporations function in the tradition of secular, distinctively neighborhood-based CDCs. They provide deliberate action and activities designed to build the capacity of a specific geographic locale or self-identified collective, also termed "place-based approaches" (Bratt & Rohe, 2004; Green & Haines, 2002). The parish boundaries of a local church can serve to target revitalization efforts to a manageable geographic space and the common bonds of church membership can enhance the development of social capital (Silverman, 2001).

The research presented here suggests that the community development corporation founded by the Archdiocese of Philadelphia was intended to be a vehicle to continue the historic anchoring and mediating functions of urban parishes while also forging a new model for supporting communities in the face of persistent blight, concentrated poverty, and the aging of parish residents.

Methods

Grounded theory formed the theoretical framework for the study presented in part here, an inductive process in which empirical data are analyzed for the purpose of defining and understanding concepts in a specific context (Glaser & Strauss, 1967). The process of building grounded theory prompted an analysis of how ideology informs power, and power influences institutional decisions (Martin & Turner, 1986). Second, it prompted a discussion on issues of internal and external legitimacy, an area that was not previously considered in the framing of the study.

Exercising the grounded theory approach also yielded a working knowledge of the interaction between the archdiocese, the community development corporation, and the urban communities in which it functions. The reflexive nature of this approach gave permission to revise and construct explanations from the practices being observed and from the narratives of interviewees (Creswell, 1994). By first considering the narratives that operate within these entities, the author could give voice to emerging concepts and groupings of ideas that might not be captured in a news report, program evaluation, quantitative study on program capacity, or other document (Merriam, 1998). This person- and practice-based approach is equitable and activist-oriented, recognizing the inherent value of participant perspective (Williams & Demerath III, 1991; Yanow, 2000). Furthermore, this form facilitated the acquisition of meaning from human interaction, a practice that is valued in community development research (Hustedde & Ganowicz, 2002).

Data Collection and Analysis

Using both exploratory and descriptive processes, the study aimed to contribute to knowledge, policy, and practice relating to community development. Field research was conducted in the Philadelphia metro region and included interviews, document collection, and direct observation of the institution site, and participant observation in the CDC neighborhood projects was supplemented by newspaper accounts and archival records such as organizational charts, budgets, and census data.

Rubin and Rubin's *Qualitative Interviewing: The Art of Hearing Data* (1995) was the guide for the interview approach and coding method. Five interview groups were defined: community stakeholders, current CDC staff, current Archdiocesan staff, founding figures, and CDC board members. The interview protocol was adapted to address each group. For example, current CDC staff was asked how they came to be involved in the organization and were probed more directly for specific details relevant to the questions, such as number of units in a development. Community stakeholders were people who worked at other CDCs, provided funding to the archdiocesan CDC, or who led a group or parish in a neighborhood where the CDC is operational. The group of founding figures included former CDC staff, those who were involved in decision-making within the archdiocese at the time of the CDC founding, and community leaders present in meetings in which the formation of the CDC was discussed. Eighteen interviews were conducted from February to July 2007. The interviews were then transcribed and the transcripts utilized for coding and analysis.

Case Context

The religious pluralism present in William Penn's colonial Philadelphia made it possible for the Catholic Church to develop a strong foundation in the city (Nash, 2006). However, anti-Catholic and anti-immigrant sentiment perpetuated by nativists eventually affected Catholics seeking outlets for education, employment, socialization, and even banking (Bennett, 1988). Local parishes and diocesan entities soon became alternative institutions, mediating exclusion and oppression. Parochial schools provided a choice from the Protestant influenced public education system. Catholic-sponsored social services met other needs associated with immigration and assimilation, including language training, basic emergency care (food and shelter), and support for widows and orphans (Kotkin & Speicher, 2003).

By the 1950s, what Gerald Gamm (2001) refers to as the "exceptional" presence of the Archdiocese of Philadelphia was diminished by the effects of migration and de-industrialization. Like other northeast cities, Philadelphia experienced significant suburbanization (Kiley, 2004) that led to waves of parish and school closings. Nonetheless, during this same period, Catholic-sponsored social services and the Church's engagement in public affairs broadened. Multiple family service agencies were created across the Philadelphia region, offering everything from help with adoption to assistance for adjudicated youth to English as a Second Language classes. Voting and politics were of a particular concern to the Archdiocese of Philadelphia and of the national Catholic Church, especially as it related to the subject of abortion.

Despite demographic changes and recent scandals, the Archdiocese of Philadelphia remains one of the largest concentrations of Catholics in the country. It encompasses a five-county region that includes the city of

Philadelphia (whose boundaries comprise the county limits) and four less dense suburban counties. According to reports from the archdiocesan Office of Research and Planning, registered parishioners in this region of 4 million people numbered 1.16 million in 2010, representing approximately 400,000 households (Archdiocese of Philadelphia, 2011). In 2010, these households were served by 268 parishes and 367 priests and 52,000 students were enrolled in K–8th grade parochial schools.

The Church's community development corporation was founded in 2001 as the Office for Community Development of the Archdiocese of Philadelphia. It currently has an operating budget of $850,000 and employs six staff: a part time director, two project developers, a corridor manager and a corridor maintenance worker. The activities of the Office for Community Development are similar to those of secular, non-affiliate CDCs. Since its founding, the agency has developed new bricks-and-mortar projects, rehabilitated infill housing for low-income families to achieve homeownership, and coordinated economic development projects in a particularly blighted inner city commercial corridor. In addition, the Office for Community Development adapted a former boys' high school for low income senior housing in one urban neighborhood, has initiated a similar project in a former parochial school, and is in discussions with parishes throughout the region about schools, convents, rectories, and worship spaces that have been closed.

Much like other CDCs, funding for these projects has come from city, state, federal government grants or tax credits, private donors and foundations, corporate partners, and revenue generating programs or projects (such as developer's fees, program fees, etc.). However, in the case of the Office for Community Development, it has also leveraged Catholic Charities and the Catholic Campaign for Human Development resources. Catholic Charities funding is generated by an annual archdiocesan appeal in each local parish. The funds are then allocated to the Church's central office to distribute to social service and charitable programs as needed. The Catholic Campaign for Human Development is a national fundraising initiative whose monies are designed to be distributed to agencies that work at the grassroots level. This Campaign is largely concerned with enhancing the advocacy skills of marginalized persons.

Discussion

The case study research suggests that the Office for Community Development of the Archdiocese of Philadelphia is unique in its structure as both a community-based organization and a unit of the authority of the regional Catholic Church. The resulting dual nature has implications for functionality, extending to capacity and neighborhood impact. Institutionalization of community development activities has brought perceived credibility, but the organization struggles with how to resolve issues of internal and external legitimacy. The following discussion addresses each of these findings in greater detail and concludes with two key recommendations that suggest implications for community development research and practice.

Dual Nature and Functionality

When comparing the Office for Community Development of the Archdiocese of Philadelphia with other community development corporations, the first major difference that stands out is the dual relationship between the parent institution and the subsidiary or affiliate organization. The Office is one of three other agencies organized under what is called the Secretariat for Catholic Human Services, including Catholic Social Services (CSS), Catholic Health Care Services, and Nutritional Development Services (NDS). Comparatively, the Office for Community Development functions on a different scale than these other entities. For example, CSS posted revenue of $114 million in 2010, 82 percent coming from government contracting for programs like out of school time care, adoption, and shelter facilities for homeless persons (CSS, Annual Report, 2011). Catholic Health Care Services operates six skilled nursing homes and an array of other services and properties for the elderly and infirm. It reported over 500,000 resident days in 2010 and net revenue of $127 million (CSS, Annual Report, 2011). Nutritional Development Services (2011) provides school lunches and other government-supported meals to over 100,000 unduplicated persons in the archdiocese's five-county service area (www.ndsarch.org).

According to staff interviewed for the study, the ability of the Office for Community Development to receive the developers' fees for bricks-and-mortar projects is intrinsically complicated by these relationships. In its current form, the CDC functions as a de facto developer with some of the financing for staff positions being channeled or "sub-granted" through these other larger agencies of the archdiocese. Maintaining a steady stream of income could ease dependency on archdiocesan charitable funding and allow for greater staffing capacity to engage local residents in each of the communities where the projects are located.

The dual nature of the archdiocesan CDC is perhaps most obvious in the governance structure where the head of Catholic Human Services is also the president of the board of directors of the Office for Community Development. As a result, the community development corporation is accountable to the larger regional "parent" institution and its stakeholders, which include clerical authorities and professional lay staff as well as donors and funders. This configuration is markedly different than a board of neighborhood residents and leaders, something more typical of a traditional place-based CDC created to empower local residents.

As standard practice, the Office partners their development projects with the local Catholic parish, although the resulting housing units and programming are not restricted to Catholics. The parish partnerships often assure that local community organizing affiliates and neighborhood coalitions are courted in the development planning, ultimately resulting in their support for the projects. In the words of one Office for Community Development staff member, "Many CDCs have to work to establish a community base. One of our biggest advantages is that we are part of an organization that already has a monumental base."

The value of the local parish as a base of community support was continually recognized in the study interviews as one of the strongest assets of the Office for Community Development. This built-in community can gather together at the church structure for planning meetings like a design charrette or for financial literacy programming without the need to pay for space. Priests can publicize programming in each Mass and through parish bulletins. Two priests who served in parishes where the archdiocesan CDC has developed projects described this process in action. To them, the partnership makes sense. It helps the Office advertise its programs while ensuring that their parishioners have access to opportunities that will improve the quality of life in their homes and neighborhoods.

The "institutional footholds" in Philadelphia are the backdrop to the new work and on occasion are also the resources through which the work is pursued. In many cases, these were the same entities that once anchored or rooted the Roman Catholic Church in urban neighborhoods. For example, in one target neighborhood, the parish leadership team in conjunction with an Alinksy style community organizing affiliate contributed significantly to the process of developing the transitional housing facility and convening support for the addition of a community center to that project. In another neighborhood, it was the local parish priests who approached the archdiocese after their parishioners expressed interest in senior housing that would allow residents to age in place. The Office for Community Development was tasked with responding to their request. As a result, a closed Catholic high school in their community was adapted for senior housing. In this way, an institutional foothold continued as a conduit for service delivery, albeit in a different form. Adaptive reuse of properties for senior housing is currently the most popular, and fundable, strategy the CDC is using in a campaign for "Preserving Parish Neighborhoods."

Interviews with external stakeholders yielded a good deal of discussion of how to engage both parishioners and non-Catholic community members in the actual work of the Office for Community Development. The most commonly held assertion, among both internal and external stakeholders, was that because this CDC does not serve a specific geographic target area, it would be difficult to define who the community constituency would be. Although the Office for Community Development has (to date) conducted most of its programming in North Philadelphia, it did develop a low-income senior housing project in South Philadelphia and is currently considering projects in other counties within its borders. This expansive geographic scope seemed to most interviewees to render it impossible to distinguish how a resident would represent the area on the board. A staff member pointed out:

> As you can see, we are kind of unique in that most community development corporations would select an area bounded by certain streets, north, south, east and west, and then work in that area. We have expanded, if you will, our work but have functioned differently. We have remained dynamic to function that way.

Perhaps in contrast to the views of external stakeholders and even staff, clergy interviewed for this study described the relationship between the archdiocese and the Office for Community Development as a natural choice for organizational form because of the Church's long history of hierarchical structure. An archdiocesan staff clergy described this arrangement as providing for an "economy of resources and energies." He went on to liken the role of the archdiocese in the relationship to an airport control tower. "There is a central control tower that could help make sure the individual flights or individual actions or individual motions are not going to collide, but are rather going to be in harmony and in tandem with each other." He continued with this caution that the current arrangement could result in dissonance:

> The tension with all that is always to make sure that we don't, by going into the tower to control things, lose connection with the people on the ground and the needs on the ground, and the day-by-day activities, and the minute-by-minute activities that need to be incorporated into major decisions.

The clergyman's response illustrates the presence of "institutional isomorphism" discussed by DiMaggio and Powell (1983). In their work, they examine the ways in which organizations relate to each other. One of their predictors of future organizational change is the degree to which one organization depends on the other. The stronger that bond, the greater the likelihood that the dependent organization will become more like the independent organization in "structure, climate and behavioral focus" (p. 154). In the case of the Office for Community Development, the CDC is heavily reliant on the structure, authority, and resources of the parent institution, that is, the central church authority for the region. Embodiment of institutional culture by staff, board members, and archdiocesan leadership leads to increasing similarities between the norms of the CDC and those of the archdiocese.

Institutionalization and Legitimacy

In the early stages of the CDC's formation, there was desire to make the most of any good will that the initiative might engender with the public due to a growing distrust of Catholic leadership. Securing control of the messaging around the Office for Community Development ensured that the work was associated with the larger parent institution, a practice common when processes are implemented to create a new normal (McMullen, 1994). In this case, the emerging reality was one of positive action by the central church authority to benefit the people of the city. When asked about institutionalizing the community development function that the archdiocese undertook at the start of the 21st century, one archdiocesan leader said:

> Think about what was going on in the Church at the time; this [the formation of the CDC] was a potential win-win for everyone. For the neighborhood, for the city, and importantly, for the Church. There wasn't a lot of good news coming out of the archdiocesan offices at the time. Clergy sexual abuse. Nationally there wasn't a lot of good news. One of the areas in looking back we could always say is that we have a good track record as a church in how we serve the community—social services, human services.

This practice, of shaping the public message, is what Kowalewski (1993) describes as "impression management." His research on the Catholic Church's attempts to coordinate communication at the onset of the clergy abuse scandal situates the control as a way to preserve the identity of Catholics in a constantly changing environment. Ongoing coverage of the CDC's projects has been promoted consistently, and throughout the stages of planning and construction, by the archdiocesan communications office and coordinated with the archdiocesan weekly newspaper. Reinforcing the organizational identity of the archdiocesan community development corporation seems to have achieved the desired result. The Office has generated numerous regional news stories since its inception in 2001. National Catholic press has covered project developments and the funding relationships between the CDC and private investment through tax credits.

Much of the discussion on legitimacy came from the portion of interviews in which the subjects were asked about the rationale for institutionalizing the community development function (instead of leaving it up to local parishes or social services), the organization's relationship to the archdiocese, the impact of the Office for Community Development on Philadelphia neighborhoods, and the goals and vision for the Office in the years to come. There was agreement that institutionalizing the community development function had resulted in credibility, power, resources, and visibility. The result of institutionalization was an organization that could do work that parishes could not, even though they were aware of the need. There was no doubt in the interviewees' minds, whether internal or external stakeholders, that there are valuable aspects of being affiliated with the archdiocese. There was almost a mythic sensibility around this area.

Interviewees identified responsiveness and flexibility as considered strengths of the Office for Community Development, when contrasted with the other agencies of the Archdiocese in Philadelphia. Many of the archdiocese's social programs are focused on specific service populations in institutionalized care settings (health care, adjudicated youth, disabilities, seniors). Thus, the CDC stood out to those interviewed as a dynamic agency, one that can adapt more quickly and perhaps even more liberally to changing demographics, funding streams, and private investment trends.

In assessing how the organizational model or nature affects functionality, the issue of legitimacy remained preeminent. Some of those interviewed thought that coupling a grassroots type organization with a central institution yielded greater objectivity. A local Catholic priest in one of the target communities believed a parish might be myopic in its focus, whereas the archdiocesan CDC can achieve more balanced outcomes for a greater measure of the population. In reference to a united plan for community development across the parish campus, the priest suggested, "I think you can do that if you are official, if you are a CDC, if you have the whole archdiocese behind you, and you are not an individual parish that can be perceived as sinking in its own self-interest."

For external observers, it appears that the relationship is valuable for the resources and visibility it must bring. There was a perception from the outside of unlimited resources, unlimited potential, and unlimited staffing. Yet the CDC staff disagreed. They may receive local and state funding more quickly because of their reputation as part of this large institution, but they still must execute the projects within the scope of their small staff. Moreover, internal stakeholders (staff and board) are expected to leverage the parent/subsidiary relationship for influence, but not to exploit what the parent institution sees as tight resources that must be shared with other agencies and initiatives under the umbrella of the archdiocese. These other priorities include Catholic education, sacramental formation activities, and care for elderly clergy, etc.

Addressing Vacant Church Property through Adaptive Reuse

While internal stakeholders interviewed for the study focused on the legitimacy of the CDC within the larger institutional structure of the Archdiocese of Philadelphia, the external stakeholders were most interested in what the CDC might do about the increasing roster of vacant properties the Church accumulated each time a parish, school, convent, or rectory closed. Nationally, blighted buildings are one of the foremost concerns facing both urban planners and community residents. Adaptive reuse—the reinvention of a space for a use other than its original purpose—is an increasingly popular practice, particularly in the urban context where the infrastructure is shifting and changing (Cantell, 2005). Repurposing is also seen as a green or environmentally friendly practice (Bullen & Love, 2009; Langston, Wong, Hui & Shen, 2008).

Rather than building new where fresh resources are expended and new environmental impacts are realized, adaptive reuse has resurrected blighted and forgotten spaces (National Trust for Historic Preservation and Partners for Sacred Spaces, 2009). For example, residential and commercial space has been carved out of many former industrial properties (Duckworth, 2010); in other instances, former parochial schools now house charter schools or apartments (Welch, 2009). The downside to adaptive reuse is that it can be expensive and tedious. In the age of modern construction, it can often be less costly and faster to build new (Kostelni, 2006).

One defining decision within the institutional structure seemed to position the CDC to pursue revitalization through adaptive reuse. In 2002, the Archdiocese of Philadelphia's Tenth Synod of Bishops made a decision that offered the Office for Community Development the right of first refusal for vacant church property (Tenth Synod, 2002a,b). However, only two properties have been secured and only one has been successfully redeveloped in the years since the decision.

While the Synod expressed the desire for the archdiocese to utilize properties in this way, the requisite next steps to create a formal or codified process for pursuing adaptive reuse did not take place. According to those interviewed, including CDC staff and external stakeholders with knowledge of the internal politics, support for carrying out the actual community development activities associated with the Synod's decision ended with the retirement of the Cardinal whose leadership initiated the formation of the Office. More recently, the political will to codify the practice and operationalize the Synod's decision seems to have been overshadowed by ongoing clergy abuse trials and parochial school closings. This, ironically, will produce an even broader array of available properties.

Conclusions

Deepen Citizen Participation to Increase Accountability and Effectiveness

There is a rich body of work on the contributions of neighborhood residents in community development planning and practice (Manzo & Perkins, 2006) as well as the role citizen participation plays in fostering self-efficacy and local control (Glickman & Servon, 1998; Silverman, 2005). The Office for Community Development has relied on parishes in the project neighborhoods to host planning meetings and design charettes, cultivate good will among other neighbors for zoning changes, and be a base of recruitment for the eventual residents or users of the properties. These activities represent important "instrumental participation" at one end of the Citizen Participation Continuum described by Silverman (2005). Wouldn't a role in governance be the next logical step to institutionalizing community development while at the same time result in greater grassroots participation?

A more intentional, activist relationship between parishes and neighborhoods to the Office for Community Development could make the work of the organization more relevant to a greater number of city residents and move it beyond public relations to truly collaborative or participatory community building. Solidifying these attributes could also reap benefits in terms of new sources of funding and partnerships that place a value on this kind of accountability. Furthermore, the participation of community members, such as that encouraged by other CDC models, could diversify the cultural capacity and social capital available to the staff when determining project goals and locations.

Embrace the Dual Nature to Advance Adaptive Reuse

The potential for adaptive reuse of dozens and dozens of vacant church properties is the most provocative idea to emerge from this case study. Interview after interview with internal stakeholders revealed a desire to see the Church present and active in neighborhoods while external stakeholders expressed concern about the continual closure of buildings throughout the region, most especially in already blighted neighborhoods. Securing formal access to the vacant properties is a first step to operationalizing this idea, something that could be facilitated by the centralized, hierarchical nature of the parent institution. Parishes must report annually on the status of their facilities and this information could be mined more aggressively to create a platform for reuse projects.

New technology, such as sustainability index software or SINDEX, can guide communities and experts in a cost-benefit analysis when weighing the merits and challenges of vacant properties for adaptive reuse (Langston et al., 2008). While a smaller CDC might not have the resources or expertise to handle this kind of technology, a larger institution with many multi-million dollar subsidiaries could share the responsibility for purchasing and maintaining the tools. Consideration must also be given to the scope of the reuse. Will it be a full-scale preservation of a historic property? Or, as is the case with the reuse of some church properties, does the shell remain intact while the interior is altered? These decisions become part of a larger dialogue around place making and can engage the community losing the space (such as the parishioners of a closed church), the residents who live in the geographic area, and perhaps even future or prospective users of the redefined space (Clark, 2007). This possibility further reinforces the need for participation that ultimately could lead to inter-group perception of legitimacy, something that the archdiocese and its parishes will require to weather the current climate.

Note

1 This chapter was originally published in the journal *Community Development*, 43(4): 251–263.

References

Archdiocese of Philadelphia. (2011). Summary of data for Archdiocese of Philadelphia 2007– 2011. Retrieved from http://archphila.org/pastplan/Rtp1/A.pdf

Bane, M.J., Coffin, B. & Thiemann, R. (Eds.). (2000). *Who will provide? The changing role of religion in American social welfare*. Boulder: Westview Press.

Bennett, D.H. (1988). *The party of fear: From nativist movements to the new right in American history*. Chapel Hill: The University of North Carolina Press.

Berger, P.L. & Neuhaus, R.J. (1977). *To empower people: The role of mediating structures in public policy*. Washington, DC: American Enterprise Institute.

Bratt, R.G. & Rohe, W. (2004). Organizational changes among CDCs: Assessing the impacts and navigating the challenges. *Journal of Urban Affairs*, 26, 197–220.

Brodie, J. (2000). Imagining democratic urban citizenship. In E.F. Isin (Ed.), *Democracy, citizenship and the global city* (pp. 110–128). London: Routledge.

Bullen, P. & Love, P.D. (2009). Residential regeneration and adaptive reuse: Learning from the experiences of Los Angeles, *Structural Survey*, 27, 351–360.

Cantell, S. (2005). The adaptive reuse of historic industrial buildings: Regulation barriers, best practices and case studies (Masters thesis). Retrieved from http://historicbellingham.org/ documents_reports_maps/adaptive_reuse.pdf

Catholic Social Services. (2011). Annual report, Philadelphia, PA. Retrieved December 16, 2011, from http://www.catholicsocialservicesphilly.org/documents/css_annual_report_2010. pdf

Clark, J. (2007). 'This Special Shell': The church building and the embodiment of memory. *Journal of Religious History*, 31(1), 59–77.

Creswell, J. (1994). Research design: *Qualitative and quantitative approaches*. London: Sage.

DiMaggio, P. & Powell, W. (1983). The iron cage revisited: Institutional isomorphism and collective rationality in organizational fields. *American Sociological Review*, 48, 147–160.

Dionne, E.J. & Chen, M.H. (2001). *Sacred places, civic purposes: Should government help faith-based charity?* Washington, DC: Brookings Institution.

Dolan, J. (1985). *The American Catholic experience*. Garden City: Doubleday.

Duckworth, L.C. (2010). Adaptive reuse of former catholic churches as a community asset (Masters thesis). Retrieved from http://scholarworks.umass.edu/cgi/viewcontent.cgi?article¼1001&context¼larp_ms_projects

Gamm, G. (1999). *Urban exodus: Why the Jews left Boston and the Catholics stayed*. Boston: Harvard University Press.

Gamm, G. (2001). The way things used to be in American cities: Jews, Protestants, and the erosion of Catholic exceptionalism, 1950–2000. In A. Walsh (Ed.), *Can charitable choice work? Covering religion's impact or urban affairs and social services* (pp. 39–55). Hartford: The Leonard E. Greenberg Center for the Study of Religion in Public Life.

Gittell, R. & Wilder, M. (1999). Community development corporations: Critical factors that influence success. *Journal of Urban Affairs*, 21, 341–362.

Glaser, B.G. & Strauss, A.L. (1967). *The discovery of grounded theory: Strategies for qualitative research*. New York: Aldine Publishing.

Glickman, N. & Servon, L. (1998). More than brick and sticks: Five components of community development corporation capacity. *Housing Policy Debate*, 9, 497–539.

Gornik, M.R. (2002). *To live in peace: Biblical faith in the changing inner city*. Grand Rapids: William B. Eerdmans.

Green, G. & Haines, A. (2002). *Asset building and community development*. Thousand Oaks: Sage Publications.

Hustedde, R.J. & Ganowicz, J. (2002). The basics: What's essential about theory for community development practice? *Community Development*, 33(1), 1–30.

Kiley, C.J. (2004). Convert! The adaptive reuse of churches (Masters thesis). Retrieved from http://dspace.mit.edu/bitstream/handle/1721.1/35692/56409883.pdf?sequence¼1

Kostelni, N. (2006). Charter schools take root and real estate deals flower, *Philadelphia Business Journal*. Retrieved from http://www.bizjournals.com/philadelphia/stories/2006/ 10/02/story3.html?page¼all

Kotkin, J. & Speicher, K. (2003). God and the city, *The American Enterprise*, October/November, 34–39.

Kowalewski, M.R. (1993). Firmness and accommodation: Impression management in institutional Roman Catholicism, *Sociology of Religion*, 54, 207–217.

Langston, C., Wong, F.K.W., Hui, E. & Shen, L.Y. (2008). Strategic assessment of building adaptive reuse opportunities in Hong Kong. *Building and Environment*, 43, 1709–1718.

Livezey, L. (2000). *Faith in the city: Public religion and urban transformation*. New York: New York University Press.

Manzo, L. & Perkins, D. (2006). Finding common ground: The importance of place attachment to community participation and planning. *Journal of Planning Literature*, 20, 335–350.

Martin, P.Y. & Turner, B.A. (1986). Grounded theory and organizational research. *The Journal of Applied Behavioral Science*, 22, 141–157.

McGreevy, J. (1996). Parish Boundaries: *The Catholic encounter with race in the twentieth-century urban north*. Chicago: University of Chicago Press.

McKinney, R.I. (1971). The black church: Its development and present impact. *The Harvard Theological Review*, 64, 452–481.

McMullen, M. (1994). Religious polities as institutions. *Social Forces*, 73, 709–728.

Merriam, S.B. (1998). *Qualitative research and case studies applications in education*. San Francisco: Jossey-Bass.

Moberg, D.O. (1962). *The Church as a social institution: The sociology of American religion*. Englewood Cliffs: Prentice Hall.

Nash, G.A. (2006). *First city: Philadelphia and the forging of historical memory*. Philadelphia, University of Pennsylvania Press.

National Trust for Historic Preservation and Partners for Sacred Spaces. (2009): http://www.preservationnation.org/issues/historic-houses-of-worship/case-studies.html

Nutritional Development Services. (2011). Philadelphia, PA. Retrieved November 6, 2011, from www.ndsarch.org

Owens, M.L. & Smith, R.D. (2005). Congregations in low-income neighborhoods and the implications for social welfare policy research. *Nonprofit and Voluntary Sector Quarterly*, 34, 316–339.

Price, M.J. (2000). Place, race, and history: The social mission of downtown churches. In L.W. Livezey (Ed.), *Public religion and urban transformation: Faith in the city* (pp. 57–81). New York: New York University Press.

Ramsay, M. (1998). Redeeming the city: Exploring the relationship between church and metropolis. *Urban Affairs Review*, 33, 595–626.

Rubin, H.J. & Rubin, I. (1995). *Qualitative interviewing: The art of hearing data*. Thousand Oaks: Sage Publications.

Silverman, R.M. (2001). CDCs and charitable organizations in the urban south: Mobilizing social capital based on race and religion for neighborhood revitalization. *Journal of Contemporary Ethnography*, 30, 240–268.

Silverman, R.M. (2005). Caught in the middle: Community development corporations (CDCs) and the conflict between grassroots and instrumental forms of citizen participation. *Community Development*, 36, 35–51.

Smith, D. (2001). Churches and the urban poor: Interaction and social distance. *Sociology of Religion*, 62, 301–313.

Tenth Synod of the Archdiocese of Philadelphia. (2002a). Decrees of the Tenth Synod of the Archdiocese of Philadelphia. Philadelphia: Archdiocese of Philadelphia.

Tenth Synod of the Archdiocese of Philadelphia. (2002b). Glossary of the Tenth Synod of the Archdiocese of Philadelphia. Philadelphia: Archdiocese of Philadelphia.

Welch, B. (2009). Sustainable urban infrastructure: How feasible is the adaptive reuse of parochial schools to house charter schools? Paper presented at the 39th annual meeting of the Urban Affairs Association, Chicago, IL.

Williams, R. & Demerath, N. III. (1991). Religion and political process in an American city. *American Sociological Review*, 56 (August), 417–431.

Wuthnow, R. (1998). *Loose connections: Joining together America's fragmented communities*. Cambridge: Harvard University Press.

Wuthnow, R. (2006). *Saving America? Faith-based services and the future of civil society*. Princeton, NJ: Princeton University Press.

Yanow, D. (2000). *Conducting interpretive policy analysis*. Newbury Park, CA: Sage.

6

ANCHOR INSTITUTIONS AND DISENFRANCHISED COMMUNITIES

Lessons for DHS and St. Elizabeths

Margaret Cowell, Virginia Tech
Heike Mayer, University of Bern

Introduction

The District of Columbia's Ward 8 neighborhood is one of the most underserved areas in the entire Washington region. For decades its residents have seen below-average employment, educational attainment, and household incomes. Virtually cut off from the economic gains that the broader region has seen in recent years, Ward 8 has suffered greatly with very few employment opportunities and very few amenities. Today, the neighborhood stands at an important juncture; the area will soon become home to the headquarters of the United States Department of Homeland Security (DHS), one of the fastest growing organizations within the federal government. This new anchor institution, set to open in 2014 on Ward 8's St. Elizabeths campus, will undoubtedly affect the residents in the surrounding neighborhood. The extent to which these effects are positive will be determined, in part, by plans being put into place today.

As part of a research team exploring the potential for an innovation hub for one half of the St. Elizabeths campus, we have been tasked with researching the broader homeland security economy and its implications for the Washington region, the District of Columbia, and, most importantly, for Ward 8. What follows below is an exploration of the DHS economy, the Ward 8 community economy, and the intersection of the two. We draw upon other anchor institution examples from Baltimore, Cleveland, and Danville to understand how local and federal leaders may better incorporate the surrounding community in the development process and foster sustained and mutually beneficial relationships thereafter.

Anchor Institutions

From Ft. Bentonville, AR to Dartmouth, NH, communities across the nation have long had intense and complicated relationships with their economic anchors. Many local economies are inextricably tied to a single corporation, a factory, a public sector outpost, an educational institution, a military base, or some other important entity. Such anchor institutions are defined as "large organizations, typically educational, medical or cultural, that are deeply rooted in their local geographies and that play an integral role in the local economy" (ICIC, 2010). Traditional anchor institutions include schools, universities, hospitals, government facilities, utilities, corporations, large churches, sports and entertainment facilities, and other cultural facilities.

The case is often made that anchor institutions are "magnets for economic development" from both direct and indirect sources (Birch, 2007). The direct benefits may be derived from the revenue that anchor institutions generate as a community's largest employer (Harkavy & Zuckerman, 1999), from their landholdings (Appleseed Inc., 2003), and by their procurement of goods and services from the local community (Alperovitz et al., 2009). Indirect benefits may be derived from the attraction of knowledge workers and their families (Fulbright-Anderson et al., 2001), workforce development programs (Nelson & Wolf-Powers, 2010), and the purchase of goods and services in the surrounding area by residents and non-residents (Yates, 2009). These indirect and direct gains can have substantial effects on the surrounding community by drawing resources in from outside of the region, procuring goods and services from the local community, and training the local workforce (ICIC, 2010).

The motivations of anchor institutions may differ dramatically from one case to the next. While many of these institutions choose to locate where profits may be maximized or output increased, others choose or remain committed to locations based on the perceived needs of the community, historical associations, or financial incentives. A museum may be wedded to a certain location because of a unique local history and a coast guard facility may be located near an important port or waterway. In both cases the institution is inherently anchored in the community, thereby becoming an important player in the local economy.

In recent years, many of these institutions have also been seen as important players in the revitalization of key urban areas, including previously abandoned or underutilized spaces and neighborhoods (Hahn et al., 2003). In light of economic restructuring, widespread disinvestment, and suburban outmigration, some communities have looked to anchor institutions to help reverse these trends or lessen their effects (McKee, 2010). Exemplary anchor institution cases are noted for their contributions to revitalization in their home communities and for the symbiotic relationships that sometimes develop between anchor and community (Work Foundation, 2010; DeVol et al., 2003; Appleseed Inc., 2003).

Anchor institutions, however, do not generally invest for purely altruistic reasons; many invest because improving their own communities also has some positive effect on their own institution. Improvements they make in the surrounding community may help them compete for the best employees, students, patients, and patrons. As ICIC has noted, "their ability to attract the best resources hinges not only on their own health but also on the health of their surrounding communities" (ICIC 2010). While such close connections often lead to positive economic investment that is rooted in the local economy, it can also mean that a community is tied to the economic fate of that anchor and its local partners for better *or* worse. Just as a team may rely too heavily on their star player, there are a myriad of risks involved when a community also puts all its eggs in one proverbial basket.

Along with the known risks of a highly specialized economic base, reliance on anchor institutions can also put communities at risk in a number of other ways. In general, the partnership between a community and its anchor institution is positive, with the anchor acting as a key driver of economic development and community revitalization (Cisneros, 1995; ICIC, 2010). But in some instances that relationship is more complicated or marred by strained relationships or exploitative practices (McKee, 2010). Fulbright-Anderson et al. (2001) found that while anchor institutions can contribute much in the way of physical and social changes within a neighborhood or community, they also sometimes cause conflict and garner ill will. Strained relationships may arise when anchor institution revitalization efforts collide with the interests of nearby residents, who often live in distressed and oppressed neighborhoods (Cromwell et al., 2005; Lowe, 2008). Though much has been said about individual anchor institutions and their revitalization efforts in general, we still know little about what makes for a successful relationship between anchor institutions and historically disenfranchised communities like the one surrounding the St. Elizabeths campus.

Increasing our understanding of what determines the nature of these relationships between anchors and host communities is at the forefront of scholarly pursuits in the economic and community development fields and is a primary motivation for this particular case study (CEOs for Cities, 2007). In this research, we ask what can we learn from other cases so that local and federal leaders may better incorporate the community in the St. Elizabeths development process and foster sustained and mutually beneficial relationships in the future. First we begin with an introduction to the case.

St. Elizabeths

In 2010, the Department of Homeland Security (DHS) began a multi-billion dollar campaign to consolidate the majority of their Washington-area operations

FIGURE 6.1 Washington, DC and St. Elizabeths (source: National Capital Planning Commission, The DHS Consolidation at St. Elizabeths Master Plan Amendment)

on one campus in the District of Columbia (Figure 6.1). The campus, known as St. Elizabeths, is located in the southeast quadrant of DC and overlooks the Potomac and Anacostia Rivers. The St. Elizabeths campus is located in Ward 8, one of the most impoverished sections of the District. The campus includes dozens of historic buildings (many in disrepair) that once housed the first federal psychiatric hospital in the United States. Intersected by Martin Luther King Boulevard, St. Elizabeths includes two campuses: the West Campus (182 acres), which is owned by the Federal Government and the East Campus (118 acres), which is owned by the District of Columbia (Figure 6.2). Current plans call for DHS facilities to occupy the majority of the West Campus and a series of commercial, education, residential, and civic developments on the East Campus.

The goals of this consolidation effort are numerous. First and foremost, DHS leaders see this as an important opportunity to streamline their operations and reduce the number of occupied buildings, which presently total 70 buildings in 46 locations across the Washington, DC region. Former DHS Undersecretary for Management Elaine Duke, notes that "extreme dispersion imposes significant inefficiencies in our daily operations that can be magnified considerably at the

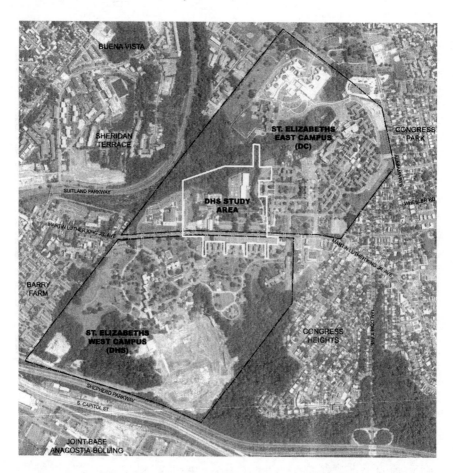

FIGURE 6.2 St. Elizabeths Facility, East and West Campuses (source: National Capital Planning Commission, The DHS Consolidation at St. Elizabeths Master Plan Amendment)

most important moments...".[1] Consolidation at the St. Elizabeths campus is expected to increase efficiencies, improve communication, and contribute to an emerging "One DHS" culture to optimize department-wide prevention, response and recovery capabilities.

Another important goal of this consolidation effort is the adaptive reuse of a historic mental health facility and its spacious grounds. The challenge in doing this is that many of the buildings on both the East and West Campuses have been neglected over the last few decades. With the exception of one functioning mental health hospital on the East Campus, the majority of the buildings have been abandoned and boarded up for mothballing purposes. In 2002, the National Trust for Historic Preservation listed the campus as one

TABLE 6.1 Selected demographic characteristics, Washington Metro Area, DC, and Wards 7 & 8, 2010

	MSA	DC	Wards 7 & 8
Population	5,332,297	588,433	143,649
Civilian labor force	2,978,188	321,466	60,488
Employed	2,818,975	291,830	49,447
Percent unemployed	5.3%	9.2%	18.3%
Average income			
Average	$108,302	$90,580	$43,480
Median	$84,424	$56,519	$32,898
Educational attainment			
High school grad. or greater	89.6%	85.5%	79.9%
Bachelor's degree or higher	46.7%	47.2%	13.8%

Source: US Census Bureau, ACS

of America's 11 Most Endangered Places. Nevertheless, both the district and federal governments are eager to see this campus space put to good use. The opportunity to redevelop such a large plot of land and such a wealth of historic structures does not come often. As Mayor Vincent Gray has often noted, this St. Elizabeths redevelopment is a "once-in-a-lifetime opportunity"[2] for the District of Columbia.

A final goal, and one that is at the center of this particular study, is to leverage this investment in DHS as an anchor institution to create an innovation hub on the East Campus of St. Elizabeths. As part of this goal, we are working to devise an innovation strategy that will promote entrepreneurship, workforce development, and education in order to increase opportunities for the surrounding community and for the region as a whole. One of the greatest obstacles to achieving this goal is the existing disconnect between the DHS economy and the community economy of southeast DC. With a median income in Wards 7 and 8 ($32,898)[3] that is less than 60 percent of the District's median income ($56,519) and an unemployment rate of 18.3 percent as compared with 9.2 percent for the District as a whole, there are significant challenges in bridging this divide (see Table 6.1). These socio-demographic differences, coupled with the physical needs of a high-security facility in a dense urban area, present a formidable challenge for planners and government officials. Despite such disheartening figures and circumstances, the District government and DHS remain committed to the idea that this impending development can help link residents and local businesses to opportunities at St. Elizabeths.

Research Design

In an effort to make sure that these goals translate into planning and policy developments, we have been involved in a multi-year study to develop an innovation strategy for the St. Elizabeths campus and surrounding community. As part of our exploration, we have utilized data from the federal government, including the Federal Procurement Data System, and our own qualitative collection methods to better understand the DHS economy and its relationship with Ward 8, the District and the Washington, DC metropolitan region. In so doing, we point to the obvious need to look to other anchor institution examples for lessons on how to better leverage investments in this type of underrepresented community.

To develop an innovation strategy for St. Elizabeths, we turned to a variety of sources. Our local analysis is based on Department of Homeland Security documents, public documents, news reports, detailed interviews with DHS officials, focus groups with key regional and local leaders, and stakeholder engagement meetings. The interviews included conversations with approximately ten DHS leaders from various departments, including Science and Technology, Private Sector, University Engagement, Office of Policy, and the Office of Employment Services. The interviews followed a standard set of questions intended to elicit open-ended responses. Interviews ranged from approximately 60 to 90 minutes each.

Approximately 90 leaders from the public and private sector participated in a total of three focus groups. These focus groups included officials and leaders working in the fields of education, innovative technologies, and federal government contracting. The focus groups also followed a standard protocol intended to elicit open-ended responses from participants. These focus groups lasted approximately two hours each. Representatives from key regional organizations, including private sector contractors, venture capitalists, university researchers, and development corporations were included in these discussions.

Three stakeholder engagement meetings were designed to solicit feedback from local representatives working within Ward 8 in the areas of education, small business development, and workforce development. Each meeting lasted approximately two hours and followed a pre-determined set of questions designed to obtain feedback and recommendations on early research and planning efforts. Participants included local business owners, social service providers, educational service providers, school principals, workforce training program providers, and local government officials.

From the aforementioned data sources we were then able to identify opportunities related to DHS consolidation and its existence as an anchor institution emerging in three key areas. These areas (which will be discussed in the findings section below) include contracting and procurement; education;

and workforce development. Based on these emerging opportunities, we then identified ten anchor institution developments[4] with comparable physical and programmatic elements. This case study stage of the research involved secondary data analysis of plans, performance documents, and other relevant information. From these ten, we focused here on three specific cases that not only relate to these emerging opportunities but also operate within similarly disenfranchised communities. Below we present the key findings of our analysis and then discuss how lessons from other anchor institution examples might better inform the planning and implementation process for an innovation hub at St. Elizabeths.

Findings

In today's world of rapid commercialization and technology development, the Department of Homeland Security (DHS) and its many public and private partners play an increasingly large role in the homeland security economy. With nearly 220,000 employees across the country, DHS represents a significant portion of the United States workforce. Twelve percent (26,965) of those employees live and work in the Washington metropolitan area, largely in the fields of management and program analysis and administration (see Table 6.2). As DHS headquarters and many of its directorates are located in Washington, the region attracts a large number of private sector partners as well. Several of the DC region's strong industry sectors are also sectors that receive significant amounts of DHS contract activity, suggesting several potential niches for DC and regional firms to serve DHS needs (see Table 6.3). The District has high concentrations of professional and technical services, administrative services, and education services firms and workers (see Table 6.4). Sub-sectors such as computer programming and related services, security services, and universities and colleges represent particularly strong matches with DHS contracting needs. Tables 6.3 and 6.4 illustrate the potential match between DC's industry sector specialization, and the types of industry sectors to which DHS often issues contracts.

With DHS acting as the anchor, these partners and partnerships will likely continue to act as drivers for the emerging homeland security economy and the economy of the Washington metropolitan area as a whole, and hopefully, with the proper guidance, as a driver for the revitalization of St. Elizabeths and its surrounding community. Residents in the nearby area may access new employment opportunities within DHS, or with businesses that interact with DHS who may locate at the East Campus facilities. Residents of DC's Wards 7 and 8 lag behind the region in terms of educational attainment and employment, however, and may require additional education or training to access these job opportunities. We will explore this challenge in further detail below.

TABLE 6.2 Top 24 job titles for DHS National Capital Region employees, as of April 2010

Series	Job title	Total
343	Management and Program Analysis	4,227
301	Miscellaneous Administration and Program	3,638
1801	General Inspection, Investigation, Enforcement, and Compliance Series	2,469
1811	Criminal Investigating	1,996
2210	Information Technology Management	1,642
1802	Compliance Inspection and Support	1,471
83	Police	1,433
340	Program Management	878
1102	Contracting	811
80	Security Administration	808
905	General Attorney	708
303	Miscellaneous Clerk and Assistant	590
132	Intelligence	585
201	Human Resources Management	524
1895	Customs and Border Protection	495
501	Financial Administration and Program	287
1101	General Business and Industry	245
1896	Border Patrol Enforcement Series	233
560	Budget Analysis	223
801	General Engineering	215
510	Accounting	208
391	Telecommunications	201
930	Hearings and Appeals	148
326	Office Automation Clerical and Assistance	132

Source: Department of Homeland Security

Based on our analysis of employment and procurement data, as well as qualitative data collected through interviews and focus groups, we identified three main emerging opportunities related to DHS consolidation on the St. Elizabeths campus: contracting and procurement, education, and workforce development. For each opportunity area, we draw upon a case study to devise a list of practices for consideration in the St. Elizabeths redevelopment process.

TABLE 6.3 Top 15 industry sub-sectors by $ amount of DHS contracts 2005–2010

Rank	Sub-sector	Amount
1	541 Professional and technical services	$33,605,700,436
2	561 Administrative and support services	$14,670,969,540
3	334 Computer and electronic product manufacturing	$6,249,549,806
4	336 Transportation and equipment manufacturing	$6,018,266,908
5	236 Construction and buildings	$2,103,345,217
6	518 Data processing, hosting, and related services	$1,916,589,885
7	321 Wood product manufacturing	$1,373,645,368
8	517 Telecommunications	$1,124,452,349
9	611 Educational services	$1,075,451,509
10	443 Electronics and appliance stores	$831,424,604
11	333 Machinery manufacturing	$831,352,937
12	315 Apparel manufacturing	$727,828,509
13	562 Waste management and remediation services	$686,273,108
14	423 Merchant wholesalers, durable goods	$643,716,070
15	237 Heavy and civil engineering construction	$630,142,843

Source: Department of Homeland Security (2010), FDPS Procurement Data

TABLE 6.4 Top 15 industry sub-sectors in which DC has a location quotient > 1

Rank	Sub-sector	LQ
1	813 Membership associations and organizations	8.99
2	519 Other information services	4.53
3	611 Educational services	3.82
4	515 Broadcasting, except internet	3.61
5	541 Professional and technical	3.21
6	487 Scenic and sightseeing transportation	2.66
7	711 Performing arts and spectator	2.24
8	712 Museums, historical sites, zoos, and parks	2.1
9	721 Accommodation	2.03
10	511 Publishing industries, except internet	1.99
11	814 Private households	1.9
12	531 Real estate	1.65
13	561 Administrative and support services	1.44
14	622 Hospitals	1.26
15	812 Personal and laundry services	1.19

Source: Bureau of Labor Statistics, LQ Calculator

Contracting and Procurement

DHS works closely with the private sector and a significant share of its budget (more than 26 percent in 2009) is allocated to the procurement of homeland security products and services, and much of this procurement occurs in the DC region. From 2005 to 2010 the region captured more than 44 percent of homeland security spending in the nation. Homeland security contractors performed work in Ward 8 during that time period in the amount of $18,013,716. This amount represents only about 0.12 percent of total homeland security procurement activity in the District of Columbia (see Table 6.5). Thus, contracting activity in Ward 8 is very low and does not presently represent a large share of total procurement activity in the District.

Given the disconnect between the types of firms from which DHS typically procures its needed goods and services and the types of firms that presently exist in the St. Elizabeths neighborhood, the challenge will be generating and preparing local businesses and employees to take advantage of these opportunities. Based on our preliminary findings, we have recommended that *local stakeholders and the District of Columbia consider targeted efforts around small business development to increase the entrepreneurial and small business development capacity in Ward 8*. For ideas on how to encourage this type of entrepreneurship and capacity building we turn to one of our case studies: Cleveland's Health and Technology Corridor.

Despite Cleveland's severe economic struggles over the last several decades, successful redevelopment efforts and the creation of Cleveland's Health and Technology ("Health Tech") Corridor have helped to improve parts of the city and the region. The Corridor stretches along Euclid Avenue from Downtown Cleveland eastward to Case Western Reserve University (CWRU), and is supported by partners including the city's major health providers, universities, and economic development groups. In 2010, the State of Ohio declared the Corridor one of its seven Hubs of Innovation and Technology. The Corridor is anchored by CWRU, the Cleveland Clinic, Cleveland State University, Cuyahoga Community College, Louis Stokes Cleveland VA Medical Center, St. Vincent's Charity Medical Center, and the CWRU-affiliated University Hospital system. Similar to how the innovation hub is being envisioned for the East Campus of St. Elizabeths, the Corridor is home to a combination of over 100 companies, performing research and technology commercialization in the areas of stem cell and regenerative medicine, sensor systems engineering, neurostimulation, neuromodulation, tissue engineering, and imaging research.

Just as St. Elizabeths residents face formidable challenges in tapping into the DHS economy, so too did many of Cleveland's underserved populations looking to play a role in the Corridor's growth. Despite significant challenges in the Corridor, one initiative has begun to bridge that divide by employing residents and helping to stabilize a nearby neighborhood. The Evergreen

TABLE 6.5 Homeland Security procurement in the District of Columbia, Ward 8, Washington-Arlington-Alexandria MSA and the United States, 2005–2010

	2005	2006	2007	2008	2009	2010	Total	Average annual growth rate
District of Columbia	$1.2B	$2.3B	$2.4B	$3.5B	$3.3B	$2.7B	$15.5B	14.1%
Ward 8	$218,649	$9,446,304	$2,560,908	$4,399,918	$633,331	$754,606	$18,013,716	22.9%
Rest of Washington-Arlington-Alexandria MSA	$2.8B	$3.1B	$3.2B	$4.8B	$3.9B	$3.8B	$21.5B	5.2%
All other MSAs	$10.6B	$9.2B	$6.5B	$7.3B	$6.5B	$6.2B	$46.3B	–8.6%
DHS $ total	*$14.6B*	*$14.6B*	*$12.1B*	*$15.6B*	*$13.7B*	*$12.7B*	*$83.4B*	*–2.3%*

Source: FDPS

Cooperatives program, a partnership between the residents of six Cleveland neighborhoods and many of the Corridor's anchor institutions, aims to create quality jobs for residents in employee-owned companies that hire and operate locally. The Evergreen Cooperative Laundry (ECL), for example, is the region's first Leadership in Energy and Environmental Design (LEED)-certified commercial laundry facility. ECL contracts with health care anchors in the Corridor while advancing green initiatives, cutting operating costs for clients, eliminating energy and water inefficiencies, reducing the use of toxic chemicals, and eliminating hazardous wastes. Employee "owners" receive "training in operations, life-skills, sustainability and ownership principles empowering their performance at work."[5] The Evergreen Cooperative follows an organizational structure designed by the Ohio Employee Ownership Center at Kent State University. Employees are based locally and hired locally, meaning that the benefits from this initiative stay within the community. In addition to earning a living wage, cooperative owners also build equity in the firms. Expansion plans include two other cooperative businesses: Ohio Cooperative Solar and Green City Growers Cooperative.

Establishing the Cooperative was not an easy thing to do and there are plenty of lessons to learn from this case. As Yates (2009) and Alperovitz et al. (2010) note, it took many leaders and organizations and lots of careful planning to get this initiative running. Early support came from the Cleveland Foundation, which organized a larger advisory group that included other philanthropic groups, local government officials, the Chamber of Commerce, local community development corporations, CEOs from other local employee-owned firms, and representatives from the Ohio Employee Ownership Center. This leadership, and its financial backing, is seen as key to the Cooperative's success thus far. Other important facets that have been key to the Cooperative's success are its close connections with anchor institutions in the growing health care sector, and its local hiring practice, which targets neighborhood residents for training, employment, and eventually ownership.

Education

The Washington region as a whole is generally well positioned to link educated workers with the positions that DHS and its partners seek to fill. However, at this point in time, very few of those positions will be appropriate for residents of the St. Elizabeths neighborhood. Workers in this neighborhood are disproportionately employed in service and sales occupations and less likely to be employed in professional occupations than workers in the region as a whole. Not only do residents of St. Elizabeths hold relatively lower-skilled jobs, but also other socioeconomic indicators highlight significant discrepancies between residents of these neighborhoods and the residents of the wider region. Income levels in this neighborhood are lower than the comparable figure for the District and the Metropolitan Statistical Area (MSA), and the unemployment rate is significantly higher. Educational attainment rates are lower as well, especially for college degrees. These low education levels have implications for the types of jobs that local residents will be able to obtain as DHS moves to the St. Elizabeths campus. Many of the jobs at DHS, as well as jobs at specialized professional services firms that may locate on the East Campus to provide services to DHS, will have education requirements that may make it difficult for local residents to pursue these opportunities without further training (see Table 6.1).

In order to transcend this problem of educational disparities, the challenge will be to bolster educational achievement within the surrounding neighborhood and identify appropriate jobs for workers with varying levels of educational attainment. Based on our preliminary findings, we recommend that *local stakeholders devise a series of educational pathway options for residents to meet the educational and experience requirements of either DHS or its partners in supporting industries.* For insight into how these pathways might operate we turn to another one of our case studies. In Baltimore, two biotechnology parks are examined: Science + Technology Park and BioPark.

Baltimore has encouraged the creation of two biotechnology research parks to serve as anchor institutions in its efforts to develop this fledgling industry and spur community redevelopment. The University of Maryland's (UMD) BioPark in West Baltimore was launched in 2003 and has completed about a third of its planned 1.8 million square feet of lab and office space. The BioPark currently employs about 500 employees in science, business development and marketing, legal services, lab technology, health care, and administrative support. Its location and university affiliation have allowed it to take advantage of an Emerging Technology Center that provides "go-to-market" business services through UMD's business school and an Intellectual Property Legal Resource Center staffed by law school faculty and students. The BioPark's tenants include domestic and foreign firms, American Red Cross labs, the Institute of Genomic Research's Institute for Genome Sciences, and a number of spinoffs from local universities including JHU. While the BioPark has seen relative success in recruiting tenants, it plans to open additional buildings "about every 24 months according to market demand."[6] Upon completion of all planned development, the BioPark will house about 3,000 employees.

Meanwhile, Johns Hopkins University (JHU), the state's largest private employer, the Annie E. Casey Foundation, and the East Baltimore Development Inc. (EBDI) have invested in the JHU Science + Technology Park, located just north of the JHU Hospital in East Baltimore. Plans for 1.1 million square feet of office and lab space in five buildings and the redevelopment of 50-plus adjacent acres into new housing, shops, restaurants, parking, and other amenities have not materialized or have simply been abandoned. Access to JHU's world-class faculty and facilities were anticipated to attract tenant companies, but as of yet, the one building that has opened is only 80 percent occupied. According to the *Maryland Daily Record*, 422 workers are currently employed at the Park. While plans for the Science + Technology Park have been scaled back, JHU continues to construct a new biotech park in Montgomery County.

Even though both anchors have faced their share of challenges, both parks have been able to create progressive educational programs within their respective neighborhoods. The BioPark's non-profit Research Park Corporation has created a fund with tenant rent payments to purchase lab and computer equipment for the nearby Vivien T. Thomas Medical Arts Academy, a magnet health sciences high school, and offers internships for students.[7] BioPark also supports workforce development through its 4+2+2 program, which creates career pathways for students from Baltimore schools such as the Vivien T. Thomas Academy. Students earning a high school degree can enroll in a two-year Associates degree program at the Life Sciences Institute of the Baltimore City Community College, located at the BioPark since 2009. Upon completion, participants can move on to UMD-Baltimore to earn a Bachelor's degree in medical technology, and obtain the skills required for quality health sciences jobs. And on the Science + Technology Park campus, the new East Baltimore Community School will open in 2014. The new school—the first to be built in Baltimore in decades—will function as a "public contract school", receiving funds from private corporations, partnerships, and a tax increment financing plan.

By including educational facilities and associated pathways on site, both biotechnology parks offer a unique way to marry education and community within an anchor institution neighborhood. Though the parks took slightly different approaches and had varying degrees of success, some common themes can be seen in both cases. First, part of what makes these initiatives possible (and also unique) is the creative financing strategies that they employ. In both cases it was a combination of nonprofit and private funding that allowed for new educational opportunities on site. Local leaders looking to create unique educational pathways related to the DHS anchor at St. Elizabeths should look for other creative ways to leverage investments. Second, part of what has made these initiatives successful, at least initially, is the community buy-in that they have cultivated. Although some elements of the parks have been somewhat contentious, the educational initiatives have actually engendered good will in both neighborhoods. In the case of Science + Technology, a planned child care facility attached to the new school facility has been instrumental in proving that education is an important part of the park, even at an early age. And at BioPark, the linked educational pathway between an Associates and Bachelors degree has helped community members see the smaller steps that lead to a career in biotechnology or related fields.

Workforce Development

Qualitative data from DHS leaders and private sector executives point to workforce development and job training as absolutely critical components of the homeland security economy. At the present time, workforce development and job training related to DHS occur in a variety of locations and in a variety of formats. For instance, the Federal Emergency Management Agency (FEMA) offers online courses for individuals as well as direct training for state and local jurisdictions. First responder training is provided by the National Fire Academy, the Emergency Management Institute, US Fire Administration, among others. Degrees and training programs focused on homeland security are available at numerous institutions in the Washington metro area and beyond.

Though less focused on homeland security, there are also a variety of organizations already engaged in workforce development in the St. Elizabeths neighborhood. Organizations like Toni Thomas Associates, RizeUp Technology Training Center, and Youth Build have been helping to train and prepare workers in Ward 8 for several years. These groups tend to have smaller budgets and lower enrollments than other big workforce development players in the region but they represent a formidable asset for the neighborhood and its residents. To leverage these existing assets, *we recommend that local leaders encourage these existing assets to become a meaningful part of the workforce development strategy related to DHS consolidation and help these organizations respond to their new anchor institution's needs.* For guidance in how to navigate this potentially difficult transition we turn to another one of our case studies: the Institute for Advanced Learning and Research (IALR) in Danville, Virginia.

Danville's IALR is part of southern Virginia's strategy to transition its regional economy, which has suffered decades of chronic unemployment in traditional industries like tobacco processing and textiles, toward a new, high-tech industry base by providing educational services and increased research capacity for the region. Founded in 2001, IALR moved three years later into a new facility that includes 25 classrooms (including distance learning classrooms), computer and science labs, an electronic library and a large conference area. The Institute's university and college partners offer undergraduate and graduate degree programs in a variety of fields at the IALR facility. Virginia Tech, Averett University, and Danville Community College faculty offer training to undergraduate and master's students in IT, math, and chemical engineering careers. The Institute also offers workforce training in technology, teaching, and research skills. Students complete much of their required coursework online, though some is also done at university campuses and at IALR. IALR also offers certificates, online courses, classes, and learning programs for adults. The IALR facility, which opens its computer labs to the public, serves approximately 9,000 people annually, including approximately 70 employers, 4,500 students,

300 educators, 20 graduate students, and 75 small businesses.[8] In recent years, IALR has been focusing efforts on technology advancements, job creation and retention, and worker advancement.

The Danville case offers an important lesson because its stakeholders have attempted to support a distressed community by creating an anchor institution to specifically transition the regional economy to high-tech industry. Over time, the focus of IALR research has gravitated toward biotech and value-added agriculture, as this area has proven the most promising area for technology commercialization and business development, given local resources and skillsets. IALR is also notable for the educational services and outreach to local youth and residents that it provides. The Institute's outreach exposes local residents to technology being developed in IALR labs and prepares workers for positions in related fields.

This approach may serve as a model for integrating DHS and its related innovation economy into the St. Elizabeths community. Distillation of lessons from this case study tells us that a successful outreach program will need to focus on three main components. First, it should provide targeted occupational skills training programs that relate to the needs of the anchor institution *and* the surrounding community. Successful integration within the St. Elizabeths neighborhood will be more likely if workforce development programs are designed to match residents with specific occupations in DHS or in the homeland security economy more broadly. Second, the workforce development program should offer programs that target a variety of educational levels. The IALR succeeds in part because it includes training and skills-based programs for unskilled workers up to highly trained workers, thereby appealing to a broad range of community members both within the St. Elizabeths community and from outside of it. Building upon this idea of educational pathways, a third component of the workforce development strategy should be the creation of a connection or gateway to regional education institutions. In IALR this connection was established through a combination of online courses and on-site classes. For St. Elizabeths, it may take a similar quasi-informal shape or it may be something more along the lines of a shared educational facility, something akin to a homeland security university campus with regional university and college representation. The idea of a shared educational and workforce development facility was frequently mentioned during stakeholder interviews and focus groups. In the near term, there may be an opportunity for the Department to collaborate with local community colleges and universities to provide workforce development and job training at St. Elizabeths or elsewhere in the greater Washington area.

Conclusions: Challenges and Opportunities

Lessons from these and other case studies provide us with guidance as we—alongside our partners in the government, private sector, and, most importantly, the community—continue to develop an innovation plan for the St. Elizabeths campus. The case study examples discussed above highlight three important recommendations. First, we must focus our efforts on cultivating small business and entrepreneurship opportunities related to contracting and procurement for community businesses within Ward 8. An appropriate innovation plan must include proper programming, infrastructure, and support for these businesses. Anything less would fall short of the goal to prepare these businesses and employees to take advantage of the opportunities related to an emerging homeland security economy. Second, we must also focus our efforts on devising a series of educational pathways that give options to residents in meeting the educational and experience requirements of employers in the homeland security economy. In order to do this, the innovation plan must provide opportunities for local residents to increase their education and work experience in areas related to the homeland security economy. Third, we must deploy existing assets and help develop new organizations engaged in workforce development in the St. Elizabeths neighborhood. Furthermore, we must help these groups and their leaders become involved in the broader workforce development strategy component of the innovation plan. Ongoing stakeholder engagement meetings suggest that existing groups are active and willing partners. The challenge moving forward will be to help them adapt to the new realities of DHS as an anchor institution.

As we continue to develop the innovation strategy for St. Elizabeths, we are cognizant of the fact that many known and unknown challenges lie ahead. It is our hope that drawing from the successes and failures of other anchor institution developments in underserved communities will help us to identify many of the known challenges and help us navigate the many that are unknown. Our work with the aforementioned and other case studies indicates that this process will not be an easy one. The case studies suggest that the best approach will be a two-pronged approach: building an innovation economy on the one hand, and embedding this economy in a healthy community on the other. To successfully achieve this we must work to align the goals of DHS and the local community, build viable bridges between the two that move beyond the superficial, and sustain this agenda despite challenges along the way.

Notes

1 http://www.dhs.gov/ynews/testimony/testimony_1274279995276.shtm
2 http://dc.gov/DC/Mayor/About+the+Mayor/News+Room/Mayor+Vincent+C. +Gray+Names+Leaders+of+St.+Elizabeths+East+Campus+Development+ Advisory+Council
3 St. Elizabeths is located in Ward 8. However, due to data availability, some calculations refer to Wards 7 and 8. Wards 7 and 8 have similar demographics and are the only two wards located east of the Anacostia River.

4 Cleveland, Ohio; Philadelphia, Pennsylvania; Baltimore, Maryland; Danville, Virginia; San Diego, California; Huntsville, Alabama; Virginia Beach/Hampton Roads, Virginia; Berlin, Germany; and Sofia Antipolis, France.
5 Evergreen Cooperative Laundry, About Us, http://www.evergreencoop.com/About.html
6 BioPark: University of Maryland, http://www.umbiopark.com/biopark
7 BioPark: University of Maryland, Mission & History, http://www.umbiopark.com/biopark/mission-history.aspx
8 Strategic Plan, http://vaperforms.virginia.gov/agencylevel/stratplan/spReport.cfm?AgencyCode=885

References

Alperovitz, G., Howard, T. & Dubb, S. (2009). Cleveland's worker-owned boom rustbelt to recovery. http://www.yesmagazine.org/issues/the-new-economy/clevelands-worker-owned-boom

Alperovitz, G., Howard, T. & Williamson, T. (2010). The Cleveland model. *The Nation.* March 1.

Appleseed Inc. (2003). Anchor institutions and their role in metropolitan change. White Paper on Penn IUR Initiatives on Anchor Institutions.

Birch, E. (2007). Special report: Anchor institutions. *Next American City.* Summer.

CEOs for Cities. (2007). Leveraging anchor institutions for urban success. White Paper. http://www.ceosforcities.org/pagefiles/CEOs_LeveragingAnchorInstitutionsforUrbanSuccess_FINAL.pdf

Cisneros, H.G. (1995). *The university and the urban challenge.* Washington, DC: US Dept. of Housing and Urban Development.

Cromwell, P.M., Giloth, R. & Schachtel, M.R.B. (2005). East Baltimore revitalization project: Opportunities and challenges in transforming an urban neighborhood. *Journal of Higher Education Outreach and Engagement,* 10, 113–126.

DeVol, R., Koepp, R. Wong, P. & Bedroussian, A. (2003). *The economic contributions of health care to New England.* Santa Monica: Milken Institute.

Fulbright-Anderson, K., Auspos, P. & Anderson, A. (2001). Community involvement in partnerships with educational institutions, medical centers, and utility companies. Paper prepared for Aspen Institute Roundtable on Comprehensive Community Initiatives. Accessed September 1, 2011. http://www.aecf.org/KnowledgeCenter/Publications.aspx?pubguid={D6374635-8A58-484A-AE37-76198A62E1E0}

Hahn, A., Coonerty, C. & Peaslee, L. (2003). Colleges and universities as economic anchors: Profiles of promising practices. Providence: Campus Compact.

Harkavy, I. & Zuckerman, H. (1999). *Eds and meds: Cities' hidden assets.* Washington, DC: Brookings Institution Center on Urban and Metropolitan Policy.

Initiative for a Competitive Inner City (ICIC). (2010). Leveraging anchor institutions to grow inner city businesses: A resource for inner city entrepreneurs.

Lowe, J.S. (2008). A participatory planning approach to enhancing a historically black university–community partnership: The case of the e-city initiative. *Planning, Practice, and Research,* 23, 549–558.

Maryland Daily Record. (2011). Daily Record investigation: A dream derailed. January 30. http://thedailyrecord.com/2011/01/30/daily-record-investigation-a-dream-derailed/

McKee, G.A. (2010). Health-care policy as urban policy: Hospitals and community development in the postindustrial city. Working Paper. Federal Reserve Bank of San Francisco's Community Development Investment Center.

Nelson, M. & Wolf-Powers, L. (2010). Chains and ladders: Exploring the opportunities for workforce development and poverty reduction in the hospital sector. *Economic Development Quarterly,* 24, 33–44.

Work Foundation. (2010). *Anchoring growth: The role of anchor institutions in the regeneration of UK cities.* Accessed August 10, 2011. http://www.theworkfoundation.com/research/publications/publicationdetail.aspx?oItemId=270

Yates, J. (2009). The evergreen cooperative initiative: Can "anchor institutions" help revitalize declining neighborhoods by buying from local cooperatives? *Owners at Work XXI(1).*

PART II

Schools as Anchor Institutions for Inner-City Revitalization

7

BACK TO THE FUTURE

Public Schools as Neighborhood Anchor Institutions: The Choice Neighborhood Initiative in Buffalo, New York

Henry Louis Taylor, Jr., Linda McGlynn, and D. Gavin Luter, University at Buffalo

Introduction

When I grew up in North Nashville, Tennessee, African Americans mostly went to Ford Green Elementary, Washington Junior High or Pearl High. These were feeder schools that typically kept classmates together from the first grade through high school, thereby fusing them into a network of friends and acquaintances, regardless of the social status of their parents.[1] North Nashville was a cross-class community composed of blacks from across the income spectrum, including doctors, lawyers, teachers, university professors, preachers, professionals, business persons, racketeers, police, firemen, porters, janitors, waitresses and blacks who were barely able to eke out a living. Institutions, like the church and public schools, blended together these diverse social groups and transformed them into one people, despite the socioeconomic cleavages that separated them.

Back in those days, the school, even more so than the church, melded the population together and gave the community a sense of pride and *oneness*. Schools were sacred neighborhood institutions and sources of great pride. Pearl High, for example, was an iconic symbol of North Nashville, not just because of its legendary basketball teams, but also because generations of family members graduated from it. My uncle, mother and brother went to Pearl High, and so too did most of my neighbors. Older and younger family members often had the same teachers, and there existed a "community memory" of Pearl High, and its place in the life and lore of North Nashville. These "memories" bonded the community together and reinforced neighborhood traditions, mutual respect and solidarity.

Teachers were an omnipresent feature of the North Nashville landscape. You saw them on neighborhood streets and in the grocery store, pharmacy, bank and church. They led organizations, were scout masters, summer park recreation leaders, little league baseball coaches and engines of neighborhood growth and development. In North Nashville and other black communities across the United States, public schools were neighborhood anchor institutions (Hudson & Holmes, 1994; Milner & Howard, 2004).

In the post-Civil Rights era, this started to change. As inner-city public schools faltered and black neighborhood conditions worsened, the role of schools in the neighborhood and community building process changed radically. The school choice strategy was the big culprit. The school choice idea was rooted in the neoliberal view of introducing accountability through forms of market-based competition and expanded parental choice. The advocates of this school reform strategy claimed that increased parental choice would force schools to bolster academic outcomes by making them more responsive and efficient (Hoxby, 2003). Parents would become consumers with the ability to send their children to the best schools in the district. This increased competition among schools would lead to the improvement of all schools as they competed for students within an open market. The choice approach also severed the traditional relationship between schools and communities, thus ending the era of neighborhood schools and diminishing the role of inner-city schools as anchor institutions.

This strategy failed. The school choice method did not improve school performance and student academic achievement among black, Latino and Native Americans (Swanson, 2009). The persistence of the urban education crisis caused US President Barack Obama to reexamine the link between schools and neighborhoods. There is an irony evident in the paradox of the Obama Administration, with its core belief in school choice, initiating policies that seek to go "back to the future" by establishing place-based school reform strategies. At the core of both the Promise and Choice Neighborhood Initiatives is the notion of formulating strategies that essentially lead to the creation of de facto neighborhood schools, which are repurposed as community assets and anchor institutions (Khadduri, Schwartz & Turnham, 2008).

Using a social institutional and neoliberal framework, this chapter will explore this theme by examining the HUD Perry Choice Neighborhood Planning Initiative in Buffalo, New York. The chapter is divided into three sections. The first section explores the role played by the "choice" strategy in undermining the role of schools as anchor institutions, while section two examines the connection between neighborhood conditions and educational reform. In the final section, the HUD Perry Choice Neighborhood and the repurposing of schools as anchor institutions is discussed.

Public Schools as Anchor Institutions

Inner-city public schools are anchor institutions that are situated in distressed, jobless and underdeveloped neighborhoods. They are rooted in these locales because of their mission, capital investment and clientele (Harkavy & Zuckerman, 1999; Netter Center for Community Partnerships, 2008). This spatial immobility (Cox & Mair, 1988) creates an expectation that anchors will play a role in improving and developing the neighborhoods of which they are a part. This motivation of anchors is based on the interplay of mission, self-interest and sometimes government incentives. According to the Anchor Institution Task Force (AITF), for an institution to be considered an "anchor" it must be more than merely *rooted* in a neighborhood, also it must promote positive socioeconomic development and social justice in that neighborhood. Anchor institutions, then, from an AITF perspective, are obligated to play a positive role in the development of their host communities. Spatially immobile institutions typically achieve an "anchor institution" status when they realize it is in their "self-interest" to become engaged with their local community. When this consciousness is institutionalized, the investment activities of anchors become sustainable (Porter, 2010; Porter & Kramer, 2011).

Developing and institutionalizing "anchor institution consciousness" is a complex task for inner-city schools because they operate under the auspices of superintendents, school boards and, in some instances, local government. So, their actions at the neighborhood level are dependent on approvals by the central school administration. Regardless, the fate of inner-city schools and distressed, jobless and underdeveloped neighborhoods are co-mingled. The reason is that school performance, student academic achievement and neighborhood conditions are interactive (Owens, 2010; Sinha, Payne & Cook, 2005). Even if a child lives in an underdeveloped neighborhood, but attends a school outside that community, his or her academic performance will still be impacted by neighborhood conditions. Consequently, neighborhood regeneration and school reform must march in tandem. This is what Jeffrey Canada, founder of the Harlem Children's Zone, meant when he said, "Fix the schools without fixing the families and community, and children will fail; but they will also fail if you improve the surrounding community without fixing the schools" (Tough, 2004).

Schools and neighborhoods are intertwined because neighborhoods are not just *neutral sites* where everyday life and culture unfolds; rather they are catalytic places that will positively or negatively influence socioeconomic outcomes of its residents, including the children (Driscoll, 2001). The reason is that neighborhoods act on people and people act on the neighborhoods, with social institutions functioning as a mediating force betwixt and between them. For example, the neighborhood effects literature argues that poorly organized, distressed and underdeveloped neighborhoods will contribute to negative socioeconomic outcomes such as poverty, joblessness, dilapidation, poor health, food insecurity, mental illness and children with persistently low levels of academic achievement. On the flip side, highly organized, thriving and developed neighborhoods are argued to contribute to positive socioeconomic outcomes by providing the community with the capacity, resources and supports that are needed to produce a vibrant, thriving and healthy place with positive socioeconomic outcomes.

This is where education and schooling become critical factors. Inner-city schools are not immune to the challenges facing distressed neighborhoods, because the children living in such places will bring the issues that originate in their home and community with them to school (Bronfenbrenner & Morris, 1998; Dryfoos, 1994; Raikes et al., 2006). Moreover, the lack of neighborhood-based infrastructure, which specifically supports education, means that many inner-city children will not meet critical developmental milestones. This, along with the lack of other types of neighborhood-based infrastructure will negatively influence student academic achievement for inner-city children and postpone critical developmental milestones (McNeely, Nonnemaker & Blum, 2002; Sarsour et al., 2010).[2]

Given the scenario just outlined, it is in the interest of schools to become anchors that work with others to improve the conditions of life found inside distressed, underdeveloped neighborhoods, thereby eliminating non-academic barriers that thwart school performance and educational achievement. This perspective is based on the hypothesis that neighborhoods matter in determining the educational outcome of students living in distressed, jobless and underdeveloped neighborhoods. If this hypothesis is correct, then, the academic outcomes of inner-city students will not improve significantly until the neighborhoods in which they live are improved. For this reason, it is important to repurpose schools and make invaluable neighborhood assets.

School Choice

The school choice strategy is the main obstacle to achieving this task. This approach emerged in the post-Civil Rights era, starting with the busing efforts beginning in the 1960s, which sought to desegregate the schools, often under court order. The school choice movement, which grew exponentially with the rise of neoliberalism in the 1970s, is a building-centric method based on the belief that school characteristics are the prime determinant of student academic achievement. Within this framework, school performance is bolstered by creating competition among the schools, which are reconstituted as entrepreneurial institutions designed to compete in a highly competitive education marketplace (Betts & Loveless, 2005; Henig & Sugarman, 2000; Hoxby, 2003). In this setting,

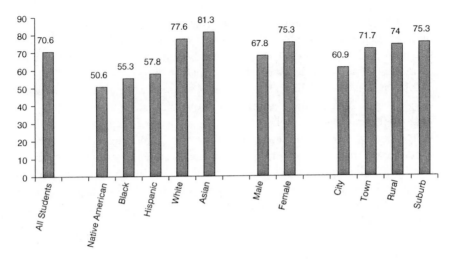

FIGURE 7.1   National Graduation Rates (Percentage), Class of 2005

students and families are reimagined as consumers with the power to choose their own school from a menu of options.[3] According to neoliberal market theory, competition will improve the quality of education by forcing "poor schools" to fail, or adopt better teaching methods and curriculum, or be taken over by those with better ideas on how to run the schools and teach the children. The neoliberal school choice model, then, would solve the education crisis.

This did not happen. The neoliberal school choice model failed to deliver on its promise of improving the quality of inner-city schools (Henig, 1994; Hursh, 2007; Swanson, 2009). The high school graduation rate is the single most important indicator of school performance in the United States. This metric makes it clear that US public schools are in a crisis mode. For example, a 2009 report by the Education Research Center indicated that three in ten students fail to finish high school with a diploma and that almost 50 percent of Native Americans, blacks and Latinos did not graduate from high school in 2005 (Figure 7.1).[4]

The education crisis is a crisis of the central city. For example, among 71 of the nation's largest metropolitan areas, the graduation rate for central cities was 59.3 percent and 77.3 percent for suburbs, a differential of 18 percent. A significant number of these central cities (22 percent) had graduation rates of 55 percent or less, including New York City, Columbus, Atlanta, Chicago, Detroit, Memphis, Nashville, Albuquerque, Wichita, Milwaukee and Cleveland. The school choice model also failed in Buffalo and other New York State central cities. In 2012, for example, Buffalo's graduation rate (four-year graduates) was 54 percent, which placed it ahead of Syracuse and Rochester, with graduation rates of 48.4 percent and 45.5 percent respectively. Nationally, the Schott Foundation (2010) for

Education listed Buffalo as one of the ten lowest performing school districts for black males in the United States, along with New York City, Cleveland, Detroit, Charleston County, South Carolina, Duval, Palm Beach, Dade and Pinellas counties in Florida and Jefferson County in Louisiana.

Merryl H. Tisch, Chancellor of the New York State Board of Regents, stressed that the education problem is more than an issue of students not graduating from high school, but it is also an issue of them graduating from high school without being ready for college or a career. He said, "New York's overall graduation rate has improved, but nearly a quarter of our students still don't graduate after four years. And too many of those students who do graduate aren't ready for college and careers" (New York State Education Department, 2012). This concern was echoed in a 2012 report by the American College Test (ACT), which indicated that 60 percent of the 2012 high school graduates are at risk of struggling in college and in their careers. African-Americans were the most at-risk group among this cohort (ACT, 2012).

The school choice movement failed because the transformation of the black institutional ghetto into a distressed, jobless, underdeveloped community in the post-Civil Rights era undermined the schooling process (Wilson, 1996). The interaction of two forces caused neighborhood decline to impact the schooling process. First, in neoliberal society, poverty and low incomes keep working class black families from purchasing the commodities needed for their children to develop the attitudes, skills and competencies required for success in school and in the workforce. Second, in the post-Civil Rights era, the rise of neoliberalism triggered the *institutional failure* of organizations servicing the black community. Social institutions are mediating institutions that are obligated to help low-income residents manage successfully the problems generated by the neoliberal economic and urban growth processes. When these institutions are dysfunctional and do not work properly, residents feel the full brunt of the negative socioeconomic forces spawned by the urban economic and growth processes. When low incomes meet institutional failure in neoliberal society the resultant outcome is social dislocation with its concomitant inadequate schools and student academic underachievement.

The guiding thesis is that poverty and low incomes do not automatically equate with hardship, misery and institutional failure. During the ghetto era, when the welfare state was a fixture of the liberal democratic order, the black community was anchored by the philosophy of racial solidarity and self-help. In this setting, blacks built an institutional framework to support and inform everyday life and culture. Collectively, these social institutions not only formed the social glue which held the community together, but also they functioned as a mediating force that lessened hardship, while simultaneously providing residents with the ability to set social norms and fight to improve their lives in a racist, class-stratified society (Bertaux & Washington, 2005; Milner & Howard,

2004). The dramatic victories against school segregation and the stunning success of the Civil Rights Movement are the metrics that provide evidence of the strength of those institutions serving the black community. For example, in Black Richmond, in the early 20th century, within a four-block area between Broad and Charity streets to the east and west and First and Fourth streets to the north and south there were a host of social institutions: Richmond Hospital, Women's Central League Training School and Hospital, Friends Asylum for Colored Orphans, Colored Workingman's Industrial Home and Nursery, YMCA, Knights of Pythias Castle, Knights of Pythias Castle Hall, Sixth Virginia Social Club, Richmond Athletic and Social Club, Hippodrome Theater, George Brown Photographic Studio, Negro Development Corporation, and Negro Historical and Industrial Association (Map 7.1). These and other institutions formed the framework that helped Black Richmond advance during the Jim Crow era and ultimately shatter the ghetto walls. The Richmond story could be repeated in just about every city where blacks lived.

Black urban life changed dramatically following the Civil Rights Movement in the late 1960s. From the late 1960s onward, the triumph of neoliberal capitalism combined with the integration movement and the demise of the welfare state to catalyze an astounding breakdown of the institutional foundation of the black community and trigger a corresponding sharp rise in black social dislocations. In this new black residential setting, operating in the context of neoliberalism society, and a weakened institutional framework, the disappearance of work, the crack cocaine epidemic and the mass incarceration movement combined to devastate the black community (Mauer, 2006).

The breakdown of the public schools, more than any other institutions, made grappling successfully with the challenges posed by neoliberal society difficult, if not impossible. Concurrently, the public schools are interconnected with other institutions in the black community. Therefore, to improve the schools and rebuild the neighborhood, it is necessary to redesign and rebuild the entire neighborhood institutional framework. To gain insights into ways to reform the schools, and re-create them as neighborhood anchors with a social purpose, within the context of redesigning the dysfunctional *social institutional infrastructure* of distressed neighborhoods, we examined Buffalo's Perry Choice Neighborhood.

The Perry Choice Neighborhood

The Perry Choice Neighborhood (PCN) is a mostly African-American community (80 percent), along with a handful of whites (14 percent) and Latinos (7 percent), which is situated in the southwestern corner of the City, near the Buffalo River (Map 7.2). The PCN is not a neutral site where everyday life and culture unfolds, but rather it is a dynamic place that influences the attitudes,

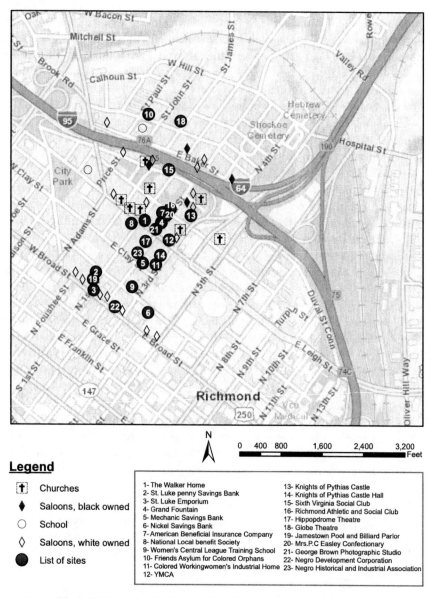

Legend

🛉 Churches	
◆ Saloons, black owned	
○ School	
◇ Saloons, white owned	
⬤ List of sites	

1- The Walker Home
2- St. Luke penny Savings Bank
3- St. Luke Emporium
4- Grand Fountain
5- Mechanic Savings Bank
6- Nickel Savings Bank
7- American Beneficial Insurance Company
8- National Local benefit Society
9- Women's Central League Training School
10- Friends Asylum for Colored Orphans
11- Colored Workingwomen's Industrial Home
12- YMCA
13- Knights of Pythias Castle
14- Knights of Pythias Castle Hall
15- Sixth Virginia Social Club
16- Richmond Athletic and Social Club
17- Hippopdrome Theatre
18- Globe Theatre
19- Jamestown Pool and Billiard Parlor
20- Mrs.P.C Easley Confectionary
21- George Brown Photographic Studio
22- Negro Development Corporation
23- Negro Historical and Industrial Association

MAP 7.1   Black Richmond, Virginia in 1920s [Institutions overlaid on 2010 Map]

values, beliefs and aspirations of the people living there. The PCN is bounded by Sycamore Avenue to the north, South Park Avenue to the south, Michigan Avenue to the west and Smith Street to the east. The neighborhood is situated in a gritty landscape of vacant land, modest working class cottages, abandoned houses and building and factories, along with commercial and retail establishments.

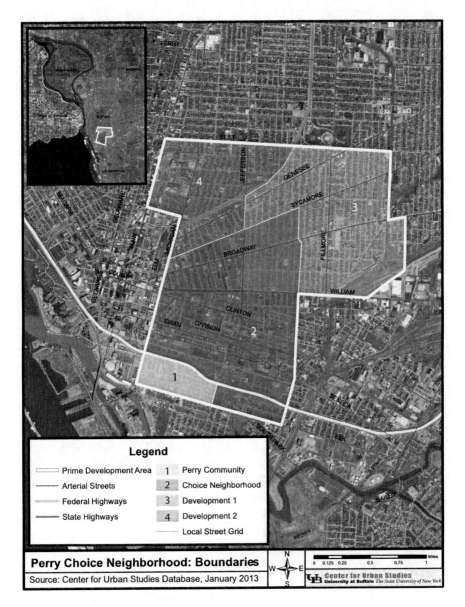

MAP 7.2 The Perry Choice Neighborhood and Environs

Most PCN residents live on the economic margin. The neighborhood has a jobless rate of 58 percent and 42 percent of the population live below the poverty line. The median household income is only $19,620 and a staggering 42 percent of households earn less than $15,000 annually. For blacks and other PCN working class groups, the lack of affordable housing is a huge problem, which depresses their already low wages. According to HUD, the acceptable definition of affordability is for a household to pay no more than 30 percent of their income for housing. In the PCN, 48 percent of the population living in rental units pays 35 percent or more of their income on housing, with 38.3 percent paying 50 percent or more of their income on housing. This lack of affordable housing is a significant hardship for PCN families, and it reduces the amount that families can spend on other basic commodities, such as food, medical care, clothing, transportation, and telephone service.

In neoliberal society, the residents' low educational levels chain them to the economic margins, because a correlation exists between education attainment and median annual earnings. Simply put, annually, those with higher levels of education will earn markedly more than people with lower levels of education. For example, a person with a Bachelor's degree will make about $25,000 a year more than a person with less than a high school diploma (US Census, 2006–2010). In 2010 about 61 percent of PCN residents had a high school diploma or less (26.1 percent). About 29 percent of the population had "some college, but no degree," while only a handful of residents had college degrees. Thus, it is not likely that most PCN residents, without obtaining specialized skills training, will be able to improve considerably their economic plight. They are situated at the bottom of the City's economic order.

Poverty, Low Incomes and Schooling

Williams Julius Wilson argues that from the late 1960s onward, the disappearance of work undermined black life and culture and destabilized the inner-city schooling process. In his analysis of Chicago he noted that, "For the first time in the twentieth century most adults in many inner city ghetto neighborhoods are not working in a typical week" (Wilson, 1996). Wilson's observations certainly mirrored the Buffalo experience. Life on the economic margins combined with institutional failures to create serious educational challenges for PCN residents. For example, these residents did not have the fiscal resources to provide their children with the real-life experiences, academic enrichment and social supports necessary for them to develop the resiliency, aspiration, skills and competencies required to succeed in school and in life. The CEO of the Buffalo Hearing and Speech Center said that top early learning centers spend from $12,000 to $15,000 per child, but inner-city early learning programs do not even begin to approach these spending levels (J. Cozzo, Personal communication, 2012). The government does provide subsidies and vouchers, but they are too low, so PCN parents cannot use them to purchase access to high quality early learning programs. There are numerous licensed and unlicensed daycare centers in the Perry Choice Neighborhoods, but these are not the type of high quality academic based centers that will get children ready for first grade.

This is just part of the problem. These parents/caregivers also do not have enough money to take their children on vacations and field trips that will enrich their lives, expand their horizons, and trigger their curiosity and desire to learn. Many residents cannot afford a computer or access to the internet, or fill up their home with books and magazines. Indeed, many parents/caregivers do not know how to create a literacy-rich home environment that encourages their child to read, problem-solve and become excited about learning new things (Raikes et al., 2006). Moreover, many parents/caregivers do not even know the appropriate way to dialogue with their children or how to read to them properly. These conditions are the result of institutional failure operating in the context of low incomes. The outcome is that most PCN children will reach first grade not ready to learn, thereby placing them at great risk to dropout or not finish high school ready for college or entry into the workforce.

There are other problems that erect obstacles to school performance and student academic success. In distressed, jobless and underdeveloped neighborhoods even the physical environment contributes to the construction of non-academic barriers to school performance and student academic success. For example, in these communities, the unhealthy housing units and the dilapidated, unkempt and foreboding visual appearance of the neighborhood functions as a disincentive to learning, growing and developing. The average PCN dwelling unit was built in 1947, more than sixty years ago. Many of them are out-of-date, unsafe, unhealthy and do not even provide children with a good place to read and study. As part of the Choice Neighborhood Planning Grant, the University at Buffalo (UB) Center for Urban Studies conducted focus groups with K–12 students who lived in the Commodore Perry Homes. The children at Perry were mostly in middle and high school, and they attended almost ten different schools. In addition to these children, focus groups were also held with students attending East High school. The participants ranged in age from 12 to 17 years.[5] The children attending these focus groups complained about not having access to computers or quiet places to study, either at home or in the community. They also complained about the rundown appearance of the neighborhood and about landlords who are slow to fix things when they are broken. In this setting, children often feel alienated, helpless and hopeless, and this places them at risk for making bad decisions or yielding to temptations, such as joining gangs, engaging in premature sex, and using drugs and alcohol.[6]

The Social Institution Framework

Before discussing Obama's Choice Neighborhood strategy, we want to return the discussion to the dysfunctional institutional structure found in the PCN. By social institutional structure, we are referring to all those neighborhood institutions that form a system that is meant to promote upward mobility, self-sufficiency, or improved quality of life, including those institutions that provide activities such as literacy training, early learning, primary education, adult education, job training, day care, youth services, physical and mental health services, transportation, economic development, safety and security, and other programs and activities for which the community demonstrates a need (Choice Neighborhoods Grant Program, 2012).[7] This system is composed mostly of non-profit community-based organizations and private companies that must compete with each other for limited grants and contracts, which fund their operations, in a highly competitive supportive service marketplace. There are some institutions that are funded by government, but their budgets are very unstable, and they must augment their finances by competing for grants and contracts.

The highly competitive nature of this battle for funding causes many organizations to retreat into silos and prioritize the survival of their organizations over the delivery of services. Concurrently, the PCN social institutions are there to help the residents grapple successfully with a range of urban issues. Also, as part of the HUD Choice Neighborhood Initiative, the UB Center for Urban Studies was required to conduct a Needs Assessment of the PCN. According to the survey, most residents did not even know the type of supportive services that existed in the neighborhood. This, combined with the absence of a good intra-neighborhood transportation system, meant that residents rarely used the supportive service institutions found in their own neighborhood. Concurrently, a number of neighborhood-based institutions did not even track the number of neighborhood residents that used their services. Most did not even have an outreach program to attract residents to their services. These institutions were in the neighborhood, but treated it as nothing more than the site where they were located. A big reason is that the clientele of many institutions came from outside the neighborhood, and those that serviced a neighborhood market seemed to have a niche and did not have the resource-base to expand. The neighborhood-based institutions worked mostly in silos and had little or no understanding of how their services impacted the neighborhood and/or its residents. Indeed, there was not a single institution in the neighborhood that systematically measured their impact on neighborhood life and culture. The result is the PCN neighborhood social institution structure does not provide the individuals, children and families with the supports they need to grapple successfully with the challenges they face.

The plight of the neighborhood's early learning institution framework will illustrate this point. The existing PCN early learning network consists of a handful of Head Start and Early Head Start programs, along with a Parent–Child Home Program, about 22 licensed daycare centers, and an indeterminate number of unlicensed daycare centers. There are two major problems with the institutional network. First, Head Start is the most sophisticated of these early learning programs, but they can only service a small number of children. In metropolitan Buffalo, the Community Action Organization of Erie County (CAO) operates 63 Head Start and Early Head Start programs. These programs, however, provide services for only about 1,102 children. In the PCN alone, there were 1,422 children of five years of age and younger living in the community. Most important, according to Nate Hare, executive director of the CAO, it is virtually impossible to get new Head Start applications approved (Personal communication, 2012).

There are about 300 children attending the licensed daycare centers in and near the PCN, but most of the centers have not been certified by QUALITYStarsNY, which is a system for determining high quality daycare centers. We do not know how many children are in unlicensed programs, but we suspect that many more children attend these unlicensed daycare programs or they stay at home with their mother or caregiver. In both of these settings, we believe that the children are not getting the type of stimulation and experiences that would get them ready to read and excited about learning. There is a very strong Parent–Child Home Program (www.parent-child.org) operating in the PCN, but the organization does not have the resources to expand its operations. The PCN early childhood institutional framework is a dysfunctional one that is not preparing most PCN children to enter first grade ready to learn. As long as this institutional framework is not working properly, African-Americans are going to struggle in Buffalo schools, no matter what type of reform system the various schools adopt.

The really bad news is that many of Buffalo's inner-city primary schools are inadequate. Consequently, even if a PCN child gets to first grade ready to succeed, the absence of a pre-K to primary school transitional program will cause many of these students to lose ground before they reach fourth grade. Standardized tests show that the cognitive benefits that are derived from their participation in early intervention programs quickly erode and vanish by fourth grade. Scholars refer to this as "fade-out" – "the gradual convergence in test scores of the children who participated in early learning programs with comparable children who had not" (Strategic Research Group, 2011; Wilson, 1996).

The purpose of this section has been to use examples of the PCN early learning network and elementary school issues to demonstrate the problem of failed inner-city institutions. Similar examples could have been drawn from any set of institutions in the PCN: health, youth development, food security, job training and employment, economic development, and transportation. All these institutions have failed in their responsibility to provide effective and efficient services to residents in the PCN; and these failed social institutions represent a huge problem in distressed, jobless, and underdeveloped neighborhoods.

The Obama Choice Neighborhood Strategy

The Obama Administration recognized that failed social institutions were part of the landscape of inner-city communities (Whitehouse.gov: Administration, Executive Office of the President, Office of Urban Affairs, Initiatives, Neighborhood Revitalization Initiative; online). Implicit in the establishment of the White House Neighborhood Revitalization Initiative was the view that community-based social institutions have failed to design the type of interconnected solutions that were required to solve problems such as concentrated poverty, unemployment, broken homes, violence, crime and failing schools. So, shortly after his election in 2008, President Obama launched the White House initiative to tackle this issue. He approached the problem by recreating the federal–local partnership through the establishment of place-based initiatives anchored by the interweaving of school reform and neighborhood regeneration. The Obama strategy was informed by five interrelated principles:

1   Interdisciplinary – to address the interconnected problems in distressed neighborhoods;
2   Coordinated – to align the requirements of federal programs so that local communities can more readily braid together different funding streams;
3   Place-based – to leverage investments by geographically targeting resources and drawing on the compounding effect of well-coordinated action;
4   Data- and results-driven – to facilitate program monitoring and evaluation, to guide action needed to make adjustments in policy or programming, and to learn what works and develop best practices; and
5   Flexible – to adapt to changing conditions on the ground.

Operating within this context, the Choice and Promise Neighborhood Initiatives were implemented as projects designed to demonstrate the practicality of a regeneration strategy based on the interplay of neighborhood revitalization and school reform. These two initiatives were essentially the same, but differed in terms of emphasis and target population. Choice seeks to revitalize those neighborhoods with a significant concentration of dilapidated public housing or assisted housing units, while Promise targets those distressed communities without such a concentration of public or assisted housing. Within this scenario, both programs are comprehensive place-based strategies informed by the credo *you cannot reform schools without transforming the neighborhoods of which they are a part.*[8] In this regard, it is best to think of Promise and Choice not as one initiative, but as multiple initiatives anchored around the transformation of a particular place.

To fund these place-based strategies, Obama sought to restructure the operations of several key federal departments, so their investments would be more closely aligned with his place-based initiatives. This increased efficiency would make the federal investments more effective. Concurrently, Obama sought incentivized collaboration, especially cross-sector ones, among non-profits at the neighborhood levels. He did this by providing organizations extra points on grant applications if they were working in collaboration with partners in high priority place-based initiatives. This approach was based on the notion that interconnected social problems demanded interconnected solutions. For this to happen, non-profits would have to abandon their silos and work in collaboration with others. The inaugural Choice and Promise Neighborhood request for proposals were announced in early 2011, and the Buffalo Municipal Housing Authority (BMHA) in partnership with the UB Center for Urban Studies applied for the Choice planning grant.[9] That spring, the BMHA was one of 17 inaugural planning applicants selected from a pool of 119 aspirants.

The Perry Choice Neighborhood Planning Initiative

The Choice Neighborhood Initiative, although operating within a HUD framework, still gave locales considerable leeway to design their solutions. In the Perry Choice Neighborhood (PCN), the planning team placed school reform at the core of its theory of neighborhood change, with the goal of interweaving school reform, neighborhood regeneration, and institutional redesign. The reason is the development of social capital and young people are the essential ingredients for the neighborhood change process. Within this context, the education process is the key link in the transformation process. Without changing the schools, you will not change either the neighborhoods or the broader society in which it is embedded.

The reason is that the development of social capital is viewed as the essential ingredient in the neighborhood change process. Without transforming the educational system, then, it is not possible to develop a sustainable strategy for bolstering the neighborhood's social capital. Thus, only by changing the neighborhood's education trajectory can the community be transformed from a distressed, jobless and underdeveloped neighborhood into a desirable mixed-income community of opportunity.

The Education Strategy

In Buffalo, the interweaving of school reform and neighborhood development is very difficult because of school choice. This challenge notwithstanding, the prime goal of the planning team is to strengthen select public schools within the PCN and repurpose them as anchor institutions with a social purpose mission. Then, as the academic performance of these schools improves, parents/caregivers will increasingly choose them over other school options, thereby transforming these "choice schools" into "de facto neighborhood schools."

Buffalo Public Schools are plagued by a host of in-school and out-of-school issues, including demoralized teachers, high stakes testing, low test scores, high suspension rates, absenteeism and other issues. At the same time, the students attending these low-performing schools are beset with a host of non-academic barriers to academic success, which *originate* in the distressed, jobless and underdeveloped neighborhoods where they live. These barriers not only include the stress of living in neighborhoods characterized by crime, violence, family instability and hard times, but also issues that stem from lack of exposure to broad cultural and life experiences, poor academic preparation, and insufficient interest in learning and studying. Therefore, one of the keys to improving student academic performance is the elimination of non-academic barriers to academic success.

In many respects, the planning team also felt that many building-centered problems were indirectly related to a combination of neighborhood-based problems faced by the students, on the one hand, and budgetary, pedagogical and other issues spawned by neoliberalism. Against this analytical backdrop, the planning team decided the best way to attack the problem of underperforming schools was to eliminate non-academic barriers to academic success and to bolster the resiliency, skills and competencies of the children. Over time, the team would gain the type of support in the neighborhood, the schools and the district, which would make engagement over these broader building issues possible. Most important, this strategy would make possible the repurposing of the schools and transformation into neighborhood anchor institutions. Toward this end, the planning team established an education strategy centered on five outcomes.

1   All PCN children enter first grade ready to learn.
2   Non-academic barriers to academic success are eliminated as factors influencing educational outcomes among PCN children.
3   Children develop the attitudes, skills and competencies required for success in school and life.
4   Children graduate from high school ready for college or entry into the workforce.
5   School reform and neighborhood revitalization are interwoven in the PCN.

The team adopted an education pipeline strategy to reach these outcomes. The pipeline approach was based on creating a continuum of programs and activities that would envelop the child from birth to college or entry into the workforce. The goal was to create critically conscious students that would graduate from high school ready for college or entry into the workforce. Strategically, the pipeline aimed to guide children from birth to college and/or entry into the workforce. In this regard, the pipeline's credo is "The purpose of education is to prepare students both to earn a living and to create a world worth living in." The idea is to develop students with critical consciousness and a strong desire to build a better world and create a good society.

The planning team called their approach the "mini-education pipeline." They chose this name because the pipeline was embedded in a specific neighborhood, and within this context, it intentionally sought to move the children from the neighborhood to college or entry into the workforce.[10] The pipeline approach had three interactive goals. The first was to construct a bridge between the school and neighborhood. The idea was to develop interaction relationships between parents/caregivers, neighborhood-based service providers, and leaders of the neighborhood revitalization movement and school principals, teachers and staff members. The second was to develop a network of high quality learning programs that would prepare students for first grade. Research shows that unless children enter the first grade academically and socially ready to learn, they will be at risk to struggle academically, end up in prison, live their lives on the economic margin, or die prematurely. The third goal was to connect the pipeline to a series of neighborhood-based youth development programs, including those that promoted the development of a safe and secure neighborhood. Within this framework, a mini-education pipeline was established with five interactive components (Figure 7.2).

1   *The Early Learning Network* – The early learning network consisted of about 22 Head Start and Early Head Start programs, along with 22 licensed daycare centers. Rather than launch new programs, the planning team made the decision to strengthen existing pre-school programs by hiring reading specialists, who could work with daycare providers on strategies to develop language abilities and pre-literacy skills, as well as working with parents/caregivers on improving the home learning environment and developing the literacy skills of their children. A "feeder" system will be established that funnels children from the early learning network into the pipeline primary schools.

2   *The K–12 Pipeline, which provides a range of academic enrichment and supportive service programs* – The K–12 pipeline consists of two primary schools and two high schools. A variety of academic enrichment and supportive services are offered in these schools and interactive links are built between the schools and parents/caregivers, as well as between the school and supportive service organizations in the neighborhood.

3   *BMHA-UB Summer Academic Camp on Neighborhood Development* – An academic summer camp was established to lessen the loss of learning during the summer and to strengthen the academic skills and competencies of middle-school students from pipeline schools by involving them in project-based learning activities related to improving conditions in their community.

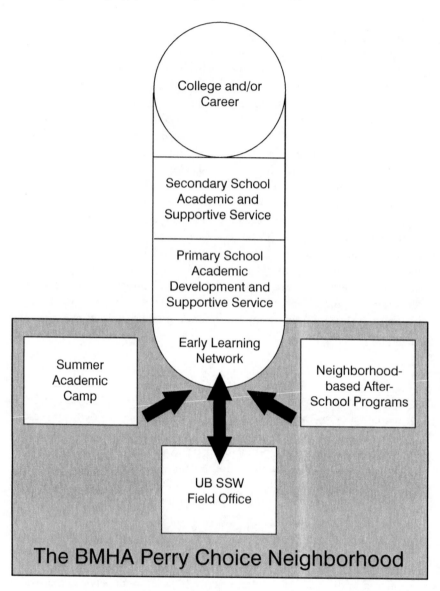

FIGURE 7.2   The Mini-Education Pipeline

4   *The Neighborhood-based Extended Day Network* – Extended-day programs are hugely important in the lives of students. However, for various reasons, many students do not attend school-based extended-day programs. Therefore, to capture these students, three different neighborhood-based extended day programs were established in the PCN.

5   *The School–Neighborhood Bridge* – The school–neighborhood bridge consists of a series of neighborhood-based programs that reinforce and strengthen the mini-education pipeline. These programs include the BMHA-UB Case Management and Service Coordination Unit, the PCN Youth Council, the Citizen Action Parent Institute, the Interventionists, a youth violence and gang prevention program, and other youth development and neighborhood-based health initiatives. A coordinator is responsible for creating strong interactive relationships between the participating schools and the members of the school–neighborhood bridge.

Building the Mini-Education Pipeline

A fundamental goal of the mini-education pipeline is to bolster the academic performance of the four participating schools and to repurpose them as anchor institutions with a social purpose mission. In this way, once these schools are improved, parents/caregivers will increasingly choose them over other options. To realize this complicated task in practice, the PCN must overcome three interactive obstacles: the Buffalo education regime; building the education collaborative in a neoliberal city; and funding the mini-education pipeline.

The Buffalo Education Regime

Education regime theory is a model that seeks to explain how educational decisions are made at the local level. The urban education regime is the engine that drives the city's schooling and education process. The federal government constructs the broad framework within which educational reform unfolds at the state and local levels. Although state governments possess the resources and authority to directly shape urban education policy, they typically leave these issues to the local education regime. In Buffalo, and elsewhere, all decision-making and education change occurs within the context of this governing framework. So, it is the education regime that defines the district's educational problems and decides how to address them. It determines how educational resources are to be accessed and in what ways they are to be distributed. Given its power and authority, the only way to effect sustainable educational change in the Buffalo Public Schools is to operate within this framework.

To bring about change in educational policy, then, an organization must have an inside and outside strategy. The inside strategy involves gaining influence within the educational regime, while the outside strategy involves using protest, in all its iterations, to influence policy and increase the leverage and power of progressive groups operating within the region. The intentional goal of the BMHA-PCN planning team was to become part of the education regime, thereby placing it in an optimal position to influence power.

The interplay of three factors made it possible for the planning team to achieve this goal. First, and most important, the Buffalo education regime was reconstituted in 2011, following the dismissal of the superintendent of schools, Dr. James Williams. The re-formed regime constituted what Shipps (2008) called a "performance regime," which is based on social-purpose politics and composed mostly of coalition partners who shared core beliefs and commitments and are willing to remain loyal to those ideals regardless of their differences over other issues (Wallace, 2008). The emergence of the new regime was triggered by a ground swell of dissatisfaction over Buffalo's failing schools. The uproar led to Williams' dismissal in August. Shortly afterwards, *Say Yes to Education* was brought to Buffalo by a group of business and civic leaders. *Say Yes,* a national non-profit organization, founded in Philadelphia in 1986, promised to dramatically increase high school and college graduation rates and to provide students who graduate from a Buffalo Public School (traditional or charter) with up to 100 percent of the tuition needed to attend college, regardless of the family's income (www.sayyestoeducation.org/). *Say Yes* convinced local business leaders, government officials and local foundations to invest $18 million to support the initiative, and quickly emerged as leader within Buffalo's new education performance regime.

Say Yes changed the discourse over education in Buffalo. It anchored its reformed strategy within a social purpose framework, which linked school reform to stimulating economic development and getting middle-income families to stay or relocate in the City. *Say Yes* argued that by using their strategy to fix public schools, the City would reduce crime, increase property values and attract middle-income residents to the City. To implement their strategy in the schools, *Say Yes* created an inner-council composed of three school reform groups, including *Say Yes,* Closing the Gap in Student Performance, a local group comprised of the United Way of Erie County, Buffalo Public Schools, and Catholic Charities, and the Buffalo Promise Neighborhood, an initiative funded by the US Department of Education and led by the M&T Bank.[11] Also joining the inner-council were two representatives from the Office of the Superintendent of Schools. This inner-council implemented the *Say Yes* reform strategy in Buffalo schools. From the planning team's perspective, the *Say Yes* inner-council, because of its connection to implementation of the school reform strategy, was a critical component of the City's education regime. So, the planning team sought to join it. The planning team's request to join the inner-council was readily accepted by *Say Yes.*

The BMHA-UB partnership provided the mini-education pipeline team with the stature and prestige it needed to be accepted by council members. Most important, the mini-education pipeline strategy was complementary to the educational model used by the other groups. All four groups, including *Say Yes,* believed in a pipeline strategy that centered on enveloping children from distressed neighborhoods in a continuum of academic enrichment and supportive service programs and activities from birth to college or entry into the workforce. The complementary nature of the four groups' approaches to education reform served as the glue which held them together, despite some differences between the various models.

Building Collaboratives in the Neoliberal City

The second barrier that had to be overcome was the building of a cross-sector collaborative (Anderson-Butcher, Lawson, Iachini, Flaspohler, Bean & Wade-Mdivanian, 2010; Bryson, Crosby & Stone, 2006; Selsky & Parker, 2005). The ability to provide a comprehensive menu of academic enrichment and supportive services for children from birth to graduation from high school is beyond the scope of any one agency, organization or discipline. The mini-education pipeline strategy, therefore, was based on the necessity of building a cross-sector collaborative among four public schools and a host of non-profit service providers. The goal was to bring together service providers from the early learning network, the four public schools, the neighborhood-based extended-day programs, and the summer academic camp under a single administration structure. For the pipeline to be successful, these disparate organizations needed to plan and work together as a team.

Building such a collaborative in the neoliberal city is extremely difficult. The reason is that neoliberalism imbues society with competitive market principles (Read, 2009). As such, non-profits are expected to be enterprising and entrepreneurial organizations engaged in a fierce competitive struggle with each other for limited resources. Under neoliberalism, to offset the loss in services caused by government spending cuts, grants and contracts are made available to non-profits and private companies, which must compete for them in a fiercely competitive education marketplace. This competitive landscape of neoliberalism promotes and reinforces siloism, which causes agencies and organizations to work independently of each other and to come together only when such partnerships or collaborations provide them with a competitive advantage.

In this setting, the building of a cross-sector collaborative not only required overcoming the traditional issues of turf, politics, distrust, and building a common vision, but also necessitated tackling the competition issue head-on. So, to build the collaborative, in addition to following the principles of developing effective collaborations, the planning team offered its potential partners three reasons why they should join the pipeline. First, joining the mini-education pipeline would provide them with a competitive edge in the struggle to secure grants to fund their operations. At both the federal and state levels, organizations, agencies and institutions working in Choice and Promise Neighborhoods are given extra points, thereby giving them an edge over competitors. Second, the planning team told the service providers that by planning and working together as a team, their individual programs could be greatly enhanced. Lastly, the pipeline planning team said the education landscape in Buffalo was rapidly changing and that service providers could best protect their interest by being part of a collaborative, directly tied to the education regime (Shipps, 2008). This approach worked, and the planning team was able to build a collaborative composed of 45 non-profit organizations.

It should be noted that the planning team appealed to the self-interest of the service providers, while placing the mini-education pipeline within the broader context of providing a viable solution to the City's education crisis. This approach appealed both to the survival and social purpose instincts of the service providers. Hence, they would not only be able to participate in a highly innovative school reform strategy, but also acquire a competitive edge in the struggle to gain the funding for their programs. Lastly, the ability to bring this collaborative together was also directly related to the role played by the UB Center for Urban Studies. The perceived *neutrality* of the UB made it an ideal group to build a collaborative in such a fiercely competitive environment. Had the lead organization for the pipeline been a member of one of the "competing" partners, it is doubtful if such a collaboration could have been built.

Funding the Mini-Education Pipeline

The third obstacle was forging a locally based financial strategy to fund the initiative. The funding needed to provide inner-city schools with the academic enrichment and supportive services generally comes from grants and contracts given by government and foundations, which are awarded in a highly competitive educational marketplace. Most of the academic enrichment programs and supportive services are then provided by non-profit organizations and private companies that are the recipients of that funding. The neoliberal quest to create "small government" has led to the increased reliance on non-profits and businesses to deliver a range of educational services. The mini-education pipeline must compete with others in this market for the resources to fund its strategy.

To rationalize this competitive process at the federal level, the Obama Administration developed a process that gives a competitive advantage to those organizations delivering services in place-based initiatives. Toward this end, the White House formulated an interagency strategy designed to engage the White House Domestic Policy Council, White House Office of Urban Affairs, and the Departments of Housing and Urban Development, Education, Justice, Health and Human Services and Treasury in support of local solutions to revitalize and transform neighborhoods. Obama argued that struggling schools located in communities with problems that feed into and perpetuate each other could not be transformed without an integrated, place-based strategy. To facilitate the development of this type of strategy, the president called upon the White House to work closely with five key federal departments to align their place-based investments with programs being developed at the local level. This approach to funding gave those organizations working collaboratively on place-based initiatives a competitive advantage over other grant applicants in the education marketplace.

In 2012, New York State adopted a similar strategy. Using language almost identical to the Obama Administration, the Cuomo Administration established the New York State Community, Opportunity and Reinvestment Initiative Solicitation of Interest.[12] This program seeks to build the well-being of communities and assure that all New Yorkers will have the opportunity to thrive in a safe and stable community from a supported childhood to a productive adulthood. The idea is for the state to work closely with local communities to better coordinate and align their resources with communities targeted for transformation. This place-based approach to funding has created an environment that provides the mini-education pipeline with a competitive advantage in the search for funding. At the same time, securing funding to support the multiple components of the program will be extremely difficult. Neoliberalism constructs a setting where funding to support programs takes place in a hyper-competitive marketplace where there are only a few winners. Locally, this funding environment is made more complex by the dominance of major groups, such as *Say Yes to Education*, Catholic Charities and United Way, along with a large number of non-profits and private companies that compete with each other for limited resources. In this setting, it will be difficult to secure a funding base sufficient to launch the mini-education pipeline and even more difficult to sustain that initiative over time.

Conclusion: Repurposing Neighborhood Schools as Anchor Institutions

The big question driving this chapter is how we get back to the future. That is, how do we reconnect schools to the neighborhoods in which they are located and repurpose them as anchor institutions? The mini-education pipeline strategy provides some clues to this challenge. Two things must happen to repurpose the neighborhood schools as anchor institutions. The first is that inner-city schools, including the principals and teachers, must understand the important role their school can play in the redevelopment of the neighborhood in which it is located. Concurrently, a strong, interactive relationship must be established between the school, the parents, residents, stakeholders and the network of academic enrichment and supportive service programs operating in the neighborhoods. These two elements must happen simultaneously, and the relationship between school and neighborhood will gradually be cemented as school performance and student academic achievement improves.

The process of building the mini-education pipeline is designed to build and cement this relationship, thereby recreating the school as an inner-city neighborhood asset and a social-purpose anchor institution. In building the pipeline, the goal is to establish enrichment programs and supportive service programs both inside the school and in the neighborhood. For example, at the primary school level, the pipeline will establish both school-based and neighborhood-based after-school programs, which are interrelated. This way, the extended day program will be able to create enrichment opportunities for those students that choose not to attend the in-school program. In both the high schools and primary schools, service learning programs will be established to build and strengthen the bonds between the school and neighborhoods. During the summer, the BMHA-UB Academic Camp will recruit students directly from the neighborhood and engage them in projects designed to improve neighborhood conditions.

The school-based supportive service program will work closely with the neighborhood-based supportive service team, which will be headed by the University at Buffalo School of Social Work. The plan is for site coordinators for the participating pipeline schools to work closely with the BMHA-UB Case Management and Service Coordination Unit, so that they can collaboratively tackle the problems facing children and their families. Over time, varied projects will be developed that are aimed at building close relationships between the school and neighborhood. For example, each year, Futures Academy, a participating pipeline primary school, holds a neighborhood Clean-a-Thon. The students, teachers and residents form brigades that clean up the neighborhood during the morning hours. In the afternoon, they have a block party, replete with food, dancing and games.

These and similar activities will raise the visibility of the school within the neighborhood, while simultaneously recreating it as an important neighborhood asset. As the school performance increases and as the academic achievement of the students is bolstered, an increasing number of parents/caregivers will choose the neighborhood school over other options. In this way, the Choice school strategy will be used to create a de facto neighborhood school. Of course, the mini-education pipeline is in a nascent stage of development and faces many obstacles before it achieves the goal of repurposing the pipeline schools and establishing them as neighborhood anchor institutions. Nonetheless, the strategy is sound and this is an experiment worth monitoring.

Notes

1 These are the reflections of Professor Henry Louis Taylor, Jr.
2 By neighborhood education infrastructure, we mean enrichment programs, high quality early learning centers, quiet places to study, computer access, and neighborhood-based tutoring and homework assistance.

3 Some cities have created voucher programs that allow private schools to be added to this menu of school choices.

4 Graduation rates are calculated using the Cumulative Promotion Index method with data from the US Department of Education's Common Core of Data, 2009.

5 For the purposes of this study, the term children refers to young people between the ages of 6 and 18 years. Children younger than this are considered preschoolers.

6 Outlaw culture is a concept that covers a broad range of anti-social behavior from vandalism, bullying, harassment, and the justification and rationalization of criminal activity. Outlaw culture rejects the black communal norms and community building, while promoting predatory individualism, conspicuous consumption operating within the context of neoliberal market values, gangsterism and gang life (Mark Naison, "Outlaw Culture and Black Neighborhoods," 1 RECONSTRUCTION, 4, 1992, p. 128).

7 Of course, there are some institutions, which are designed to provide services for a neighborhood, but are not located in it. These institutions are considered part of that dysfunctional and failed institutional framework.

8 Interestingly, the Obama administration does not account for the role played by school choice in complicating this quest to connect school reform to neighborhood revitalization.

9 BMHA selected the Choice Initiative over Promise because of its control over a significant number of public housing units in need of major repair.

10 In the late 1990s and 2000s, school reformers begin to focus increasingly on the development of pre-K through 12 education pipelines, which were designed to ensure that students successfully made their way through the schooling process without getting derailed. Groups started to emerge, such as the Strive Partnership in Cincinnati, Alignment Nashville, Say Yes to Education and similar programs around the country, which are based on a full-service community school model. While building on these models, including the community schools method, the BMHA-PCN Mini-Education Pipeline approach focuses on the building of a pipeline that extends from the neighborhood to college and/or a career and employs a hybrid of the community school model.

11 Buffalo Promise Neighborhood (2011). Project Narrative for Buffalo Promise Neighborhood. Buffalo, NY: Author. Retrieved from http://www2.ed.gov/programs/promiseneighborhoods/2011/u215n110046narrative.pdf

12 New York State Department of Health (2012). Online: http://www.health.ny.gov/funding/soi/opportunity_and_reinvestment_initiative/opportunity_and_reinvestment_initiative.pdf

References

ACT (2012). *The condition of college and career readiness 2012*. Iowa City: IA: Author. Retrieved from www.act.org/readiness/2012

Anderson-Butcher, D., Lawson, H.A., Iachini, A., Flaspohler, P., Bean, J. & Wade-Mdivanian, R. (2010). Emergent evidence in support of a community collaboration model for school improvement. *Children & Schools, 32*(3), 160–171.

Bertaux, N. & Washington, M. (2005). The "Colored Schools" of Cincinnati and the African American community in Nineteenth-century Cincinnati, 1849–1890. *The Journal of Negro Education, 74*(1), 43–52.

Betts, J. & Loveless, T. (2005). *Getting choice right: Ensuring equity and efficiency in education policy*. Washington, DC: Brookings Institution Press.

Bronfenbrenner, U. & Morris, P. (1998). The ecology of developmental process. In W. Damon (Series Ed.) & R. Lerner (Vol. Ed.), *Handbook of child psychology: Vol. 1: Theoretical models of human development* (5th edn, pp. 992–1028). New York: Wiley.

Bryson, J.M., Crosby, B.C. & Stone, M.M. (2006). The design and implementation of cross-sector collaborations: Propositions from the literature. *Public Administration Review, 66,* 44–55.

Choice Neighborhoods Grant Program (2012). 77 *Federal Register* (10 May 2012). Online. Available http://www.gpo.gov/fdsys/pkg/FR-2012-05-10/pdf/2012-11305.pdf

Cox, K. & Mair, A. (1988). Locality and community in the politics of local economic development. *Annals of the Association of American Geographers, 78*(2), 307–325.

Driscoll, M.E. (2001). The sense of place and the neighborhood school: Implications for building social capital and for community development. In R. Crowson (Ed.), *Community development and school reform* (p. 19–42). New York: JAI/Elsevier.

Dryfoos, J. (1994). *Full service schools: A revolution for health and social services for children, youth, and families.* San Francisco, CA: Jossey Bass.

Harkavy, I. & Zuckerman, H. (1999). *Eds and meds: Cities' hidden assets. The Brookings Institution Survey Series, 22.* Washington, DC: The Brookings Institution, Center on Urban & Metropolitan Policy.

Henig, J R. (1994). *Rethinking school choice: Limits of the market metaphor.* Princeton, NJ: Princeton University Press.

Henig, J. & Sugarman, S. (2000). The nature and extent of school choice. In S. Sugarman & F. Kemerer (Eds.), *School choice and social controversy: Politics, policy and law* (pp. 68–107). Washington, DC: Brookings Institution.

Hoxby, C. (2003). *The economics of school choice.* Chicago, IL: University of Chicago Press.

Hudson, M.J. & Holmes, B.J. (1994). Missing teachers: impaired communities: The unanticipated consequences of *Brown v. Board of Education* on the African American teaching force at the precollegiate level. *The Journal of Negro Education, 63*(3), 388–393.

Hursh, D. (2007). Assessing "No Child Left Behind" and the rise of neoliberal education policies. *American Educational Research Journal, 44*(3), pp. 493–518.

Khadduri, J., Schwartz, H., and Turnham, J. (2008). *Policy roadmap for expanding school-centered community revitalization.* Columbia, MD: Enterprise Community Partners.

Mauer, M. (2006). *Race to incarcerate.* New York: The New Press.

McNeely, C.A., Nonnemaker, J.M. & Blum, R.W. (2002). Promoting school connectedness: Evidence from the National Longitudinal Study of Adolescent Health. *Journal of School Health, 72*(4), 138–146.

Milner, H.R. & Howard, T.C. (2004). Black teachers, Black students, Black communities, and Brown: Perspectives and Insights. *The Journal of Negro Education, 73*(3), 285–297.

Netter Center for Community Partnerships (2008). *Anchor institutions toolkit.* Philadelphia, PA: University of Pennsylvania. Retrieved from http://www.upenn.edu/ccp/anchortoolkit/

New York State Education Department (2012). Education Department releases high school graduation rates; overall rates improve slightly, but are still too low for our students to be competitive. [Press release] Retrieved from http://www.oms.nysed.gov/press/GraduationRates2012OverallImproveSlightlyButStillTooLow.html

Owens, A. (2010). Neighborhoods and schools as competing and reinforcing contexts for educational attainment. *Sociology of Education, 83*(4), 287–311.

Porter, M. (2010). *Anchor institutions and urban economic development: From community benefit to shared value.* Presentation from Inner City Economic Forum Summit 2010, Washington,

DC. Retrieved from http://www.icic.org/ee_uploads/publications/Anchor-Institutions. PDF

Porter, M. & Kramer, M. (2011). Creating shared value. *Harvard Business Review, 89*(1/2), 62–77.

Raikes, H., Luze, G., Brooks-Gunn, J., Raikes, A., Pan, B.A., Tamis-LeMonda, C.S., Constantine, J., Tarullo, L.B. & Rodriguez, E.T. (2006). Mother-child bookreading in low-income families: Correlates and outcomes during the first three years of life. *Child Development, 77*(4), 924–953.

Read, J. (2009). A genealogy of homo-economicus: Neoliberalism and the production of subjectivity. *Foucault Studies, 6*, 25–36.

Sarsour, K., Sheridan, M., Jutte, D., Nuru-Jeter, A., Hinshaw, S. & Boyce, W.T. (2010). Family socioeconomic status and child executive functions: The roles of language, home environment, and single parenthood. *Journal of the International Neuropsychological Society, 17*, 120–132. doi:10.1017/S1355617710001335

Schott Foundation. (2010). *Yes, we can: The 2010 Schott 50-state report on public education of black males.* Cambridge, MA: Author. www.blackboysreport.org.

Selsky, J.W. & Parker, B. (2005). Cross-sector partnerships to address social issues: Challenges to theory and practice. *Journal of Management, 31*(6), 849–873.

Sinha, S., Payne, M.R. & Cook, T.D. (2005). A multidimensional approach to neighborhood schools and their potential impact. *Urban Education, 40*(6), 627–662.

Shipps, D. (2008). Urban regime theory and the reform of public schools: Governance, power, and leadership. In B.S. Cooper, J.K. Ciubulka & L.D. Fusarelli (eds), *Handbook of Education Politics and Policy* (pp. 89–108). New York: Routledge.

Strategic Research Group (2011). *Assessing the impact of Tennessee's pre-kindergarten program: Final report.* Columbus, OH.

Swanson, C. (2009). *Cities in crisis 2009: Closing the Graduation Gap, Educational and Economic Conditions in America's Largest Cities.* Bethesda, MD: Editorial Projects in Education. Available: http://www.edweek.org/media/cities_in_crisis_2009.pdf

Tough, P. (2004, June 20). The Harlem project, *New York Times Magazine*, pp. 44–49, 66, 72–75.

US Census Bureau. (2006–2010). Buffalo City, Erie County, New York, B20004 Median Earnings In The Past 12 Months (In Inflation-Adjusted Dollars) By Sex By Educational Attainment For The Population 25 Years And Over [Data]. 2010 American Community Survey 5-Year Estimates. Retrieved from http://factfinder2.census.gov

Wallace, D. (2008). Community education and community learning and development. In: T. Bryce and W. Humes (eds., pp. 742–751). *Scottish education: Beyond devolution.* Edinburgh: Edinburgh University Press.

Wilson, W.J. (1996). *When work disappears: The world of the new urban poor.* New York: Random House.

8

ASSESSING THE STATE OF THE VILLAGE

Multi-method, Multi-level Analyses for Comprehensive Community Change

John M. Wallace, Jr. and Samantha N. Teixeira
University of Pittsburgh

Introduction

A growing body of research reveals that "place matters" for the academic, social, emotional and physical health and well-being of children. Consistent with the growth in research, there has also been an increase in programs and social policy that promote "place-based" strategies to address the holistic well-being of poor children. At the federal level, the most prominent recent policy strategies designed to benefit poor children and their families are President Obama's Promise Neighborhood and Choice Neighborhood initiatives. Motivated, at least in part, by the success of Geoffrey Canada's Harlem Children's Zone (www.hcz.org), Promise Neighborhoods, administered by the Department of Education, focuses on education and schools as primary loci of community development.[1] Choice Neighborhoods, administered by the Department of Housing and Urban Development, complements Promise Neighborhoods, with a specific focus on housing (i.e., mixed income housing), transportation, public services and job access.[2]

Despite the appeal and potential of Promise and Choice Neighborhoods as strategies to impact positively the life chances of poor children, the magnitude of the problem of child poverty, coupled with funding restrictions, constrain their scope and scale to a few locations around the nation. And so, although these federal placed-based strategies to comprehensively address the needs of poor children have significant potential as demonstration projects and models, they cannot begin to address the problems of the more than 16 million poor children and their families around the nation (Institute for Research on Poverty, 2011).[3] Despite their limitations, however, these federal initiatives appear to have catalyzed other efforts, and in fact, what some have called a "movement" of holistic place-based initiatives that seek to reduce and eliminate poverty and its consequences for children in communities around the country. The purpose of the present chapter is to describe one of these initiatives—the Homewood Children's Village in Pittsburgh, PA, with a particular focus on the way in which research—theoretical and empirical, qualitative and quantitative—has informed the initiative's design, early implementation and ongoing growth and development.

Background[4]

Homewood is a one square mile neighborhood located on the east end of Pittsburgh, Pennsylvania. At its peak, in the 1940s and early 1950s, Homewood was an ethnically and racially diverse middle income community of more than 31,000 residents, with a thriving business district, strong public schools, tree-lined streets and well-maintained homes. Today, Homewood is an economically challenged, racially segregated neighborhood (96 percent African American) whose population has decreased by nearly 80 percent to only 6,442 residents (of whom 1,798 are children under 18 years of age) (United States Census, 2010). Although Homewood has a rich history and retains numerous assets, it is also plagued with many of the social problems that characterize economically disadvantaged communities across the nation. These problems, all of which have been found to have significant adverse outcomes on children's well-being, include high rates of school failure, unemployment, welfare dependency, crime and vacant and abandoned properties.

Designed explicitly to address the myriad social problems that adversely impact the lives of children, the Homewood Children's Village (the "HCV" or the "Village") is a place-based, child-centered, comprehensive community initiative inspired by Geoffrey Canada's internationally acclaimed Harlem Children's Zone. The vision of the HCV is that Homewood is a community "where every child succeeds!" and its mission is, "to simultaneously improve the lives of Homewood's children and reweave the fabric of the community in which they live." The HCV was born out of a search to identify a replicable, evidence-based strategy to address the numerous problems that confront the children and families who live, learn, work and worship in Homewood. The HCV began in 2008 as a data-driven community-based participatory research partnership between the University of Pittsburgh's School of Social Work and Operation Better Block (OBB), a Homewood-based community organizing non-profit. Over time, the HCV partnership has grown to include a diverse group of Homewood residents, leaders of Homewood non-profits, and public, private and non-profit leaders from around the greater Pittsburgh community. Below we describe the organizational structure of the HCV and the theoretical and empirical research that undergirds its development and implementation.

HCV Organizational Structure and Strategy

Organizationally, the HCV is comprised of *administrative offices*; *initiatives* that deliver programs and services to Homewood's children along the HCV's cradle-to-college-to-career developmental continuum; *networks* that convene and coordinate services for children; and *collaboratives* that support broader community initiatives that directly and indirectly impact children.

The HCV's *administrative offices* (i.e., the Office of the President/CEO, the Office of Evaluation and the Office of Community Affairs) provide vision, raise funds, evaluate and market the HCV's work. The HCV *initiatives* collaborate with others to deliver direct services to children. For example, the Full Service Community School coordinates educational, academic, arts and cultural enrichment, social services and health and wellness programs. The Office of Promise Fulfillment works within the Full Service Community School Office and in partnership with other providers, to deliver educational support services to students, and to increase the number and percentage of students who graduate from high school, who are eligible to participate in the city's college scholarship program—the Pittsburgh Promise—and who enroll in, and graduate from, college or other post-secondary academic institution. Currently, the Pittsburgh Promise provides eligible students—those who earn a minimum grade point average of 2.5 and have 90 percent attendance—up to $40,000 to attend any accredited post-secondary institution in the state of Pennsylvania.

In addition to the direct services that the HCV provides through its Full Service Community School and the Promise Fulfillment Offices, it convenes and helps to coordinate and manage services delivered through three *networks* of service and program providers. These networks—the Early Learning Network, the Faith, Family and Out of School Time Network and the Health and Wellness Network—engage key existing service providers, government agencies and funders to implement and evaluate evidence-based interventions included on the HCV's cradle-to-college-to-career continuum.

Consistent with the second part of its mission, to "reweave the fabric of the community" in which Homewood's children live, the HCV is actively involved in various strategic *collaboratives* that focus on community and economic development and social policy issues that directly and indirectly impact children (e.g., transit-oriented development, crime and the vacant and abandoned properties surrounding Homewood's schools). The Homewood Economic and Community Development Collaborative focuses upon the built environment of Homewood and connecting the Homewood community to the regional economy of the city of Pittsburgh. The Research and Policy Collaborative brings together the HCV, various schools, offices and departments at the University of Pittsburgh (e.g., Social Work, the Office of Child Development, Family Medicine) and other local colleges and universities (e.g., Carnegie Mellon) to provide research support, to strengthen the internal research capacity of the HCV and to provide insight into emerging best practices in service delivery, program evaluation, collaboration and relevant social policy.

In sum, the HCV does four things that comprise its 4Cs—it *convenes* existing services providers, *coordinates* their services along the cradle-to-college-to-career developmental continuum, builds partners' *capacity* to deliver and evaluate evidence-based interventions, at scale, with fidelity and *collaborates* with other non-profit organizations, government, and businesses to address issues that directly and indirectly impact children and the neighborhood in which they live and learn.

The HCV's Theoretical Frameworks

Two theoretical models underpin the work of the Homewood Children's Village. The first model, focused on the *contexts* in which children develop, is Urie Bronfenbrenner's bioecological systems theory (Bronfenbrenner, 1979, 2005). Bronfenbrenner's theory focuses on the five nested ecological contexts in which child development occurs (i.e., microsystems—like peer networks, families, classrooms; mesosystems—like school; exosystems—like parents' workplaces; macrosystems—the broader cultural, social, belief systems and opportunity structures; and the chronosystem—change or stability over individual's life course and across historical time (Bronfenbrenner and Ceci, 1994)).

The second theoretical model that informs the work of the Village is James Comer's theory of child development. Comer's theory focuses on the developmental *pathways* along which children need to grow to be holistically healthy. According to Comer, these pathways are physical, ethical, social, psychological, linguistic and cognitive. Students' well-being on these pathways determine their "availability" to learn and to succeed academically (Comer, Joyner and Ben-Avie, 2004). Comer's work emphasizes the importance of children's development, nested in their social contexts, with a particular focus on their primary relationships (i.e., parents, peers, and school faculty, staff and administrators).

Undergirded by bioecological systems theory and Comer's theory of child development, the HCV identifies and integrates the best evidence-based practices and practice-based evidence to design, implement and rigorously evaluate its cradle-to-college-to-career developmental continuum for Homewood's children.

The State of the Village Multi-Level Multi-Method Assessment

Consistent with the multi-level theoretical models that guide the work of the HCV, faculty and students from the University of Pittsburgh's School of Social

Work, in partnership with the HCV, Homewood residents, and other local non-profits, initiated a collaborative multi-level, multi-method data collection and analysis process. The purpose of this process was to create a comprehensive, data-based portrait of Homewood and to provide the foundation for the multiple levels of intervention required to build a sustainable child-centered comprehensive community initiative. A central goal of the assessment process was to analyze and report qualitative and quantitative data, collected at the individual, family, school, and neighborhood levels, to inform the work of the HCV.

Guided by the multi-level theoretical framework, the research team aimed to collect data across multiple ecological systems levels and points across the lifespan. Consistent with a community-based participatory approach, these methods were designed to simultaneously collect data and engage community residents in the research and intervention process. Below, we outline some of the research methods and individual projects that comprised the State of the Village Assessment, which began in 2008 and continues through to the present (i.e., 2012). Each project description begins with background information about the specific data collected, followed by an outline of the methods, where applicable, the process by which residents were engaged and a brief summary of the results.

Secondary Analysis of Census and Other Existing Data

Beginning in 2008, as we laid the foundation for the HCV, the chapter's co-authors sought to identify existing data on conditions in Homewood, with a particular focus on children. The intent of this effort was to establish a baseline of the magnitude and extent of the challenges that faced Homewood's children and families and to also identify and mobilize the individual and institutional resources available to address these challenges.

Methods

The baseline secondary data we identified and analyzed included the following: 1) Census and administrative data on Homewood's demographics, housing and neighborhood conditions; 2) school performance data including academic and behavioral outcomes for students; 3) Allegheny County Department of Human Services data describing service use in the areas of mental health, abuse and neglect, and assistance for low income families (i.e., TANF, SNAP); 4) crime and violence data from the Pittsburgh bureau of police; and 5) data on Homewood's organizational assets from existing lists and neighborhood resource guides. These data were compiled and analyzed largely by students and faculty from the University of Pittsburgh.

Results

According to the Census, demographically, 32 percent of Homewood families (and more than 60 percent of its children) live below the federal poverty level; nearly 90 percent of its public school students are eligible for free or reduced lunch (A+ Schools, 2012); 26 percent of adults have not earned a high school diploma; only 45 percent are in the workforce; roughly 40 percent of those who work earn less than $15,000 per year; more than 50 percent lack transportation; 62 percent are renters; 72 percent of Homewood's children are being raised by one parent; and 28 percent of all live births in Homewood are to teenagers.

Academically, Homewood's schools are failing. In 2009, when the data collection for the State of the Village Assessment began, Homewood's elementary school, Faison K–8, was in its second year of School Improvement and its high school, Westinghouse (grades 9–12), was in Year 2 of Corrective Action.[5] Because of its high dropout rate (58 percent),[6] Westinghouse was identified as a "dropout factory" (i.e., a high school in which 60 percent or fewer students graduate).[7] The cumulative grade point average for the school's 12th graders was 1.76, far below the 2.5 criteria required for the Pittsburgh Promise scholarship. In fact, in 2009, Westinghouse had the lowest percentage of "Promise ready" students in the district (i.e., 39 percent versus 67 percent for the rest of the city's high schools).

Test score data revealed that Homewood's children enter kindergarten significantly behind[8] and that the magnitude of the "proficiency gap" grows over time. More specifically, in 2009, only half of Homewood's 3rd graders were proficient in reading (47 percent) and math (52 percent); even fewer 8th graders were proficient (38 percent in reading and 22 percent in math); and among 11th graders only a quarter (25 percent) were proficient in reading and about one-tenth (13 percent) were proficient in math.[9] Comparatively, students in 99 percent of Pennsylvania's K–8 schools and high schools scored higher than students in Homewood's Faison K–8 and Westinghouse 9–12.[10]

Data from the Allegheny County Department of Human Services, on family and community support needs in Homewood, revealed that Temporary Assistance for Needy Families (TANF) cash assistance and food stamp eligibility rates are more than double those for the City of Pittsburgh (TANF 10 percent and food stamps 21 percent).[11] Further, Homewood has one of Allegheny County's highest out-of-home placement rates for abused, neglected or abandoned children (188 in 2007) and the largest number of children referred to the Allegheny County Juvenile Court Probation office (145 in 2007).[12]

Crime data revealed that Homewood also has had the largest number of homicides (76 between 1997 and 2009) in Pittsburgh, the largest number of gangs of any neighborhood in Pittsburgh and has among the highest violent crime rates in the city (i.e., drug, gun and overall violent crime rates are, respectively, 1.7, 4.0 and 2.5 times those of the city taken as a whole).[13]

Resident Surveys

An important supplement to the Census and human services administrative data are data collected directly from residents. Between July and December 2009, Operation Better Block Inc. (OBB), a Homewood-based community organizing non-profit, partnered with researchers from the University of Pittsburgh to design and implement a community-wide survey known as the 1,000 Conversations Campaign. The purpose of the campaign was to engage a significant number of Homewood residents in brief interviews to ascertain their needs, concerns, and aspirations for the neighborhood. It was also hoped that the survey would help to better understand and prioritize concerns of most importance to residents and guide future directions for research and interventions.

Methods

Pitt researchers worked with OBB administrators to identify, train, and mobilize a data collection team comprised of block club members, community volunteers, staff, and interns. Respondents were a convenience sample of Homewood residents interviewed face-to-face and by telephone. The OBB interviewers asked respondents to answer five questions and recorded their answers verbatim on printed questionnaires. Overall, a total of 1,003 interviews were completed. Student interns from the University of Pittsburgh's School of Social Work coded the interviews, identified key themes and entered the responses into a database. The research team analyzed the survey data and produced a one-page, community friendly report of the findings that OBB staff distributed to the community.

Results

Homewood residents overwhelmingly identified two issues as the most pressing problems in the neighborhood—crime (50 percent) and abandoned properties (27 percent). Issues that garnered additional support included the need for businesses and for safe and productive activities for young people. Specifically, in their qualitative comments, many residents noted the intersection between the large number of vacant homes, crime, and drug activity in the neighborhood. They reported that the vacant homes were not only an eyesore but that they also contributed to social disorder and fear among residents.

Systematic Social Observation of Homewood Properties

Based on direct observation of the problem of vacant land, coupled with residents' concerns about the intersection of crime, safety and vacant and abandoned properties, the Pitt research team reviewed the literature on property assessment, and vacancy, as well as existing instruments and processes that past research has used to evaluate the condition of properties. In light of the concerns about the impact of vacant properties on crime and safety, and the particular interest in the impact of these properties on children, we designed a property evaluation instrument to assess the safety and condition of properties along the routes that children take to, from and around Homewood's schools.

Methods

The systematic observation data were collected through the use of a hybrid ecological assessment instrument that combined systematic social observation methodologies with property level measures based on building inspection protocols. Measures included an assessment of features of the overall block as well as each individual property on the block including residential and non-residential buildings and vacant parcels. The Pitt researchers partnered with OBB staff and community volunteers to design and pretest the instrument to ensure that it was culturally and geographically relevant to Homewood. A member of the Pitt research team then used the instrument to train Homewood residents, University of Pittsburgh students and youth from a Homewood-based after school program to assist in the systematic property assessment data collection.

Results

In total, the data collection included 1,509 properties in a 56-block area surrounding Homewood's schools. The majority of the residential buildings in the areas surveyed were occupied ($n = 587$, 76 percent). Vacant and boarded buildings represented the next largest segment of those surveyed at 14 percent ($n = 110$). Buildings that were vacant and not boarded fell into two categories: those that were in very poor condition and open to entry and those that appeared recently vacated that appeared empty but not open to entry. Fifty-seven buildings (7 percent) were vacant and not boarded. Raters were unsure about the occupancy of 26 buildings (3 percent). The bulk of properties surveyed were in good ($n = 377$) to fair ($n = 362$) condition. Data were missing for one property and 128 properties (15 percent) were in poor condition.

The results of the assessment, particularly information related to the properties that were vacant and not boarded and in poor condition, were used to a spur data-driven community organizing projects like Homewood's Dirty Thirty, outlined in the action and intervention section.

Focus Groups

The HCV engaged a consultant to design a comprehensive plan for child-, youth- and family-centered development and programs—A Children Youth and Family Master Plan for Homewood. The consultant conducted a series of focus groups with various groups of Homewood stakeholders to learn more about key issues that were important to Homewood residents across a number of life domains.

Methods

Three focus groups were conducted with middle school students (n = 33) and high school students (n = 22) from Homewood's schools. Three other focus groups included adult samples of parents of Homewood students. The moderator used the same discussion guide for each 40-minute group and audio taped and transcribed the discussions. Participants were asked to describe their overall perception of their school, community, and available activities and support systems. The moderator worked with community gatekeepers to engage with teachers and community leaders to identify and recruit focus group participants.

Results

Youth consistently reported facing challenges at home, at school, and in their community. Students reported feeling unsafe walking in the neighborhood, educational problems including disengaged teachers and peer pressure, families that are largely uninvolved, and a lack of positive role models. Older students voiced an interest in mentoring and job-training programs as a way to supplement the lack of support and guidance they receive at home and in school. Parents reported concerns that were similar to those expressed by students and added that they felt unsupported by the broader community and alone in holding their children accountable for their behavior. Parents also wished for more structured, cultural activities for their children to help with socialization that they believed is lacking in the school and community.

Geographic and Photographic Mapping Methods

In addition to the traditional data collection and analysis methods described above (e.g., Census, surveys, focus groups), the State of the Village assessment also utilized several innovative methods designed to engage community residents in unique ways to measure the built and physical environment of the neighborhood. The first project, in partnership with the Community Robotics, Education, and Technology (CREATE) Lab at Carnegie Mellon University and the Pittsburgh Neighborhood and Community Information System (PNCIS), used GigaPan technology to document neighborhood conditions. The second project involved a participatory photo mapping effort that engaged young people in neighborhood tours and photography. Finally, we used GIS (Geographic Information Systems) to visualize data collected during the secondary data analysis to create powerful public presentations and fundraising tools. We describe the results of these non-traditional methods more fully below.

GigaPan Panoramic Photos

The GigaPan EPIC is a robotic camera mount that allows users to quickly take hundreds of photos that are then "stitched" together to create highly detailed panoramic photos (GigaPan, 2012). The technology, collaboratively developed by Carnegie Mellon University Robotics, NASA, and Google, was donated to the HCV and used to document neighborhood conditions, block by block, over the course of the summer of 2010.

METHODS

Prior to photographing the neighborhood, researchers from PNCIS and the Pitt School of Social Work met with community organization leaders to determine a focus area for the photographs and discuss any ethical concerns. The team decided that the effort should be focused on blocks surrounding Homewood's public schools in order to document the conditions most likely to affect school children. Further, they created a one-page sheet describing the effort that was distributed to residents, with business cards bearing the GigaPan website address. The researchers used the camera to take panoramic photos of blocks, stitched the photos together using the GigaPan software, posted the photos on the GigaPan website, and geotagged the photos so that they can be replicated from the exact same locations in the future.

RESULTS

Researchers photographed over 100 blocks. These photographs were geotagged and added to the GigaPan website (www.gigapan.com) where they are being used to foster an interactive conversation about community conditions. Further, large printouts (5" × 3") of the photos were displayed at the HCV community kickoff event in September of 2010. Residents annotated their hopes and concerns for the blocks displayed using sticky notes affixed directly to the photos. It proved to be a powerful discussion tool that allowed residents to point out specific concerns to community practitioners. The effort can be replicated to see how neighborhood conditions have changed or stayed similar over time.

Participatory Photo Mapping

Twelve youth were engaged in a participatory photo mapping study to assess facets of the built environment that affected their daily lives The study utilized youth-led neighborhood tours and photography to actively engage youth aged 14–16 in an assessment of their neighborhood environment.

METHODS

This study used participatory photo mapping, an approach that integrates photography, Geographic Information Systems (GIS), and walk-along interviews, to elicit input about the youths' lived experiences and to analyze spatial patterns of neighborhood use. The youth were taught to conduct thematic coding of the photographic and spatial data. Themes that the researcher noted through field notes were discussed with participants to ensure accuracy. The youth used this information to identify actionable issues and presented their findings at a resident and leadership forum to help inform community planning efforts.

RESULTS

Spatial data and data obtained during the walk-along interviews with youth suggested the importance of play spaces (parks, fields, playgrounds) in shaping the participants' childhood memories and perceptions of the neighborhood. The youth highlighted the influence of places in negative memories related to exposure to violence, drugs, and physical deterioration in the neighborhood environment. Despite these hardships, there was a distinct focus on assets including educational landmarks and institutions like libraries and community centers and the role they could play in changing negative perceptions of the neighborhood.

Geographic Information Systems (GIS) and Spatial Analysis

In order to visualize and spatially analyze the data collected during the secondary data analysis, researchers used ArcGIS software to map the data. Several different types of maps were created for different target audiences including residents, community organizations, and to approach funders.

METHODS AND COMMUNITY ENGAGEMENT

The Pitt research team compiled data from the Department of Human Services, city level administrative data, public school performance data, and observational data and merged the datasets with parcel-level spatial data in order to map the results. The first maps created were targeted toward funders and illustrated the extent to which absentee ownership prevails and tax delinquency and code violations exist. These maps spurred interest from community organizations that requested maps to bolster their neighborhood efforts (e.g., maps of block club locations and crime statistics, maps of organization-owned property). Finally, as engaged residents began to see these maps, researchers worked with individual residents to map block conditions that helped them to gather detailed data about problem properties on their blocks (e.g., map of code violations gives residents data to back up existing concerns).

RESULTS

The maps illustrated the extent of property vacancy and dilapidation in Homewood and allowed community-based organizations to identify these properties by owner. Further, the maps clearly showed the concentration of low property values and absentee ownership by showing the stark contrast between properties in Homewood and the adjacent neighborhood. These maps were powerful presentation tools and helped to spur significant investment in the HCV by local foundations. The maps were also effective tools to translate complex data to lay audiences and helped to illustrate simply things like the correlation between crimes and vacant property.

Using Data to Move From Knowledge to Action

Many of the community-based research projects described above built upon one another with the insights and findings of one project leading to the next, informed by the questions, concerns and challenges raised by residents, researchers, non-profit leaders and others. While knowledge development was and is an important goal of the research, another important goal is to move from knowledge development to action. Below we present briefly how we have used data from the assessment to design and implement interventions to address specific problems and challenges that adversely impact the well-being of Homewood's children and families.

Homewood's Dirty Thirty

Based upon resident concerns identified by the 1,000 Conversations Campaign, it was known that abandoned homes were a top neighborhood priority. In order to address this concern, the Pitt research team used a data-driven approach to identify properties that were deemed an imminent threat to neighborhood residents in general, and children in particular.

Methods

We used the property assessment database created by the systematic observation of the 1509 properties that surrounded Homewood's schools (described above), to identify properties that were both vacant and open to entry. The list of thirty properties that met these criteria (i.e., the "Dirty Thirty") was distributed to Homewood residents who had been previously engaged by Operation Better Block as members of a vacant property task force. These residents were trained to use the Mayor's 311 non-emergency phone line to report property concerns. The residents and OBB staff repeatedly called to the 311 line for each property on the list and requested that each property be remediated (i.e., that the city board up the windows and doors, remove the debris that surrounded them or demolish the property).

Results

Members of the research team took photos of each property on the list before the start of the intervention and tracked the city's responses to the 311 calls over a 30-day period. After the 30 days, the properties were then evaluated as either "improved" or "not improved" based upon the comparison of the before and after photos of each property. By the end of the 30-day intervention period, 22 of the targeted properties were boarded and one was torn down, thus conditions of 77 percent (n=23) of the properties were improved.

Safe Routes to School

The HCV and students from the Carnegie Mellon University Heinz School of Public Policy and Management partnered to conduct the Safe Routes to School project. This project addressed the issue of safety for Homewood students who walk to and from school by identifying safe routes from students' homes to the schools in Homewood and engaging the community in the development and use of these routes.

Methods

The CMU students conducted surveys and focus groups with youth and families to determine what routes were commonly used to travel to school and identify barriers that children perceived along these routes. Systematic observation was utilized to identify areas of high pedestrian and vehicle traffic. GIS software was used to identify high-risk (crime, traffic) areas and to create routes to school that were efficient, minimize risk and incorporated residents' current preferences.

RESULTS

Safe routes to school were identified and distributed to community-based organizations in a one-page, community friendly pamphlet. HCV representatives worked with the City of Pittsburgh and Pittsburgh's Urban Redevelopment Authority to tear down vacant properties that surrounded Homewood secondary school (grades 6–12) and bus transportation has been provided to students who lived more than 0.5 miles away from the school and would otherwise have to walk to and from school.

Lessons Learned and Future Directions

There are over 16 million poor children in the United States. Many of these children attend poor and underperforming schools and they and their families live in poor neighborhoods, characterized by high rates of poverty, crime and social and physical disorder. Despite these challenges and liabilities, however, many of these communities are also home to loving stable single, two-parent and extended families, long-term residents who own and maintain their homes and strong faith- and community-based organizations that are committed to improving conditions for the children and families who live, learn, work and worship there. In this chapter we have described the work being done in one of these communities, being led by a partnership between a university—the University of Pittsburgh's School of Social Work, and a newly formed child-centered comprehensive community initiative—the Homewood Children's Village.

The chapter has described the iterative State of the Village assessment and action process that the HCV/Pitt partnership uses to identify problems that are significant to the community; to design research projects to better understand the issue or problem; to engage the community in the data collection, analysis and reporting of the results of the studies; and to use the results to address the concerns. The State of the Village process illustrates how a theoretically driven, comprehensive strengths- and needs-based multi-method, multi-level community-based participatory data collection, analysis and reporting system can be used to create knowledge *and* to advance practice. The chapter also presents a transferrable model of how research can be used to design practical programs for the community that meet the residents "where they are" and begin to address their needs, desires and concerns.

Notes

1 http://www2.ed.gov/programs/promiseneighborhoods/index.html#description
2 http://portal.hud.gov/hudportal/HUD?src=/program_offices/public_indian_housing/programs/ph/cn

3 http://www.irp.wisc.edu/faqs/faq6.htm "How many children are poor?"
4 This section is adapted from Wallace and Lopez (2012).
5 Based on the NCLB's definition of Adequate Yearly Progress.
6 Pittsburgh Public Schools (2009).
7 Balfanz and Letgers, Center for Social Organization of Schools, Johns Hopkins University, 2004: http://web.jhu.edu/CSOS/images/Number_of_Dropout_Factories_and_Percentage_of_Estimated_Dropouts_who_Attended_Dropout_Factories.pdf
8 As measured by their scores on the Dynamic Indicators of Basic Early Literacy Skills test.
9 PPS data are from A+ Schools. "Report to the community: School progress report" for all K–8 and high schools, 2009. http://www.aplusschools.org/eq_reports_08.shtml and Pennsylvania data come from www.greatschools.com
10 According to the National School Performance website, www.greatschools.com
11 Allegheny County Department of Human Services. "Homewood Youth Active in DHS Systems During 2009". Pittsburgh, 2010.
12 Allegheny County Department of Human Services. "DRAFT Community profile: Homewood". Pittsburgh, 2009.
13 Pittsburgh Neighborhood and Community Information System, 2010. www.pghnis.pitt.edu

References

Bronfenbrenner, U. (1979). *The ecology of human development: Experiments in nature and design*. Cambridge: Harvard University Press.

Bronfenbrenner, U. (2005). The bioecological theory of human development. In U. Bronfenbrenner (Ed.), *Making human beings human: Bioecological perspectives on human development* (pp. 3–15). Thousand Oaks: Sage. (First published in 2001.)

Bronfenbrenner, U. & Ceci, S. J. (1994). Nature-nurture reconceptualized in developmental perspective: A biological model. *Psychological Review, 101*, 568–586.

Comer, J.P., Joyner, E.T. & Ben-Avie, M. (2004). *The field guide to comer schools in action*. California: Corwin Press.

GigaPan. (2012). About GigaPan. Available: www.gigapan.com

United States Census. (2010). https://www.census.gov/2010census/

9

YOUTH ORGANIZING FOR SCHOOL AND NEIGHBORHOOD IMPROVEMENT

Brian D. Christens, University of Wisconsin–Madison
Jessica J. Collura, University of Wisconsin–Madison
Michael A. Kopish, Plymouth State University
Matea Varvodić, Teach for America

Youth Organizing Initiatives

Youth organizing, a strategy for community change that involves leadership by young people, has become steadily more widespread during the past decade. Confirming this trend, a recent scan of the field (Torres-Fleming, Valdes & Pillai, 2010) identified 160 active youth organizing initiatives (up from 120 as recently as 2004) in the United States. Youth organizing initiatives take place in a variety of settings, including community centers, schools, churches and independent organizations. The most common issue that these groups seek to address through their organizing is education.

Fueled by increasing inequalities in education, youth organizing initiatives have taken both a practical approach – conducting research and demanding specific changes in local policies and practices – and a justice-oriented approach, arguing for young people's rights and ability to participate in civil society, and to have equal access to opportunities, including quality education and safe neighborhoods.

There is an emerging understanding among scholars and practitioners that youth organizing is a particularly potent model for working with youth. This is, in part, because youth organizing creates change at multiple levels (Christens & Kirshner, 2011). First, at a systemic level, youth organizing functions as a much-needed source of public engagement in local schools and school systems (Orr & Rogers, 2011), as well as a catalyst for changes in communities (Christens & Dolan, 2011; Mediratta, Shah & McAlister, 2009). In this way, youth organizing often has beneficial effects even for young people who are not directly involved in these initiatives. Second, at the level of individual youth development, youth organizing initiatives create unconventional and dynamic extracurricular settings in which young people – particularly low-income youth adversely affected by educational inequalities – are exposed to critical, experiential civic education (Kirshner & Ginwright, 2012). Developmental, educational and career development outcomes for these youth are often seen to improve through involvement in youth organizing (e.g., Conner, 2011). Moreover, youth organizing provides a powerful demonstration of the potential of young people to exercise power and leadership in the civic domain, and to work effectively across generations. In this way, it likely contributes to changes in perceptions of young people in their local communities. This chapter examines each of these three mechanisms and provides two illustrative case examples to make these points more concrete.

Case Example 1: Voices of Youth in Chicago Education (VOYCE)

A collaborative effort of six Chicago community organizations with long traditions of organizing and social action, Voices of Youth in Chicago Education (VOYCE),[1] was formed in 2007. VOYCE is a youth organizing collaborative that was launched with a youth participatory action research (YPAR) project on public education issues. Several of the member organizations had been doing youth and intergenerational organizing for many years. Others joined the effort due to their recognition of the need for citywide youth involvement in addressing problems with public education. The multi-organization collaborative effort attracted the support of private foundations and began working with groups of students in the Chicago Public Schools (CPS) – the third largest school district in the US.

The students' work began with training on participatory action research as a tool for social change. After publicly launching their campaign, they held meetings with school officials and reflected on their own educational experiences in order to formulate questions for the YPAR project on school settings and policies, and to make recommendations for improvement. The questions they identified concerned the curriculum of Chicago schools and the school environments. The backdrop for these questions was that the schools were among the worst in the nation in terms of graduation rates and preparation for college, with a 50 percent graduation rate and 8 percent college completion rate. Youth researchers designed a research project, surveying 1,325 other CPS students and interviewing 383 stakeholders in the CPS, including parents, students and teachers. Youth researchers then analyzed these data. They also conducted site visits to successful schools in other locations, including New York, Texas and California.

The research was published in a 2008 report titled *Student-led solutions to the nation's dropout crisis* (VOYCE, 2008). The report triangulated findings from the quantitative, qualitative, and observational research conducted by youth. The findings indicated that students in CPS generally did not find their schools' curricula relevant, that they had internalized their schools' problems including the dropout rates, that they did not see school as a stepping-stone to future academic and professional successes, and that they did not have strong relationships with school staff, or feel free to express themselves in their school environments. VOYCE called on CPS stakeholders to work with youth to identify solutions to these issues, including the adoption of district-level policies that would create better relationships in schools and a greater sense of purpose. They presented their findings and recommendations to school officials in a series of meetings, and to the broader community through large public presentations, including local and national media. These actions resulted in school- and district-level changes, as well as further refinement in the ongoing research and action.

In 2011, VOYCE released another report that focused on the issues with school disciplinary policies. The report, *Failed policies, broken futures: The true cost of zero tolerance in Chicago* (VOYCE, 2011), leveled a critique on the zero-tolerance discipline policies of the CPS. It argued that the Chicago schools' security and discipline policies were overly punitive. The report includes case examples of students whose education had been derailed by run-ins with the harsh disciplinary infrastructure of the schools for minor rule violations, such as writing on a desk or bringing a cell phone to school. The VOYCE report also descriptively analyzed educational and budget data from the district, demonstrating, for instance, that the schools' disciplinary policies were resulting in increased rates of out-of-school suspensions, but not increased perceptions of safety. The harsh disciplinary policies, the report argues, were contributing to mistrust and alienation among students, harming the relationships between students and school staff, and, in many cases, increasing school disruptions. And, of course, the increases in suspensions and expulsions had negative implications for student educational outcomes.

The 2011 VOYCE report went beyond the student perspective on disciplinary policy and analyzed budgetary data, discovering, for example, that the CPS spent $67 million in 2010–11 on safety and security. Their analysis compared this figure with expenditures on other initiatives in the district. For instance, in 2010–11, CPS spent only $1.5 million on arts education, $29 million on language and cultural education, and $35 million on college and career preparation. In combination, these areas received less funding than school security. Further, the district had more than 1,000 full-time employees in safety and security – far more than other comparable offices. The report makes the case that the direct expense of administering zero-tolerance policies pales in comparison to the costs associated with poor student outcomes, dropouts, and incarceration: "We know that it is much more cost-effective to educate students than to incarcerate them. The annual cost of educating a student in Chicago is approximately $12,880, while the annual cost of incarcerating a young person is $76,095 – almost six times the cost of their education" (p. 22). Relying on previous studies on the likelihood of arrested students dropping out and the associated increases in costs to the public, the VOYCE report estimates the arrests that occurred in the CPS in one year (2009) alone will cost Chicago $240 million in public funds over time.

Youth leaders from VOYCE have presented the findings and recommendations from their research to multiple audiences, including CPS, the Board of Education, and other Chicago elected officials. In addition, they have traveled to present their work at events sponsored by the US Department of Education. As of this writing, VOYCE's efforts have had effects on policy, including revisions in the CPS student code of conduct that include an end to automatic two-week suspensions and cutting the maximum time for all offenses in half. CPS has not entirely overhauled its approach to school discipline, but youth leaders are keeping up the pressure.

Catalysts for Community and School Improvement

As the VOYCE example illustrates, building sustainable power in community organizations to create change in local systems is among the primary goals of most youth organizing initiatives. They do this by building new networks of relationships among participants, developing leadership and research capacities, and implementing strategic approaches to grassroots issue-based advocacy. In this way, youth organizing often draws on traditions of grassroots community organizing among adults (e.g., Stoecker, 2009; Swarts, 2008), a practice that has become more widespread in neighborhoods and institutions across the US during the last thirty years (Wood & Warren, 2002). Mediratta, Shah and McAlister (2009) examined multiple organizing campaigns related to education over the course of six years, reporting their successes at influencing school policies, curricula, teacher training and parent and community engagement in the schools. While only some of these initiatives involved youth in their work, nearly all were found to be effective at improving school climates, professional cultures in schools, instructional cores, and student educational outcomes.

Conner, Zaino and Scarola (2012) interviewed 30 adult leaders in the Philadelphia schools about the influence of a particular long-standing youth organizing initiative, the Philadelphia Student Union (PSU). They found that the district leaders credited the PSU with being a critical force for change in district policies. Moreover, the PSU was viewed as a stakeholder and important ally for (or potential threat to) ongoing decision-making in the district, due to their knowledge of the issues, their public visibility, the fact that they had become a frequently sought source for journalists covering the schools, and their relationships with policy-makers. Like other successful youth organizing initiatives (e.g., VOYCE), the PSU has been able to alter power relations between local institutions and develop roles and agency for youth leaders in the local ecology of games (Long, 1958) that determines local priorities, agendas, and the distribution of resources. In this way, youth organizing represents a form of public engagement in educational systems, which is widely viewed as a critical component of educational reform and improvement (Orr & Rogers, 2011).

New approaches to improving urban public education, such as the Promise Neighborhoods[2] program, are highlighting the links between community capacity (e.g., affordable housing, access to health care, parental and community engagement) and student educational outcomes. While youth organizing similarly seeks to create change at the intersections of neighborhoods and schools, there are distinguishing characteristics of an organizing approach to educational improvement that can help to inform other approaches. These include: (1) youth organizing initiatives build new bases of grassroots power that exist outside of the formal, existing decision-making structures in local communities; (2) youth organizing efforts are grounded in a social justice orientation; and (3) unlike many other approaches to education reform and improvement, youth organizing actively involves young people in efforts to change and improve their own neighborhoods and schools.

Grassroots Power

Many approaches to changing systems begin with the assumption that a rational solution to problems can be discovered and implemented if only all stakeholders can communicate and work cooperatively. A community organizing approach to social issues insists that this is a naïve view, and that, in fact, many problems persist because of power relationships and imbalances. A change in the status quo often means that some people will win and others will lose. Change is therefore likely to be resisted, and this means that conflict is likely to occur when groups push for change (Christens, Jones & Speer, 2008). Organizing is an approach that builds civic power outside of existing local power structures and can therefore advocate for changes in policies and practices that might be too politically costly or inconvenient for elected officials or other publicly prominent positions to endorse. This often allows organizing initiatives to address issues that would not be brought to the fore if not for their insistence.

Social Justice

An organizing approach is also rooted in an orientation that views systemic disparities as issues of justice. Applying this orientation to education means that every student deserves an equal chance for educational achievement and success. Barriers to equality of opportunity include not only elements of the educational systems, but also socioeconomic and sociocultural factors that limit the opportunities available to students of color or low-income status (e.g., lack of access to health or dental care, recreational and extracurricular opportunities, family supports). These disproportionate challenges are understood as oppression. A more mainstream approach to address disparities would be to designate disadvantaged students as "at risk" and to target them for special programs and support services. While such supports are often important, an organizing approach is more likely to insist that systems reorient and transform themselves in more fundamental ways in order to effectively provide opportunities to all students.

Youth Involvement

Finally, and perhaps most notably, youth organizing involves young people themselves in the change making process. A guiding philosophy of many community organizing initiatives is that the people closest to the problem should be a part of the solution to that problem (Stahlhut, 2003). Many approaches to education reform and improvement do not involve the students of the schools in determining the direction of reforms. Failing to involve students in educational change efforts not only sacrifices opportunities to gain crucial insights from students' perspectives, it misses opportunities for youth to be agents of their own development and to work collaboratively with adult allies and decision-makers (Zeldin, Christens & Powers, in press). Studies indicate that participating in community and educational change efforts can be an impactful experience in the lives of young participants (e.g., Conner & Strobel, 2007; Kirshner, 2009), leading not only to a critical awareness of social justice issues, but also to improved formal educational outcomes.

Case Example 2: Youth United for Change (YUC)

Youth United for Change (YUC) was founded by 15 young people and one adult staff member in 1991 to explore the root causes of drug abuse in their Philadelphia community, including the lack of meaningful educational and career opportunities for youth (Youth United for Change, 2012). In 1993, YUC changed its structure and established a school-based model of youth organizing that recruited youth to work on school campaigns. Today, YUC operates five school-based chapters that organize youth in traditionally low-performing Philadelphia public high schools to demand improvements in public education. There is also a sixth chapter that engages youth city-wide and organizes young people who have been "pushed out" (dropped out) of the public education system.

Through the school chapter models, youth leaders recruit students to meet weekly after school to identify problems, conduct research on school reform, and develop campaigns. Each chapter receives support from a YUC staff organizer, but the youth volunteer leaders are at the forefront of the campaigns. For example, an initial campaign in Kensington High School focused on eliminating study hall. Youth leaders and members identified study hall as a problem because it was considered a waste of both student and teacher time. They conducted research on alternative uses for this time period (Sherwood & Dressner, 2004), drafted a petition, solicited signatures from students and teachers, and then met with the school principal to discuss proposed alternatives. As a result, study hall periods were eliminated in Kensington High School. These early victories demonstrated to youth members that research and action are capable of producing change. Subsequent successful school-based campaigns included efforts to improve school facilities, implement more rigorous academic curricula, expand after-school programming, and improve the safety of the schools.

Although YUC achieved many early successes, leaders still expressed frustration that their victories were not producing the improved educational quality that members envisioned (McAlister, Mediratta & Shah, 2009). This frustration forced YUC to reexamine its underlying theory of change and to develop a more systemic strategy to improve school outcomes. In 2001, the state of Pennsylvania pushed a district privatization proposal and takeover of the local school district's governance. This presented an opportunity for YUC to move beyond school-based issues and to participate in a district-wide coalition against the state's privatization proposal. Participating in the coalition allowed YUC to develop relationships with a variety of school reform and advocacy groups, including the Philadelphia Student Union (Conner, 2011). This alliance with Philadelphia Student Union (PSU) would prove to be particularly beneficial as YUC prepared for its most notable campaign, the Small Schools Campaign.

Amid devastating budget cuts and a district policy of consolidation into large schools of 800 to 1,000 students, YUC students led a plan to involve parents and influential community allies to address long-standing deficiencies in education and services provided in comprehensive high schools. In 2002, the citywide Small Schools Campaign resulted in a proposal to replace a large failing high school with four new schools of 400 to 500 students. Youth leaders at the Kensington High School chapter invited school officials to tour their building and convinced leaders to add their school to the list of buildings in need of repair (McAlister, Mediratta & Shah, 2009). Youth leaders then initiated a "listening campaign" to identify problems and issues with their school and solicit ideas on how the school might be renovated and improved. A vision for four small, autonomous schools that would share property emerged from the listening campaign (Suess & Lewis, 2005).

Over the next two years, members of the YUC Kensington chapter conducted research on the small schools model and traveled to Chicago, Oakland, Rhode Island and New York City to observe and further research a variety of school models. Concurrently, at the local level, members of YUC partnered with members from the PSU to actively garner support for the Small Schools Campaign. YUC also built a coalition of supporting organizations, including Philadelphia Citizens for Children and Youth, Eastern Pennsylvania Organizing Project (EPOP), Research for Action, and the Philadelphia Federation of Teachers. Collectively, these organizations developed a proposal for a new district policy on small schools and created an outreach plan to inform elected officials about the actions needed to transform public education in Philadelphia (McAlister, Mediratta & Shah, 2009). YUC advocated for a transparent public planning process. In June of 2005, YUC won a public commitment from Philadelphia's Chief Academic Officer for the creation of four small high schools to serve the Kensington community and the creation of a public planning process for the school's redesign. In September 2005, three small, theme-based high schools opened on the Kensington campus; three years later, construction on the fourth school began. The themes of the new small schools (i.e. performing arts, business, and culinary arts) were proposed by YUC students based on the results of their research.

The success of the Small Schools Campaign marked an ideological shift in focus for YUC from solely school-based issues to more structural and systemic issues in education. This ideological shift also resulted in several practical changes. For example, after the Small Schools Campaign, YUC decided to focus on more multi-year campaigns rather than campaigns based on the academic school year. The organization also began to integrate more political education for its members to situate school reform campaigns within a larger analysis of community change (McAlister et al., 2009). In addition, while school chapters continue to organize their individual school-based campaigns, they also attend monthly meetings with all YUC chapters to discuss crosscutting issues and explore potential district-level campaigns

YUC continues to spearhead school-based campaigns, but the organization simultaneously considers how district policies affect the school climate and, when necessary, advocate for district-level changes. For example, a school-wide survey led by the Strawberry Mansion chapter of YUC revealed test taking misconduct at the school. Specifically, student surveys identified that teachers were completing blank answers on students' exams and that tests were being administered in classrooms with instructional aids on the walls (McAlister et al., 2009). Surveys also demonstrated a strong dissatisfaction with the school's practice of pulling students from core subjects for test preparation. Based on this research, students produced a report documenting concerns and recommendations for improvement, met with district administrators, and presented testimony to the Philadelphia School Reform Commission which led the district to update its standardized testing practices and procedures.

YUC is a respected organization leading to tangible outcomes in the Philadelphia school district. At the district level, the organization has been influential in small schools construction on the Kensington campus. YUC is also credited with changing adult perceptions regarding youth engagement; district and school leaders now understand the benefits of engaging students in reform activities (McAlister et al., 2009). Youth engagement is also leading to positive outcomes for young people. For example, administrative data from the restructured Kensington high schools indicate an improved school climate and increased student engagement. Although the demographics of the school have remained the same, student attendance has increased, the dropout rate appears to be decreasing, state exam scores show positive trends in math and reading, and there is an increased number of students who identify as college bound (McAlister et al., 2009).

Contexts for Youth Development

As has been observed in adult organizing initiatives (Speer & Hughey, 1995), there is a reciprocal relationship between the development of organizational power and the empowerment of participants in youth organizing initiatives (Christens & Kirshner, 2011). A community organizing approach to creating change in local systems begins with the empowerment and leadership development of participants in the organizing initiative (Mediratta, Shah & McAlister, 2009). In aggregate, this strategy is critical for building the capacity of youth organizing initiatives to successfully change local systems to better support all youth, but it can also be more immediately beneficial for the personal development of youth organizers. Psychological empowerment, for instance, has been identified as a key component of resilience, leading to improved academic engagement and the avoidance of risk behaviors and psychological symptoms (Christens & Peterson, 2012). Youth organizing teaches young people how to exercise agency in the systems that affect their daily lives, providing a buffer against the helplessness and alienation that can develop when young people experience inequitable and oppressive systems without effective avenues for working for change in those systems.

There is increasing recognition across disciplines that disparities in health and education have developmental roots. Disciplines as diverse as economics (Heckman, 2011) and neuroscience (Shonkoff, Boyce & McEwen, 2009) are uncovering the pathways by which repeated childhood traumas disproportionately experienced by disadvantaged children can adversely influence development and, thereby, educational achievement through adolescence and early adulthood. Prescriptions for decreasing these disparities involve early childhood interventions and increasing the nurturing capacities of school and family contexts (e.g., Heckman et al., 2010). Less commonly examined are the ways in which some young people, including youth organizers, are responding to adverse circumstances by becoming actively engaged in their communities and schools (Ginwright, 2007). These youth gain critical awareness of the social and political environments that make it more difficult for some to succeed, and the tools necessary to work for change in these environments (Watts, Diemer & Voight, 2011). They can also find a socially and emotionally supportive extracurricular environment that supports pro-social development and healing (Ginwright, 2010). Kirshner and Ginwright (2012) recently reviewed the existing literature on the impacts of participation in youth organizing, and grouped the developmental effects among participants into three domains: (1) civic development, (2) psychosocial wellness, and (3) academic engagement. Here, we follow the same rubric for describing youth organizing as a development-enhancing context.

Civic Development

The civic domain – like family, neighborhood and school contexts – is increasingly understood as an important context for youth development (Sherrod, Torney-Purta & Flanagan, 2010). Young people who are civically engaged likely develop psychological sense of community (Evans, 2007) and social responsibility (Wray-Lake & Syvertsen, 2011). The development of civic attitudes and capacities among young people is beneficial for the future of democratic societies, since democracy requires capably and knowledgeably engaged citizens (Flanagan & Faison, 2001). Research indicates that young people who participate in youth organizing are more likely to be civically active later in their lives (Conner, 2011; Mediratta et al., 2008), and that it is a potent context for development of civic identity (Kirshner, 2009). It is also likely that young people who become engaged in the civic domain develop greater resilience (Fergus & Zimmerman, 2005), making it less likely that they will become engaged in violence and other risky behaviors.

Psychosocial Wellness

Youth organizing can be considered an empowering community setting (Maton, 2008), meaning that it likely enhances the psychological empowerment of participants. One component of psychological empowerment is the self-perception of one's own ability to lead and have influence in the civic domain. This component has been operationalized as sociopolitical control (Peterson et al., 2010), which has been empirically linked with other positive developmental outcomes for youth (Christens & Peterson, 2012). Another component of psychological empowerment is the critical understanding of social systems power dynamics and change processes that can be gained as young people participate in organizing and advocacy efforts. These gains in awareness can be understood as critical consciousness (Watts, Diemer & Voight, 2011), which is thought to be a particularly important developmental achievement for marginalized or disadvantaged young people (Kirshner & Ginwright, 2012; Watts & Flanagan, 2007). The skills and perspectives that young people gain from becoming engaged in liberation-oriented practice likely promote wellbeing (Prilleltensky, 2008).

Academic Engagement

Psychological empowerment has been found to be associated with the perception that formal education is important to one's current and future life goals (Peterson et al., 2010). Participation in youth organizing likewise appears to promote academic engagement. Students engaged in youth organizing have reported that they are more motivated to complete high school, earn better grades and to take more challenging classes as a result of their involvement in youth organizing (Mediratta et al., 2008). Students who have been involved in youth organizing appear to be more ambitious in their goals for academic and professional achievement after high school (Conner, 2011; Shah, 2011). These gains in academic engagement are likely due to the ways that youth organizing increases young people's understanding of the importance of knowledge and skills for creating change in the neighborhoods and schools. For instance, many youth organizers learn how to conduct and present research, evaluate policies, speak in large public venues, and negotiate with decision-makers. Many times, they partner with university-based researchers in these efforts (e.g., Peterson, Dolan & Hanft, 2011). These culturally-relevant educational experiences can change young people's perspective on the relevance and usefulness of education (Cammarota, 2007; Kirshner & Ginwright, 2012).

Conclusions

In this chapter, we have considered the outcomes of youth organizing initiatives at individual and systemic levels of analysis, and we have explored youth organizing as a process through descriptions of two youth organizing campaigns. As the Voices of Youth in Chicago Education (VOYCE) and the Youth United for Change (YUC) case examples illustrate, youth organizing can act as a catalyst for school and community improvement through strategic research and advocacy for changes in local policies and practices. These changes can lead to improved student outcomes, including attendance, achievement and graduation. Youth organizing differs from many approaches to educational reform and community development, however, in its orientation to power and social justice, as well as the ways in which it engages youth. Moreover, as the VOYCE and YUC examples make clear, youth organizing campaigns can create impactful extracurricular settings for the youth who participate. They encourage civic engagement and development. Numerous published accounts of youth organizing also take notice of the impressive academic and developmental trajectories among the youth leaders of these initiatives. By way of conclusion, we will explore a less direct mechanism by which we believe youth organizing is advancing social justice and wellbeing for young people, particularly in marginalized and oppressed communities. That is, youth organizing is a demonstration of the power and potential of young people as civic actors. Importantly, it is also often a demonstration of the potential of youth of color.

United States society and institutions offer young people few opportunities to be involved in decision-making regarding the systems that affect their lives (e.g., their schools and communities). Young people are often segregated from adults in much of their daily lives. Interactions between youth and adults fall largely into familial or professional categories, and youth and adults often hold negative stereotypes about each other (Camino & Zeldin, 2002; Collura, Christens & Zeldin, 2011). Age segregation can be even more pronounced for low-income youth of color, who have fewer opportunities for extracurricular activity and civic engagement than middle-class peers (Kahne & Middaugh, 2009). These trends are a disservice to young people and society on several fronts. They deprive young people of opportunities to develop and demonstrate their democratic capabilities, and they deprive social systems of intergenerational relationships, which can be a key ingredient for human development (Li & Julian, 2012). Age segregation and ageism can be considered as a self-reinforcing cycle. On the other hand, young organizing is a model for youth civic engagement that can initiate a countervailing cycle (Christens & Zeldin, 2011) in which youth and adults work together, demonstrate their capabilities, and create new expectations for youth involvement in society and institutions.

This argues for policies and institutional supports that will make youth organizing initiatives more widespread and available to greater numbers of young people and communities. Foundations (e.g., the Funders' Collaborative for Youth Organizing)[3] have increasingly taken notice of youth organizing, but many cities, towns and regions still do not have active or high-functioning youth organizing initiatives, and support for youth organizing still pales in comparison with support for other service or extracurricular activities. Since youth organizing campaigns often seek to change policies, governmental entities may be limited in the ways that they can directly support organizing activities. Foundations and local organizations (e.g., community centers; faith-based institutions; nonprofits) must take the lead in developing a stronger infrastructure of support, training, and research. For sustainability, successful youth organizing initiatives require talented and experienced staff. The payoff would be multi-faceted – youth would be better positioned to take leading roles in improving their local communities, while simultaneously improving their own chances of wellbeing and success. In addition, their actions would drive social change toward norms of intergenerational collaboration.

Finally, insights from youth organizing should be integrated into other community development strategies. Policies and institutions geared toward changing schools and neighborhoods should consider whether they might more meaningfully engage young people in their efforts. For example, efforts that seek to increase public engagement in education, like the Promise Neighborhoods initiative, or to reform education, like the Gates Foundation,[4] might consider whether their approach could be enhanced by more student voice and grassroots involvement. Further, a community organizing approach to building grassroots power, relationships, participatory research capacity, and direct action should be considered as a mechanism for promoting community autonomy and wellbeing.

Acknowledgment

The authors wish to thank Emma Tai (Coordinator, Voices of Youth in Chicago Education) for helpful comments on a draft of this chapter.

Notes

1　See http://www.voyceproject.org
2　The Promise Neighborhoods program (http://www.promiseneighborhoodsinstitute. org/) is a US Dept. of Education effort to replicate the successes of the Harlem Children's Zone (see Tough, 2008) at linking local institutions (e.g., nonprofits, churches, universities) to provide comprehensive supports for the success of low-income students.
3　See http://www.fcyo.org
4　See http://www.gatesfoundation.org/united-states/Pages/education-strategy.aspx

References

Camino, L. & Zeldin, S. (2002). From periphery to center: Pathways for youth civic engagement in the day-to-day life of communities. *Applied Developmental Science, 6*(4), 213–220.

Cammarota, J. (2007). A social justice approach to achievement: Guiding Latino/a students toward educational attainment with a challenging, socially relevant curriculum. *Equity and Excellence in Education, 40,* 87–96.

Christens, B.D. & Dolan, T. (2011). Interweaving youth development, community development, and social change through youth organizing. *Youth & Society, 43*(2), 528–548.

Christens, B.D. & Kirshner, B. (2011). Taking stock of youth organizing: An interdisciplinary perspective. *New Directions for Child and Adolescent Development, 134,* 27–41.

Christens, B.D. & Peterson, N.A. (2012). The role of empowerment in youth development: A study of sociopolitical control as mediator of ecological systems' influence on developmental outcomes. *Journal of Youth and Adolescence, 41*(5), 623–635.

Christens, B.D. & Zeldin, S. (2011). Community engagement. In R.J.R. Levesque (Ed.), *Encyclopedia of adolescence.* (pp. 479–487). New York: Springer.

Christens, B.D., Jones, D.L. & Speer, P.W. (2008). Power, conflict, and spirituality: A qualitative study of faith-based community organizing. *Forum: Qualitative Social Research, 9*(1), Art. 21.

Collura, J.J., Christens, B.D. & Zeldin, S. (2011). Broadening the frame of violence prevention through the promotion of youth community engagement. In M. Paludi (Ed.), *The psychology of teen violence and victimization, Vol 2: Prevention strategies for families and schools.* (pp. 221–238). Santa Barbara, CA: Praeger.

Conner, J.O. (2011). Youth organizers as young adults: Their commitments and contributions. *Journal of Research on Adolescence, 21*(4), 923–942.

Conner, J.O. & Strobel, K. (2007). Leadership development: An examination of individual and programmatic growth. *Journal of Adolescent Research, 22*(3), 275–297.

Conner, J.O., Zaino, K. & Scarola, E. (2012). "Very powerful voices": The influence of youth organizing on educational policy in Philadelphia. *Educational Policy.* Published online ahead of print: doi:10.1177/0895904812454001

Evans, S.D. (2007). Youth sense of community: Voice and power in community contexts. *Journal of Community Psychology, 35*(6), 693–709.

Fergus, S. & Zimmerman, M.A. (2005). Adolescent resilience: A framework for understanding healthy development in the face of risk. *Annual Review of Public Health, 26*, 399–419.

Flanagan, C.A. & Faison, N. (2001). Youth civic development: Implications of research for social policy and programs. *Social Policy Report, 15*(1), 3–14.

Ginwright, S.A. (2007). Black youth activism and the role of critical social capital in black community organizations. *American Behavioral Scientist, 51*(3), 403–418.

Ginwright, S.A. (2010). Peace out to revolution! Activism among African American youth: An argument for radical healing. *Young, 18*(1), 77–96.

Heckman, J.J. (2011). The developmental origins of health. *Health Economics, 21*(1), 24–29.

Heckman, J.J., Moon, S.H., Pinto, R., Savelyev, P.A. & Yavitz, A. (2010). The rate of return to the High/Scope Perry Preschool Program. *Journal of Public Economics, 94*(1–2), 114–128.

Kahne, J. & Middaugh, E. (2009). Democracy for some: The civic opportunity gap in high school. In J. Youniss & P. Levine (Eds.), *Engaging young people in civic life* (pp. 29–58). Nashville, TN: Vanderbilt University Press.

Kirshner, B. (2009). Power in numbers: Youth organizing as a context for exploring civic identity. *Journal of Research on Adolescence, 19*(3), 414–440.

Kirshner, B. & Ginwright, S. (2012). Youth organizing as a developmental context for African American and Latino adolescents. *Child Development Perspectives, 6*(3), 288–294.

Li, J. & Julian, M.M. (2012). Developmental relationships as the active ingredient: A unifying working hypothesis of "what works" across intervention settings. *The American Journal of Orthopsychiatry, 82*(2), 157–166.

Long, N.E. (1958). The local community as an ecology of games. *The American Journal of Sociology, 64*(3), 251–261.

Maton, K.I. (2008). Empowering community settings: Agents of individual development, community betterment, and positive social change. *American Journal of Community Psychology*, *41*, 4–21.

McAlister, S., Mediratta, K. & Shah, S. (2009). *Keeping parent and student voices at the forefront of reform.* Providence, RI: Brown University, Annenberg Institute for School Reform.

Mediratta, K., Shah, S. & McAlister, S. (2008). *Organized communities, stronger schools: A preview of research findings.* Providence, RI: Brown University, Annenberg Institute for School Reform.

Mediratta, K., Shah, S. & McAlister, S. (2009). *Community organizing for stronger schools: Strategies and successes.* Cambridge, MA: Harvard Educational Press.

Orr, M. & Rogers, J. (Eds.) (2011). *Public engagement in public education: Joining forces to revitalize democracy and equalize schools.* Stanford, CA: Stanford University Press.

Peterson, N.A., Peterson, C.H., Agre, L., Christens, B.D. & Morton, C.M. (2011). Measuring youth empowerment: Validation of a sociopolitical control scale for youth in an urban community context. *Journal of Community Psychology*, *39*(5), 592–605.

Peterson, T.H., Dolan, T. & Hanft, S. (2010). Partnering with youth organizers to prevent violence: An analysis of relationships, power, and change. *Progress in Community Health Partnerships*, *4*(3), 235–242.

Prilleltensky, I. (2008). The role of power in wellness, oppression, and liberation: The promise of psychopolitical validity. *Journal of Community Psychology*, *36*(2), 116–136.

Shah, S. (2011). *Building transformative youth leadership: Data on the impacts of youth organizing.* New York: Funders' Collaborative on Youth Organizing.

Sherrod, L., Torney-Purta, J. & Flanagan, C.A. (2010). *Handbook of research on civic engagement in youth.* Hoboken, NJ: Wiley.

Sherwood, K.E. & Dressner, J. (2004). *Youth organizing: A new generation of social activism.* Philadelphia, PA: Public/Private Ventures.

Shonkoff, J.P., Boyce, W.T. & McEwen, B.S. (2009). Neuroscience, molecular biology, and the childhood roots of health disparities. *Journal of the American Medical Association*, *301*(21), 2252–2259.

Speer, P.W. & Hughey, J. (1995). Community organizing: An ecological route to empowerment and power. *American Journal of Community Psychology*, *23*(5), 729–748.

Stahlhut, D. (2003). The people closest to the problem. *Social Policy*, *34*(2/3), 71–74.

Stoecker, R. (2009). Community organizing and social change. *Contexts*, *8*(1), 20–25.

Suess, G.E.L. & Lewis, K.S. (2005). Youth leaders carry on campaign for small schools: Two Student organizations imagine a different kind of high school. *Philadelphia Public School Notebook* (Spring). Available online at: <www.thenotebook.org/editions/2005/spring/youth.htm>

Swarts, H.J. (2008). *Organizing urban America: Secular and faith-based progressive movements.* Minneapolis, MN: University of Minnesota Press.

Torres-Fleming, A., Valdes, P. & Pillai, S. (2010). *2010 field scan.* Brooklyn, NY: Funders' Collaborative on Youth Organizing.

Tough, P. (2008). *Whatever it takes: Geoffrey Canada's quest to change Harlem and America.* New York: Houghton Mifflin.

Voices of Youth in Chicago Education (VOYCE) (2008). *Student-led solutions to the nation's dropout crisis.* Chicago: Author. Retrieved from: http://www.voyceproject.org/userfiles/file/VOYCE%20report.pdf

Voices of Youth in Chicago Education (VOYCE) (2011). *Failed policies, broken futures: The true cost of zero tolerance in Chicago.* Chicago: Author. Retrieved from: http://www.voyceproject.org/sites/default/files/VOYCE%20report%202011.pdf

Watts, R.J., & Flanagan, C. (2007). Pushing the envelope on youth civic engagement: A developmental and liberation psychology perspective. *Journal of Community Psychology, 35*(6), 779–792.

Watts, R.J., Diemer, M.A. & Voight, A.M. (2011). Critical consciousness: Current status and future directions. *New Directions for Child and Adolescent Development, 134,* 43–57.

Wood, R.L. & Warren, M.R. (2002). A different face of faith-based politics: Social capital and community organizing in the public arena. *International Journal of Sociology and Social Policy, 22*(9–10), 6–54.

Wray-Lake, L. & Syvertsen, A.K. (2011). The developmental roots of social responsibility in childhood and adolescence. *New Directions for Child and Adolescent Development, 134,* 11–25.

Youth United for Change (2012). Retrieved July 20, 2012 from http://youthunitedforchange. org/

Zeldin, S., Christens, B.D. & Powers, J.L. (in press). The psychology and practice of youth-adult partnership: Bridging generations for youth development and community change. *American Journal of Community Psychology.* Published online ahead of print: doi:10.1007/s10464-012-9558-y

10

PUBLIC SCHOOLS AS CENTERS FOR BUILDING SOCIAL CAPITAL IN URBAN COMMUNITIES

A Case Study of the Logan Square Neighborhood Association in Chicago

Mark R. Warren, University of Massachusetts Boston

Introduction

A new wave of research is showing just how much relationships matter for community well-being (Sampson, 2012). We also are developing some understanding of why urban neighborhoods and other kinds of communities vary in their levels of social capital (Sampson, 2012; Smalls, 2009). However, we continue to lack much understanding of how social capital can be built. One strand of important research has examined community organizing as an intentional social capital building strategy (Warren, 2001) while others have considered the role of community-based organizations and voluntary associations (Putnam & Feldstein, 2004; Saegert, Thompson & Warren, 2001). Some of this research highlights the importance of institutions like religious congregations or other stable community organizations as sites around which social capital can be built (Smalls, 2009; Warren, 2001).

Public schools, along with religious congregations, are perhaps the most prevalent type of institution in urban neighborhoods. They are democratically accessible and relatively stable. As such, they represent a key potential resource. However, little research has examined their role as builders of social capital (Driscoll, 2001).

This chapter explores the potential for public schools to be sites for social capital building in low-income communities. It does so by presenting a case study of the Logan Square Neighborhood Association (LSNA) in Chicago, which has developed a prominent model for organizing parent leaders in and around its neighborhood schools. Over 1,500 parent leaders have been trained and many go on to undertake collective action and develop initiatives in schools and communities. These initiatives, in turn, serve to build new kinds of relationships among and between parents, educators, and a variety of other participants in school and community life. The chapter describes and analyzes how LSNA builds social capital utilizing a base in schools and some of its effects on participants.

Public Schools and Social Capital

The level of an urban neighborhood's social capital has important influences on a wide range of indicators of family and community well-being, including crime rates, health outcomes, and child development outcomes (Sampson, 2012).[1] These and other factors associated with poverty influence how well students achieve in public schools (Duncan & Brooks-Gunn, 1997; Ginwright, 2010; Rothstein, 2004). Important new research has shown that the ability of public schools to improve in low-income, urban communities depends on the level of family and community engagement in those schools as well as the broader level of social capital in the school's surrounding neighborhood. By social capital, I mean resources like social trust that are inherent in relationships between people that help them achieve collective goals (Warren, Thompson & Saegert, 2001). In other words, school improvement depends on social trust and relationships in and around the school.

Indeed, Anthony Bryk and his colleagues identify parent and community engagement as one of the five *essential* supports to improving low-performing public schools. The researchers measured gains in student test scores in Chicago public schools from 1990 to 1996, comparing the top quartile improving schools and the bottom quartile stagnating schools. Analyzing this data, Bryk and his colleagues identified five supports necessary for improvement, including school leadership, professional capacity, student-centered learning climate, instructional guidance and family and community engagement. The authors conclude, "We found that a sustained, material weakness in any one of these subsystems [including family and community engagement] undermined virtually all attempts at improving student learning" (Bryk, Sebring, Allensworth, Luppescu & Easton, 2010, p. 96).

Bryk and his colleagues also show that the level of a neighborhood's social capital and social needs have an important influence on the ability of public schools located there to improve. Using data from the Project on Human Development in Chicago Neighborhoods, Bryk demonstrates that communities with higher levels of trust and civic engagement, all other things being equal, were best able to develop the essential supports necessary for school improvement and make effective use of those supports. Indeed, schools in communities without much social capital and with high levels of social needs proved resistant to change, leading the authors to conclude that in such neighborhoods, "A much more powerful model of school development is needed – one that melds a comprehensive community schools initiative" (Bryk et al., 2010, p. 196).[2]

Much research has examined the ways that community organizing groups and community-based organizations more broadly can positively affect the level of a neighborhood's social capital (Saegert et al., 2001; Smalls, 2009; Warren, 2001). We have little understanding, however, of the potential of public schools to be sites for building and using social capital to address both educational improvement and other community needs (Driscoll, 2001). Yet public schools are located in virtually every urban neighborhood and are democratically accessible to all families.

There are promising experiments in this direction. Some schools attempt to be community centers, engaging families and offering services. Some of these are called community or full-service schools which typically offer health and family services and afterschool programs (Dryfoos, Quinn & Barkin, 2005). Other approaches focus on facility design, building new schools that incorporate facilities like libraries and gymnasiums to serve broader community needs (Vincent, 2006). In these approaches, building social capital tends to be articulated as one of a set of goals and is sometimes a byproduct; however, because service delivery is the main purpose of these efforts, social capital building typically gets little direct attention (Warren, 2005).

Indeed, public schools are not well designed to build social capital on their own (Schutz, 2006). Educators are not trained in relationship building and many hold deficit orientations to families in poor communities, especially those of color (Valenzuela, 2010; Valenzuela & Black, 2002). Unequal power relationships also undermine more egalitarian relationships, particularly across lines of race and class (Horvat, Weininger & Lareau, 2003; Rusch, 2009). In other words, it may be difficult for a school principal and teaching force, particularly if it is largely white and college-educated, to create bridging social capital with low-income parents of color (Warren, Hong, Rubin & Uy, 2009).

However, if they are engaged in collaborative efforts with community organizing groups, schools might be able to play such a role. By community organizing, I refer to groups whose purpose is to build relationships and power for people themselves to create change in their communities. Community organizing groups are primarily locally-rooted, but can range from neighborhood to metropolitan wide. There are several statewide and national networks of organizing groups. Many trace their traditions back to the work of Saul Alinsky, the so-called "father" of American community organizing, but the organizing tradition has been influenced by the civil rights, labor, feminist and other social movements as well. Working primarily in low to moderate income communities, organizing groups place a high priority on leadership development activities and typically combine both confrontation and collaboration in their efforts to influence public and private institutions.[3]

Community organizing groups are experts in building social capital, trained in relationship building, leadership development, and collective action. They may be better suited to creating a combination of bonding and bridging social capital (Putnam, 2000; Warren et al., 2001). Some research suggests that bonding relationships among low-income parents of color may be necessary for them to build truly collaborative and empowered bridging relationships with educators (Warren et al., 2009). Rather than face a college-educated teacher on her own, a low-income parent can do so with the support and encouragement of other parents, as well as the knowledge and skills she gathers from leadership development processes.

Community organizing groups that draw upon established institutional foundations often prove more durable than ones that seek to engage individuals (Swarts, 2008; Wood, 2002). Some organizing groups engage religious congregations as institutional members. But public schools also offer potential institutional anchors to organizing and social capital building efforts (Driscoll, 2001). Schools are relatively durable neighborhood institutions where families have reason to gather. Many play an important role in community identity (Tieken, 2011).

Collaborations between local public schools and community organizing groups also promise to foster social closure (Coleman, 1988). Social closure occurs when all (or many) members of a community are connected to each other, rather than in fragmented sets. Social capital can be more effective in fostering child development and student achievement, for example, when teachers, parents, and community members are connected to each other, develop common values and goals, and work together to support student learning (Coleman & Hoffer, 1987).

The purpose of this chapter is to examine how community organizing groups can collaborate with educators to utilize public schools as institutional sites for building social capital in schools and communities. I have selected a "model" case, a relatively successful effort to identify what can be learned about the ways in which schools can play this role.

Data and Methods

Data for this case study of the Logan Square Neighborhood Association (LSNA) in Chicago comes from several research projects conducted by myself and Soo Hong, a student who was part of a larger multi-case study of education organizing efforts at the time.[4] Each project included formal interviews of participants, observations of organizational and school activities, and review of relevant documents. Interviews were conducted with a diverse set of participants, including parents, teachers, community organizers, principals and other school staff, public officials, allies, and knowledgeable independent observers. These interviews were designed to understand organizing processes from multiple perspectives. A total of 90 interviews were conducted over a period of seven years.

Observations were conducted on a variety of organizational activities in community and school settings. We observed internal organizational meetings, training and political education sessions, house meetings, direct action events and public meetings; we also visited schools where LSNA worked. These observations were designed to see organizing in action, to better understand the role of various kinds of participants, and to observe dynamics in the relationships between various stakeholders (parent leaders, paid organizers, allies, and educators). Detailed field notes were taken on about 50 of these observational activities. However, we were making informal observations all the time that we were in the field. We spent many hours walking through neighborhoods and schools, eating lunch with participants in local restaurants, and watching people interact in a variety of settings. Impressions of these observations were summarized in notes. In the end, this analysis draws upon our formal field notes and interviews, but also from all the informal observations and conversations that constitute ethnographic research.

Finally, a variety of organizational documents were collected and reviewed for additional information on organizing activities and their effects. These included LSNA newsletters, annual reports, and flyers as well as school newsletters. We also examined school level data (student demographics, test scores, etc.). We reviewed newspaper articles and other publications about organizational activities. These documents helped us understand the history of the group, its internal dynamics as well as its public activities.

Data from these sources were systematically coded and emerging themes identified. In order to increase the accuracy of the analysis, data sources were triangulated by checking wherever possible what people said in interviews against what we observed and what was stated in published accounts. During data analysis, we searched for discrepant data and alternative interpretations of emerging patterns in the analysis. We weighed all these data and alternatives in an effort to produce a balanced and nuanced account of the case.

Building Social Capital in Logan Square

The LSNA is a community organizing group founded in the 1960s.[5] It traces its roots to the work of Saul Alinsky who began his organizing tradition in Chicago in the 1930s. Like most organizing groups, LSNA is focused on building relationships and power for residents to take action around community needs. It is nonpartisan and pursues a multi-issue agenda including housing, health, safety, education and immigrant rights. It seeks to take a holistic approach to addressing the needs of families and has long appreciated the link between the quality of public education and the well-being of families and children.

The Logan Square neighborhood sits northwest of downtown Chicago. It has about 75,000 residents. When LSNA started, the neighborhood was largely composed of European immigrants. In the 1980s, however, a dramatic influx of Latino immigrants from Latin America and migrants from Puerto Rico transformed the neighborhood. Latinos became a majority of the neighborhood's residents and an overwhelming majority of students in the local schools. By the 1990s, when LSNA turned its attention to education organizing, the student body in the local public schools was 90 percent Latino; 95 percent of students qualified for free or reduced price lunch.

By the late 1980s, LSNA was looking for a way to address the educational needs of the children of new immigrants. However, LSNA's lead education organizer, Joanna Brown, describes the neighborhood schools at the time as "fortresses" disconnected from families and the surrounding community. Parents were largely absent from schools. Teachers came from outside the community, with little knowledge of the new Latino culture; they often expressed low expectations of children and sometimes fear of families. In the face of quick neighborhood transition, race, class and cultural differences between educators and families led to disconnection and sometimes conflict. Parents told LSNA organizers they did not feel welcome in the schools and many mothers reported feeling isolated in their homes in this new neighborhood (Blanc, Brown, Nevarez-La Torre & Brown, 2002).

In the late 1980s, the Illinois state legislature passed legislation that devolved important decision-making powers to elected local school councils at each Chicago public school, including the power to hire and fire principals (Katz, Fine & Simon, 1997). This created an opening that LSNA was looking for. LSNA took a highly collaborative approach that proved particularly successful. LSNA began by focusing on school construction. As the new wave of Latino immigrants grew, the school-age population in Logan Square increased rapidly in the 1980s so that local schools had become overcrowded. In response, LSNA launched a successful campaign to get the city to build annexes to five elementary schools in the neighborhood and to build two new middle schools. The campaign helped foster relationships with principals in the neighborhood's schools, which desperately needed the additional classroom space. In 1994, LSNA adopted a Holistic Plan that built on the trust established with principals to move organizing work directly into the neighborhood's schools.

Parent Mentor Program

Working with school principals, LSNA launched the parent mentor program.[6] The program was designed to address the disconnection between schools and families and to build parent participation and leadership primarily in the schools but also in the community as well. Parent mentors, mostly Latina mothers, work two hours per day in classrooms and receive a modest stipend for their work. They meet together each Friday for leadership development workshops. The program started in one school in 1996 and has now grown to eight schools with 150 parents participating each year. Over 1,500 parents have graduated from the program to date. Parents with limited English fluency are also encouraged to participate, and organizers place these parent mentors within bilingual classrooms or those with younger children. At first, many teachers resisted the idea of having parents in their classrooms, worrying that they would be "spying" on them. However, the mentors proved to be making valuable contributions to their classrooms and gradually built a positive reputation. Now, LSNA cannot fill all of the teacher requests for mentors.

The program has some key features that make it powerful. First, parents do the real work of schooling. The activities of mentors vary by classroom and depend on the relationship with the teacher. Indeed, through this program, parents build direct relationships with teachers, learn to work together and build trust and cooperation over time. In this program, parents are approached as potential leaders and the intent is to build their leadership capacity.

The weekly training sessions play a key role in the program. Parent mentors meet on Fridays in their school; once a month, the mentors from all the schools gather together for a session. Surprisingly, these sessions focus little on building skills to support learning in the classroom. Rather, they are intentionally designed for leadership development. According to LSNA organizer Joanna Brown (Hong et al., 2012, p. 5), the goal of the weekly sessions is:

> to give parents a space where they could get to know each other, support each other, and slowly build a stronger connection to the school, in essence, building a sense of community… As an organizing group, we are interested in building parents as leaders, not necessarily training them to learn how to follow the rules and guidelines of any teacher's classroom.

Each parent mentor is required to set a personal goal for themselves for the year. Some mentors set the goal of learning English, others work to pass a GED. LSNA supports the mentors in achieving these goals, which builds a sense of self-efficacy and personal empowerment.

Personal empowerment is combined with building skills for collective power and action. Mentors learn a variety of skills relevant to organizing, such as how to chair a meeting and how to speak in public. They also learn about community issues like public health and affordable housing as well as educational issues. LSNA creates many opportunities for developing leadership: talking with funders, speaking at a rally, sharing testimony in front of the state legislature, working on a door-knocking campaign, or reading with a first grader. According to organizer Joanna Brown, part of LSNA's vision is to "bring people into the leadership of actions and campaigns that fundamentally matter to our work in the community."

However, a critical result is the building of community across the mentors, what can be understood as bonding social capital. Mentors support each other in the achievement of personal and group goals. Meanwhile, they are supported and encouraged by former parent mentors who have moved on to further leadership roles in LSNA. Leticia Berrera began as a parent mentor and is now a paid organizer for the program. Berrera tells new parent mentors:

> I was right there, just like you are, sitting in this room, and I was quiet. I didn't know what to say, and there was so much that was new to me, but I had this fire and energy that just was lighting up inside me. And now here I am working with you, and this is what is possible for all of you here—that you will find a connection and make some kind of change in your life that you want to make. And we will be here to support you with those goals.
>
> We ask, "Who is a leader?" A lot of mothers like me don't think of themselves as leaders. The parent-mentor program gives us the chance to develop. We have the opportunity to go to workshops and to learn. We set personal goals and it builds our self-esteem. As soon as teachers know that parents are in school and going to workshops, they see you differently.

One LSNA organizer, describes the program as a "steppingstone for everything else" the organization does:

> These parents go on to find full-time jobs outside, or they start working in the schools as tutors or paraprofessionals, serve on school committees, lead one of our programs, or become elected on the local school councils. It's a little seed that gets planted that grows into a whole bunch of other things. As parent mentors, they build new skills of leadership and activism and this becomes the base for their work as leaders in many of our other programs or in the school and community more broadly.

Parent Leadership and School/Community Action

The community created and the leadership development experienced has led parent mentors to launch an impressively large range of organizing initiatives since the program's origins. These include:

• Community learning centers at the local schools which offer cultural and educational classes to parents and other neighborhood residents;

- Lending libraries in school cafeterias where parents can borrow books to read to their children;
- Literacy Ambassador program where teachers and parent leaders partner and visit the homes of other parents for literacy activities;
- School safety patrols at the start and close of the school day;
- Parent tutors in classrooms to provide extra tutoring to individual students;
- Grow Your Own Teacher program that provides free college education for parents to become bilingual teachers in Logan Square schools;
- Participation in local school councils where parents have decision-making power over principal hiring and some budgeting issues;
- Campaigns to support bilingual education and to increase levels of funding for public education; among others.

Some of these initiatives cross the school/community divide. The safety patrols contribute to broader neighborhood safety while the Literacy Ambassador programs reach out into neighborhood homes. In many schools, teachers do home visits. But the Ambassador program is different. In this initiative, a teacher and a parent leader team up and visit the home of another parent to conduct literacy-based activities, like reading to children. However, the host parent is required to invite several other families from the school or neighborhood to their house to participate. Typically, this is an important event and the host family often puts on lavish spreads of home-cooked food to welcome the ambassadors and guest families.

In other words, the Ambassador program is a venue to build social capital among families and with teachers, as well as promote reading and literacy. According to Leticia Berrera, one of LSNA's education organizers, "It gets teachers and parents at the same level. At home, we don't have a desk for teachers or a special chair. They sit on the floor! It's very different the next day: Parents come in and say 'hi!'." Catherine Delgado, a parent who serves as the program's coordinator at Monroe School, reports one incident that captures the spirit of this initiative. "The teachers at Ames are great. One mother had to work, so Mr. Perez, the teacher, went to her place of employment, a pizza parlor, and held the visit there. Other people in the shop got interested and joined in too."

Graduates of the parent mentor programs have also launched organizing initiatives directly into the community. For example, parents helped initiate and currently participate in LSNA's Health Outreach Team, which has connected thousands of low-income families to affordable health services and state insurance over the past five years. Parents also helped develop LSNA's newest health initiative, Active Living by Design, whose goal is to increase physical activity in the neighborhood.

Meanwhile, parents have become leaders in campaigns for affordable development in Logan Square and for immigrant rights. Gentrification is threatening the neighborhood, as it has across other Chicago communities.

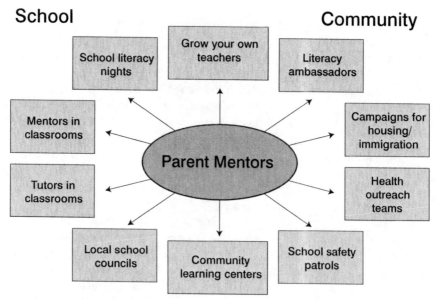

FIGURE 10.1   Parent Leadership Initiatives

LSNA has become a key part of a "balanced development" initiative that seeks to preserve affordable housing. LSNA parents also featured in a recent successful campaign to get the Illinois legislature to make undocumented immigrants eligible for driver's licenses.

Taken together, these parent leadership initiatives have created a large and diverse set of actions and activities in the schools and surrounding community (see Figure 10.1). One parent mentor, Karla Mack, describes the interconnection between leadership development and relationship building. Discussing her involvement in a door-knocking campaign to raise awareness and generate community input for a newly formed community center at McAuliffe, Mack says:

> If you would have told me a year ago that I would be knocking on the door of strangers—people I don't know—I would never have believed you. This experience gets us in contact with all these families around the neighborhood. We start to feel connected as a group and as a community, and we start to understand what our neighbors care about…and then for me, this is just raising my own level of confidence that I can oversee this project and get out there and start doing things for my community.

According to another parent mentor:

> I feel I have some power—power that I can make a difference. And even though I cannot change a lot of things in the community myself, when I am

part of a group like this, we all feel different. We feel that together, we can do this—we can do this together.

According to organizer Joanna Brown:

> Our parents don't want to play a purely supportive role in the school. Of course, they do things to support school improvement and relational dynamics, but the big picture is that they are pushing for significant changes. They want to understand what's going on in their classrooms, because then, they can be articulate about what's needed for change. They want to see teachers be pushed and challenged to shift their ways of teaching. This doesn't come from asking, it comes from organizing, and at the end of the day, it's about power. Our parents are building power and voice in the schools.

Building Powerful Relationships

Through these initiatives new relationships are created (see Figure 10.2). I have discussed bonding social capital above. On the basis of the strength of their bonding ties, parent leaders create bridging ties to a range of school and community actors, including teachers, students, principals, school administrators, police, health professionals, local public officials, and state legislators. Parents in a sense become the connector tissues for creating a degree of social closure within the community and across schools and the neighborhood.

According to Melva Patock, a longtime teacher at the Funston Elementary School:

> The [parent mentor] program really changes how teachers and parents interact with each other. We move from a place where teachers really didn't know if parents were on their side, so they tried to keep their classrooms to themselves. And now, classrooms are really open spaces for parents [and we work together].

Speaking of the Literacy Ambassador program where a teacher and a parent leader together visit the home of another parent, Patock adds:

> It's hard to build that connection with parents when you don't know them. And when you only meet them in school, you don't really have to think about it. But when you come to a student's house and you sit down together for dinner with his parents and you can see where they live, then you can really focus on the family and the community that they are a part of. You start to see everything in a different light, but especially from that student's perspective.

Social closure

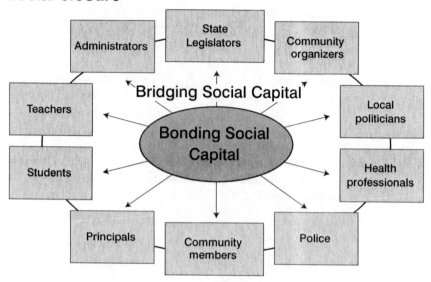

FIGURE 10.2 Social Capital in the School Community

Principals at the six elementary schools now lead an annual reading walk where the entire school community gathers at a central neighborhood location for a literacy event. In this way, principals leave the isolation of their individual school and build relationships with each other and with a variety of neighborhood participants in the walk.

However, it is the core of parent leaders organized around schools that is the engine driving community connections and actions. According to John McDermott, a housing organizer for LSNA, parents who are involved in his housing campaigns come in with a sense of power, compared with the other individuals and groups he may organize. He explains:

> We have people who walk in off the street. And we have some relationships that we build through other member groups like churches and block clubs. But the schools are these intense hubs, these intense webs of relationships. There is such a huge level of trust and relationship between the educational organizers and the parent mentors, among the parent mentors, that the parent mentors at a given school are like this already formed team. They have a common base, they have a lot in common in terms of life issues. They are moms, they have a school in common, they tend to have a neighborhood in common because they live around the school. So they are like a team that's already somewhat powerful.

In McDermott's view, the sheer mass of support from parent mentors accelerates and accentuates LSNA's work in the area of housing:

> If it weren't for the parents, a lot of these campaigns—some of them would not happen and most of them would not have the kind of power and impact that they have. On the balanced development campaign, LSNA has been one of the key members of the coalition, and when there are citywide actions or some major hearings at the City Council Housing and Real Estate Committee, the education leaders, parent mentors, and to some extent, the community center students, are really the lion's share of the turnout of the force.

For LSNA, schools have become a natural center for community life. According to Joanna Brown (Hong et al., 2012, p. 13):

> I think we should do everything [emanating out] of schools, because there's where we connect with people. By coming into the [parent mentor] program, people actually get pulled into the community; they get pulled out of their private houses, into the first public space that they've entered, many of them.
>
> Over and over again, the women themselves speak about being transformed by the experience. Many were isolated in their homes by language, culture, and small children. For many, it is their first step out into the public sphere. This works in part because the school is the safest public institution, filled with women and children.

Limitations and Challenges

This qualitative study was designed to identify the ways that LSNA builds social capital by utilizing public schools as institutional sites. It documented new relationships created and some of their effects, as reported by participants. It was not designed to measure quantitatively increases (or not) in the relationships described and their effects on family well-being in Logan Square, although there is some evidence of increases in student achievement and improved school climate in local schools.[7]

LSNA itself faces an important challenge as gentrification has begun to occur in Logan Square. From 2000 to 2010 the community experienced a population shift of almost 10,000 people as many Latinos left to be replaced with young professionals. LSNA has been working with community groups within the neighborhood and across Chicago on what it calls balanced development to protect affordable housing and help maintain the square's Latino population. But it remains to be seen if LSNA and its allies can build enough power to stop the economic forces of gentrification.

Maintaining collaboration with educators has also proven a challenge, as principal turnover is high. Each new principal must be engaged and convinced of the benefits to the school's alliance with LSNA. In order to achieve these alliances, LSNA takes a relentless collaborative approach. Indeed, it requires a delicate balance between working with schools in support of common goals and pushing schools to make necessary changes. According to LSNA executive director Nancy Aardema:

> In our work outside of schools, as is often the case with traditional community organizing groups, there is usually an external enemy, an institution or individual that you have identified and associated with a concrete problem. And if you are a strong, powerful organizing group, you are going to push up against that external enemy until you win. It's you versus them. But in schools, it's not that clear—is there a clear external enemy? In most cases, no. We have to share space with principals; in some ways, you would say we need their blessing to do the work in schools. So our strategy for working with them has to be different, more collaborative.

Discussion and Conclusion

LSNA has developed a powerful model for collaborating with schools so they can become sites for social capital building. They do this by intentional efforts to create bonding social capital among Latina parents, build their leadership capacity, and scaffold them into leading action efforts in schools and the broader neighborhood. Through the strength of bonding social capital, these parent leaders create new bridging ties with educators and a variety of other community actors, leading to a degree of social closure. In the end, as we found in our fieldwork, parents are everywhere.

How broadly applicable is a community organizing model for collaborating with educators and utilizing public schools as institutional sites for social capital building? LSNA's parent mentor program has received much attention recently, including being featured on NBC's 2012 "Education Nation" summit. Many organizing groups and schools in Chicago and across the nation are attempting to replicate the parent mentor model by adapting it to their local conditions. To date, although they appear promising, we do not have a careful study of these replication efforts.

Meanwhile, the field of community organizing is growing and the number of organizing groups working to improve public education through parent and youth collective action is increasing. A recent effort put the number of community organizing groups engaging in public education reform to number over 500 (Warren, 2010). New research is documenting the growth in sophistication of these efforts and their expansion in scope and scale (Mediratta,

Shah & McAlister, 2009; Warren et al., 2011). The vast majority of these groups seek ways to collaborate with local schools and educators. From this point of view, an organizing model that utilizes schools is growing in potential.

On the other hand, community organizing groups, while increasing in number and capacity, still remain relatively small and under-resourced even as they try to address a broad range of community concerns (Walker & McCarthy, 2012; Wood, Partridge & Fulton, 2012). Although the vast majority seek to collaborate with public schools, they vary widely in how they seek to do so (Warren et al., 2011). Many do organize parents, young people and other community members in and around schools. Some, however, organize mainly around congregations or neighborhoods for policy change in public education.

Current trends in public education present both opportunities and obstacles to forming collaborations. Federal policy has become favorable to supporting community schools.[8] The federal government's Promise Neighborhoods initiative, modeled to an extent on the Harlem Children's Zone, also reflects an appreciation of the need for schools to collaborate with community-based organizations to holistically address the needs of children. The US Department of Education now requires community engagement as part of its school turnaround funding for the lowest performing schools.[9]

Meanwhile, however, public schools are under enormous pressure to narrow their work in pursuit of increasing measurable student achievement, particularly in reading and mathematics scores (Ravitch, 2010). Although collaborations with community organizations to build family engagement and social capital promise school improvement, pressure to produce results in the short term undermine the willingness of many to put time and energy into alliance building. Some districts are closing traditional public schools and encouraging charter schools. Chicago itself closed over 40 schools as part of the mayor's Renaissance 2010 plan (Lipman, 2011) and more since, but so far, LSNA's allied schools have remained open. Of course, some community organizing groups might partner with new charter schools to build family and community engagement (Warren, 2005),[10] but the contentious atmosphere that has been created could undermine the conditions for collaboration between educators and communities (Lipman, 2011).

Broadly speaking, an approach to public schools as centers of democratic and community life requires the transformation of our current paradigm for public education. The dominant paradigm today places a narrow focus on increasing student achievement (Ravitch, 2010). A collaborative approach requires a return to and a revitalization of the American democratic tradition in public education (Dewey, 1915, 1938 [1916]; Oakes & Rogers, 2005). In this approach public education does not simply provide a service; public education also represents a vital democratic institution. In the words of George Counts (1978 [1932]), who challenged progressive educators to become part of the social reform movement of the 1930s, if schools are to become vital centers for community development, they must "dare" to become part of the effort to build a new social order.

Acknowledgments

I am grateful to Soo Hong who conducted much of the research that forms the basis for this chapter. The Ford Foundation and the Charles Stewart Mott Foundation provided funds to support some of this research.

Notes

1   I am aware that Sampson uses the concept of collective efficacy; while there are important differences with the concept of social capital, I believe they are close enough for the purposes of this chapter.
2   See also Misra, Grimes & Rogers (2013).
3   For an overview of community organizing, especially as it relates to public education, see Warren, Mapp & Community Organizing and School Reform Project (2011).
4   For further details and other findings from the first round, see Warren (2005); for the second round, see Warren et al. (2009); for the larger multicase study, see Warren, Mapp & Community Organizing and School Reform Project (2011).
5   For a fuller account of LSNA, see chapter 6 of *A Match on Dry Grass* (Warren et al., 2011) and Soo Hong's (2011) book-length account, *A Chord of Three Strands*.
6   For an excellent, extended account of the parent mentor program that draws out its lessons for engaging parents in public schools, see *A Chord of Three Strands* (Hong, 2011).
7   Between 1997 and 2002, student performance on the Iowa Test of Basic Skills in math and reading improved at all LSNA-affiliated schools, from an average of 28% scoring at or above the national norm in math in 1997 to an average of 39% in 2002. Meanwhile, the percentage scoring in the bottom quartile on the math tests fell at all schools, dropping from an average of 41% to 26%. Reading scores showed similar gains. Meanwhile, 71% of teachers in a staff survey of LSNA schools reported improved discipline as a result of parent mentors (Blanc et al., 2002, p. 22). Five LSNA schools reporting to the Annenberg Challenge all showed declines in disciplinary referrals, some as large as 37% (p. 22).
8   See information and resources available from the Coalition for Community Schools at: http://www.communityschools.org
9   See the guidelines at: http://www2.ed.gov/programs/sif/index.html
10 Charter schools are a diverse phenomena, including mission-driven and for-profits, and the evidence for their effects on surrounding neighborhoods is mixed (Frankenberg, Siegel-Hawley & Wand, 2011).

References

Blanc, S., Brown, J., Nevarez-La Torre, A. & Brown, C. (2002). Case Study: Logan Square Neighborhood Association *Strong Neighborhoods, Strong Schools, The Indicators Project on Education Organizing*. Chicago: Cross City Campaign for Urban School Reform.
Bryk, A.S., Sebring, P.B., Allensworth, E., Luppescu, S. & Easton, J.Q. (2010). *Organizing schools for improvement: Lessons from Chicago*. Chicago: University of Chicago Press.

Coleman, J.S. (1988). Social capital in the creation of human capital. *American Journal of Sociology, Vol. 94 (Supplement)*, S95–S120.

Coleman, J.S. & Hoffer, T. (1987). *Public and private high schools: The impact of communities.* New York: Basic Books.

Counts, G.S. (1978 [1932]). *Dare the school build a new social order?* Carbondale: Southern Illinois University Press.

Dewey, J. (1915). *The school and society.* Chicago: University of Chicago Press.

Dewey, J. (1938 [1916]). *Democracy and education: An introduction to the philosophy of education.* New York: MacMillan.

Driscoll, M.E. (2001). The sense of place and the neighborhood school: Implications for building social capital and for community development. In R.L. Crowson (Ed.), *Community development and school reform* (Vol. 5, pp. 19–42). Amsterdam: JAI.

Dryfoos, J.G., Quinn, J. & Barkin, C. (2005). *Community schools in action: Lessons from a decade of practice.* New York: Oxford University Press.

Duncan, G.J. & Brooks-Gunn, J. (1997). *Consequences of growing up poor.* New York: Russell Sage Foundation Press.

Frankenberg, E., Siegel-Hawley, G. & Wand, J. (2011). Choice without equity: Charter school segregation. *Education Policy Analysis Archives, 19(1)*, 1–92.

Ginwright, S.A. (2010). *Black youth rising: Activism and radical healing in urban America.* New York: Teachers College Press.

Hong, S. (2011). *A cord of three strands: A new approach to parent engagement in school.* Cambridge: Harvard Education Press.

Hong, S., with Warren, M.R. & Mapp, K.L. (2012). *Building Parent Leadership through Community Organizing: The Logan Square Neighborhood Association's Parent Mentor Program in Chicago.* Cambridge: Harvard Educational Publishing Group.

Horvat, E.M., Weininger, E.B. & Lareau, A. (2003). From social ties to social capital: Class differences in the relations between schools and parent networks. *American Educational Research Journal, 40(2)*, 319–351.

Katz, M.B., Fine, M. & Simon, E. (1997). Poking around: Outsiders view Chicago school reform. *Teachers College Record, 99(1)*, 117–157.

Lipman, P. (2011). *The new political economy of urban education: Neoliberalism, race and the right to the city.* New York: Routledge.

Mediratta, K., Shah, S. & McAlister, S. (2009). *Community organizing for stronger schools: Strategies and successes.* Cambridge: Harvard Education Press.

Misra, K., Grimes, P.W. & Rogers, K.E. (2013). The effects of community social capital on school performance: A spatial approach. *The Journal of Socio-Economics, 42*, 106–111.

Oakes, J. & Rogers, J. (2005). *Learning power: Organizing for education and justice.* New York: Teachers College Press.

Putnam, R.D. (2000). *Bowling alone: The collapse and revival of American community.* New York: Simon & Schuster.

Putnam, R.D. & Feldstein, L. (2004). *Better together: Restoring the American community.* New York: Simon & Schuster.

Ravitch, D. (2010). *The death and life of the great American school system: How testing and choice are undermining education.* New York: Basic Books.

Rothstein, R. (2004). *Class and schools: Using social, economic and educational reform to close the black-white achievement gap.* Washington, DC: Economic Policy Institute.

Rusch, L. (2009). Rethinking bridging: Risk and trust in multiracial community organizing. *Urban Affairs Review, 45(4)*, 483–506.

Saegert, S., Thompson, J.P. & Warren, M.R. (Eds.). (2001). *Social capital and poor communities*. New York: Russell Sage Foundation Press.

Sampson, R.J. (2012). *The great American city: Chicago and the enduring neighborhood effect.* Chicago: University of Chicago Press.

Schutz, A. (2006). Home is a prison in the global city: The tragic failure of school-based community engagement strategies. *Review of Educational Research,* 76(4), 691–743.

Smalls, M.L. (2009). *Unanticipated gains: Origins of network inequality in everyday life.* New York: Oxford University Press.

Swarts, H.J. (2008). *Organizing urban America: Secular and faith-based progressive movements.* Minneapolis: University of Minnesota Press.

Tieken, M. (2011). *Our only hope: The roles of schools in two rural Southern communities.* (Dissertation), Harvard University, Cambridge, MA.

Valenzuela, R.R. (2010). *Dismantling contemporary deficit thinking: Educational thought and practice.* New York: Routledge.

Valenzuela, R.R. & Black, M.S. (2002). 'Mexican Americans don't value education!' On the basis of the myth, mythmaking and debunking. *Journal of Latinos and Education,* 1(2), 81–103.

Vincent, J.M. (2006). Public schools as public infrastructure: Roles for planning researchers. *Journal of Planning Education and Research,* 25(4), 433–437.

Walker, E.T. & McCarthy, J.D. (2012). Continuity and change in community organizing: A report to organizers.

Warren, M.R. (2001). *Dry bones rattling: Community building to revitalize American democracy.* Princeton: Princeton University Press.

Warren, M.R. (2005). Communities and schools: A new view of urban education reform. *Harvard Educational Review,* 75(2), 133–173.

Warren, M.R. (2010). Community organizing for education reform. In M. Orr & J. Rogers (Eds.), *Public engagement for public education: Joining forces to revitalize democracy and equalize schools* (pp. 139–172). Palo Alto: Stanford University Press.

Warren, M.R., Thompson, J.P. & Saegert, S. (2001). The role of social capital in combating poverty. In S. Saegert, J.P. Thompson & M.R. Warren (Eds.), *Social capital and poor communities* (pp. 1–28). New York: Russell Sage Foundation Press.

Warren, M.R., Hong, S., Rubin, C.L. & Uy, P.S. (2009). Beyond the bake sale: A community-based, relational approach to parent engagement in schools. *Teachers College Record,* 111(9), 2209–2254.

Warren, M.R., Mapp, K.L. & Community Organizing and School Reform Project. (2011). *A match on dry grass: Community organizing as a catalyst for school reform.* New York: Oxford University Press.

Wood, R.L. (2002). *Faith in action: Religion, race and democratic organizing in America.* Chicago: University of Chicago Press.

Wood, R.L., Partridge, K. & Fulton, B. (2012). *Building bridges, building power: Developments in institution based community organizing.* Jericho, NY: Interfaith Funders.

11

BUILDING SCHOOLS AND COMMUNITY CONNECTIONS

Outreach and Activism for New Schools in Southeast Los Angeles

Greta Kirschenbaum Brownlow,
California State University, East Bay

Introduction

> I know our job is to build schools, but we sometimes think very narrowly about education. Kids live in a community; they live with their families...everything is connected.
>
> (LAUSD School Board Member)

About 15 years ago, the Los Angeles Unified School District (LAUSD/ District) embarked on the largest public school construction program in US history. Conceived as the major component in the District's undertaking to relieve classroom overcrowding and return students to neighborhood schools operating on traditional calendars, the multi-billion dollar program set out to deliver approximately 167,000 new classroom seats by 2015 (LAUSD, 2009). Throughout the course of program implementation, community participation has occurred both by District invitation and through grassroots grit. This research looks at the forms and outcomes of such participation to understand whether and how a combination of District outreach and community activism has built a foundation for sustained school–community connections in Southeast Los Angeles. Such connections, I contend, will prove crucial to building and growing urban public schools that successfully serve as both centers of educational attainment and anchors of community development.

Underlying this research are the assumptions that parent and community engagement is important in building and sustaining academically successful schools, and that successful, well-integrated schools can be assets to neighborhood communities. This is not to say that parental and broader community involvement is a panacea for languishing urban schools and communities. Rather, as corroborated by research demonstrating how community involvement and organizing positively impacts schools (Henderson & Mapp, 2002), students benefit most from other types of school improvement measures, like enhancing instructional quality, providing schools with adequate resources, and increasing rigor and accountability, when parental involvement and community connections are present. Conversely, healthy schools can help strengthen communities by providing physical neighborhood resources and by creating or enhancing the types of intracommunity connections that help build social capital (Noguera, 2001).

Given the community's crucial role in school improvement efforts, and the function of quality, well-used schools as neighborhood assets, it is important for several reasons to consider whether and how districts employ school facilities planning as an opportunity to engage key stakeholders. First, community participation in school development presents community stakeholders with the opportunity to envision and articulate the function of schools for their children and their neighborhoods. Additionally, outreach around school planning allows districts to gain local insight and foster long-term community commitment to building and maintaining quality schools. Lastly, community outreach around school planning opens a door for parents and other community members to become active champions of community-based school reform.

This chapter argues that while further research is required to determine whether outreach and activism in the Southeast will result in sustained community–school connections, process outcomes to date demonstrate an enhanced potential for community-based school reform that must be captured by the District and its partners, and hold important lessons for future facilities improvement programs, within and beyond LA.

For, even as LAUSD's big construction push comes to a close, and the availability of funding for new schools has ebbed along with a crippled economy, continued facilities investments will be required by school districts in California and beyond. Such expenditures will be needed not only to accommodate population growth, relieve school overcrowding, eliminate deferred maintenance, and keep up with the normal life cycle of building systems and components, but also to enrich education through modernized facilities aligned with innovations in teaching and learning (UC Berkeley, 2012). As demonstrated herein, these future facilities investments will create important opportunities for fostering the type of parent and community engagement in schools that can blossom over time into a broader movement for educational reform.

Methods

The findings presented herein are based on qualitative data gathered over approximately one year during visits to the Los Angeles area. I focused on

Southeast LA as a case study of the District-wide process, because it encompasses an entire Sub District, Local District 6, wherein many school construction projects were undertaken early in the District's process. Further, the Southeast cities represent an area wherein enormous economic and demographic shifts have occurred since the last new LAUSD schools were built, and where as a result, new and better quality schools were greatly needed.

During the course of my research, I visited and toured ten new school sites, most of which had been operating for more than one year, conducted 50 interviews, and attended numerous community meetings and events. As part of a team of researchers examining the effects of the construction program on student achievement, I also attended several internal meetings of LAUSD Facilities Division staff. Interviews were conducted both in person and by phone with various stakeholders, including parents and other local community members, teachers, principals, government officials, and LAUSD staff and leadership. All direct quotations included herein are extracted from transcripts of these interviews; names have been changed to preserve participant anonymity. Lastly, I facilitated group discussions with students at two Southeast high schools, and gathered additional background data by reviewing public meeting transcripts, articles related to school construction in the LA area, and demographic data for LA County, the Southeast cities, and LAUSD.

Theoretical Underpinnings

To understand the outcomes and possibilities that this process has advanced, I employed two areas of literature: participatory planning and community organizing for school reform. Concerned with the mission and methods employed in soliciting public involvement, participatory planning literature embodies debates regarding the ability of the participatory process to represent a diversity of opinions and to influence the quality of plans, the effectiveness of participatory planning as a means of community empowerment, and the capacity of local government agencies to develop and implement programs that authentically engage participants. Community organizing literature, on the other hand, explores a more activist approach to civic engagement by providing insight into how community engagement around schools emerges to engender public schools that are both sites of educational achievement and "institutional sites for strengthening and revitalizing urban communities" (Warren, 2007: 16).

Planning research effectively articulates how various mechanisms for government-initiated participatory processes can maximize stakeholder participation, mitigate for inequities (both in the process itself and in the sociopolitical realm in which it is undertaken), and improve project outcomes by community expertise (Arnstein, 1969; Forester, 1999; Hibbard & Lurie, 2000; Innes & David, 2005). This literature also successfully demonstrates what can happen when preferred practices are not employed, and/or where participation becomes ritual rather than meaningful. What it generally disregards, however, is participatory planning specific to schools. Similarly, while community organizing literature strongly illuminates the importance of parent and community organizing around education by documenting its effects on students' achievement, district policy, and individual and collective capacity for creating community change, it fails to provide much in the way of empirical studies looking at activism around school planning and its potential for building sustainable, multifaceted community engagement in schools.

To an extent, "community school" advocates – who encompass both planners and scholars of community organizing – help fill the gaps in both areas of literature. They do so by articulating crucial school–community connections through studies of how community engagement in school planning and programming can help redefine relationships between schools and communities, thus creating more effective schools and healthier neighborhoods (Baum, 2003; Blank et al., 2003). Increasingly, architects and designers aligned with the community schools camp also support smart school planning by demonstrating how facilities design can maximize student learning (Bingler, 1999; Dyck, 2002; Lippman, 2007). Yet, while some of these works acknowledge the relationship of school facilities to the surrounding community, few discuss how and to what end the public could shape schools, from the outside in, through the school planning process. It is the intent of this research to augment the current literature related to both school planning and community-centered school improvement in a way that illuminates the possibilities for change that arise when institutional process meets grassroots organizing in an evolving and dynamic participatory landscape.

Research Context

Southeast LA and Local District 6

Situated just south of Downtown LA amidst the floodplains of the lower Los Angeles and San Gabriel rivers, the Southeast blossomed during the early 20th century into a thriving mix of industrial and suburban development, helping to transform the area into the Detroit of California. Yet, while the Southeast cities, including Bell, Cudahy, Huntington Park, Maywood, South Gate, and Vernon, played a pivotal role in the development and prosperity of the LA region, subsequent deindustrialization led to their eventual loss of tax base and subordination to the larger, politically and economically dominant City of LA. With job loss began white flight from the area, a trend that continued as the immigrant population flourished in successive decades. Between 1975 and 1980, the Southeast cities' population (including adjacent Bell Gardens and Commerce) grew from 180,000 to 222,000, almost 5 percent a year, as new residents arrived from Mexico and other Latin American countries. Part of a larger occurrence of immigration during the 1970s and 1980s, this population influx both dramatically changed the face of the Southeast and greater LA and resulted in increasingly unmet demands for social services, including the need for more schools.

Encompassing the Southeast cities, Local District 6 is reflective of the predominantly blue-collar, Latino, and immigrant character of the area. According to the 2010 US Census, an average of 96 percent of documented residents in each of the Southeast cities are of Hispanic or Latino origin.[1] Similarly, Latino students comprised 98.5 percent of the student population in Local District 6 during the 2007–08 school year (LAUSD 2009). With the exception of Vernon, which has remained a predominantly industrial city with few residents, each of the area cities has documented foreign-born populations of between 33 and 42 percent. In 2007–08, District 6 Latino students were primarily of Mexican and Central American descent, and almost half were English Language Learners.

These trends have significant implications not only for instruction but also for the District–community communication required for collaborative school and neighborhood change. For instance, the fact that many parents are unfamiliar with the structure of US schooling affects their ability to participate in their children's education. Further, parental and community involvement in schools can be thwarted when parents feel alienated from District processes, either due to language or cultural barriers, or because they believe they lack the time, financial resources, or expertise needed for meaningful involvement.

Given the demographic composition of Southeast LA, it is not surprising that a significant proportion of LAUSD's most severely overcrowded schools historically have been located within Local District 6. In fact, most students in California's overcrowded schools are Latino English learners, and most overcrowded schools are in poor neighborhoods (UCLA/IDEA, 2003). Also, for LAUSD and other California districts, school overcrowding is indicated not by a few extra students, but by substantial over-enrollment,[2] which can result in reduced student achievement, increased violence, and unsafe physical conditions.

LAUSD long addressed overcrowding with portable classrooms or by busing students to alternative schools across the District and away from their neighborhoods. The District also instituted multi-track calendars such as Concept 6, a year-round school operation strategy that has long been a source of controversy in the Southeast – both because it effectively robs students of instructional days,[3] and because multi-tracked schools tend to disproportionately enroll low-income students of color. Corroborating parent concerns, studies show that students who attend schools operating on Concept 6 calendars suffer marked disadvantages over students attending traditional calendar schools, including truncated and lost instructional time, limited access to courses and specialized programs, ill-timed breaks, less access to extracurricular activities and enrichment programs, and poorer academic performance (Oakes, 2003). Disadvantages associated with involuntary busing, including impediments to parental involvement, limited access to after-school activities, disincentives to kindergarten enrollment, and poorer achievement, also have been identified (Oakes, 2003: 39).

Rebuilding Trust and Building Schools

Given the limitations of traditional remedies to school overcrowding, LAUSD sought to capitalize on a combination of state and local bond funding to support school construction and renovation throughout the District. The influx of new school construction funds began in 1997, when voters allocated $2.4 billion for school construction and modernization. In subsequent years, voters approved six additional local and State bond measures, the latest of which provided $7 billion for repairs and upgrades. With the onset of the 2008 economic recession, the District's ability to access local bond funds became limited. However, with the help of special bond structures made available under the federal American Recovery and Reinvestment Act of 2009, LAUSD was able to sell more than $4 billion of General Obligation Bonds, ultimately allowing the District to have 129 of its planned 131 new K–12 schools up and running by the fall of 2012 (LAUSD, 2011).

Community Outreach

Construction of so many new schools within a relatively short timeframe was facilitated by a District reorganization that created the New Construction Branch within LAUSD's Facilities Services Division.[4] Paving the way for New Construction's bricks and mortar program, LAUSD's Community Outreach Department was charged with implementing a public involvement program that would build public understanding, participation, and partnership around new school construction. In its practical application, LAUSD's outreach approach was by no measure groundbreaking. Yet, the sheer scale of the effort within a climate of strained community–District relations necessitated a degree of process normalization that had not previously been undertaken in LA, and that is not generally pursued by large urban districts undertaking school building or renovation projects.

Early attempts to relieve existing campuses and return students to neighborhood schools set a shaky stage, as project missteps and related public relations blunders spurred doubt in the District's ability to respond to community needs. In particular, fallout from the Belmont Learning Center project, which enabled construction of a $160-million high school subsequently declared unsuitable for student occupancy, left many community stakeholders skeptical about LAUSD's ability to successfully execute new school projects. Widespread public dissatisfaction also was fed by LAUSD's apparent lack of public accountability, demonstrated by its failure to engage with the public and its overall dismissal of school conditions in many neighborhoods.

Over time, LAUSD's lack of community engagement only intensified the tensions created by Belmont and other compromised projects. As Diego, an LAUSD organizer[5] described of past District practices,

> Definitely around facilities there was never, like well, how would you like this new school to look? Or, where do you think it should go? I don't think there was any of that. The school district just came and said, we're gonna put a school here, and here's the paper that you need if you want to go to court and fight us. There was no community meeting – like everybody come and hear about this new school…People festered for so long, they were so angry for so long because of things we had already done.

This dynamic created a tough challenge for fledgling Community Outreach staff, dispatched to communities to procure buy-in and input around new school construction. Describing the tone at some of the initial public meetings, another District organizer illuminated the initial difficulties faced by LAUSD organizers and helped explain the impetus for the formation of Community Outreach as a discrete department within the Facilities Division.

> When we first started, it was surprising to me that the District didn't have a community relations team or group that was out there in the community. So, in the beginning…we would get just everything, everything. Where you were the meeting facilitator, but also the piñata at the party, and everyone would just take your stick and go after the facilitator, right?

With some egg on their faces, District organizers ultimately made progress in achieving stakeholder buy-in by building community trust. They did so by reaching out to communities and becoming a presence throughout the life of each project. From site selection through ribbon cutting, organizers distributed notices, held and attended community meetings, and provided regular and strategic briefings to "key stakeholders."

Such interaction provided an important opportunity for community members to influence school siting and design, and ultimately to advocate for new schools that would not only provide educational benefits, but also be situated and designed to become community assets.

Residents perceived early on, for instance, that new school construction could provide an opportunity to rid their communities of undesirable uses, such as blighted structures or businesses attracting drug traffic and prostitution. As one former LAUSD School Board staff member described,

> ...there was a lot of sites during Phase I that the community wanted us to redevelop. So, they would call the Board member's office, or they would lobby Community Outreach, and they would say, there's this cluster of apartments that are just blighted, and there's a lot of criminal activity there – can you consider that as a potential site?

This and other, similar accounts corroborate the notion that "good" planning should tap into local knowledge. In this case, that knowledge speaks also to an important goal of organizing for school reform: that school and community improvement should occur in concert. Hence, both to inform District process and to advocate for community redevelopment, activist community members in the Southeast demonstrated a vested interest in doing the work of building schools.

The Power of Politics

Despite notable gains in trust and community involvement, critics claimed that the potential of the Outreach process was stunted both by a lack of institutional will on the part of the District, and by a lack of political capacity within the communities of the Southeast. Critics of the District claimed, for instance, that LAUSD's own reticence toward community engagement limited what Community Outreach could accomplish in terms of authentic engagement and capacity building. In other words, LAUSD's ability to lay the foundation for sustained school–community connections was constrained from the outset by institutional struggles over the extent to which community involvement should take place, and what form it should take. As Steven, a school architect and community activist, surmised,

> The District frustrates the process of participatory planning from the outset. By the time LAUSD gets to the point that they are ready to talk to the community, they are talking in either or terms about the site...the public is therefore not truly engaged in the shaping of its schools or its communities.

Further limiting the process' transformative potential, Outreach garnered little power, according to some LAUSD staff, beyond the ability to delay decisions or seek additional community input on projects generating sustained public controversy. As explained by Linda, a member of the New Construction team,

Organizers don't have that much power. They basically just set up community meetings and hold ribbon-cutting ceremonies.

Elaborating on the relative efficacy of Community Outreach, one School Board member commented,

They are good people, but we (LAUSD) don't really know authentic engagement. We don't take seriously, or treat as important, community perspective as compared to official data compiled by the District.

Other skeptics claimed that even if the District could overcome such incapacities, embedded within which are the inherent bureaucratic limitations of the school planning process, the communities of the Southeast seemingly lack the depth of capacity to leverage school planning as an opportunity for sustainable school and community improvement. For while a number of fledgling Community Based Organizations (CBOs) mobilized around new school development in the Southeast, some saw these efforts more as a relatively unorganized reaction to District decisions than as proactive and promising community activism. Commenting on the capacity of local CBOs to affect long-term change in the educational landscape, Selena, a Southeast activist, opined,

I think that organizations like that (need to) evolve…into being either about social advocacy, school advocacy, or membership organizations that are welcoming and create a better power base. Or, they end up being the same people, the same group, always advocating for the same thing, but not really developing…Facilities are just not enough. They haven't gotten beyond that, and quite frankly, they don't want to get beyond that.

Selena, along with other critics, also pointed to insularity as a limiting characteristic of the most prominent CBOs fighting for new and better schools in Southeast LA.

My experience has been that if you are not part of the club, you are not welcome at the table, and your ideas don't matter. And that is a real indication of lack of forward thinking and insight…it's a lack of capacity to understand that there's a bigger picture, and if we're really about building momentum, that group that I think is now maybe 30 people, should be 300, it should be 3000.

In addition to this failure to develop sufficiently broad-based agendas and alliances, Selena also noted a tendency among many Southeast school activists to, conversely, align themselves too closely with the District.

So, what happens in these systems, and I've seen this happen over and over again, the people who are most vocal and most challenge the system are the ones who get co-opted by it. They are the ones who first get hired to basically control them. So, my perception of who gets hired into these community outreach positions is very much in line with that. It's very much people who are connected politically or have the potential to be connected politically, get brought into the fold, are hired to control the masses…I think the lack of political consciousness, and political development, and actual political savvy, has really hurt the community.

What Selena and other critics of Southeast schools activists have identified is a "narrow sectarianism" (Shirley, 1997: 27) on the part of activists, that, when combined with a tendency toward "redistributive" rather than "transformative" empowerment on the part of the District, may keep local community activists from fully cultivating the "generalized reciprocity and social trust" needed to engender broad reaching collaboration around school and neighborhood change. As articulated by Kennedy and Tilly (1990), redistributive empowerment implies a more temporary, context-based solution, wherein the faction of activists working within the institution (i.e., District) run the risk of being co-opted. Whereas, transformative empowerment allows for a more "countercultural collectivism," which may be limited in terms of short-term gains, but holds greater potential for permanently altering the school–community agenda (Kennedy & Tilly, 1990).

The District's promotion of redistributive versus transformative power also plays out in its tendency both to co-opt certain individuals and to align with those CBOs that are perceived as unthreatening. Anna, a former School Board staffer, illuminated this dynamic with her perspective on LAUSD's overall motivation for engaging community.

Sometimes you have to escalate strategies…but with the District, they're not open to mobilizing. They're not really open to activism; and, then you bring in an edgy strategy. That is going to turn them off. So, in many meetings, where we were going to have controversial projects, we would personally call Padres Unidos and let them know, this is what's coming down the pipeline, and this is why, and this is how you could influence this. We were less inclined to call other groups because of some of the strategies that they have used to publicly shame the District.

Anna's perspective provides valuable insight into how LAUSD orders stakeholder participation. Unfortunately, such an approach not only forestalls the development of transformative power, but also limits the District's own institutional evolution and ability to best serve its constituents. In combination, such limiting conditions ultimately may hinder the potential for collaborative school and community change.

Measures of Success: Building a Foundation for Sustained School–Community Connections

The ray of light in an arguably problematic political and institutional climate is that despite the impediments characterized above, District Outreach and concomitant community activism have resulted in positive school and community outcomes that are aligned with the District's own goals: to educate the community on the complexity of building new schools; to identify real opportunities for community input; to develop a support base for new schools; and, to establish the foundation for community participation beyond completion of new schools.[6]

Community Education

Despite a somewhat cynical beginning, where new school projects were notoriously abandoned or monumentally over budget, valuable learning has occurred as a result of the Outreach process. Community activists have learned, for instance, how to most effectively make demands on the District. As one District staff member described,

> Now people are used to the process and make demands…what I love the most is when community members recite the process. They know; they are empowered now. It's different day.

Other staff members too attested to the vast difference in community capacity to engage in public process between the inception and near conclusion of the construction program. Importantly, while such empowerment aligns with Outreach goals, it clearly goes beyond the scope intended by LAUSD leadership. More specifically, while the District's aim was to educate the public about *this* process, community stakeholders ultimately have become educated in how to participate in *the* process. In other words, as stakeholder understanding of the school construction process has evolved over time, so has the capacity of community stakeholders for applying their expanded cultural and political capital to new and different challenges.

Creating a Community Forum

Outreach also has provided a forum for community stakeholders to express concerns beyond those directly related to school construction. This is illustrated by transcripts of dozens of District-sponsored community meetings that served not only as an opportunity for public comment on proposed school projects, but also as a forum for community members to voice their general concerns about LAUSD and its schools. Acknowledging that the process has filled a void in opportunities for communication between the District and the communities it serves, one School Board member revealed,

> There is no other forum for people to complain…when you are engaging parents at a school site, no matter what the meeting is about, parents will take the opportunity to speak their minds.

Anna, a former Board staff member concurred, and expanded on the importance of providing a forum for community stakeholders to air their concerns, the benefits of Outreach in this regard, and the connection of mutual awareness to community activism.

> …other people are hearing their concerns and they're saying, yeah, that's true. And, maybe that's building an awareness that they already have. But, they're able to air that awareness and make other people aware that, you know, this isn't normal…I don't think we've ever done a good job of going out into the community. So, to have the District leave Beaudry[7] and go out to the community, I think that's one of the benefits.

Thus, despite an effort at outreach that, in the words of the Board member quoted above, "felt more like compliance," the community was able to make itself heard on topics of critical importance that reached above and beyond new school siting and design.

Developing a Base of Support

Beyond opening long-obstructed lines of communication, the process of building new schools in Southeast neighborhoods has helped to develop support for schools by creating increased opportunities for parent involvement and enhancing city–school connections.

Parent Participation

One of the effects of busing students across the District has been that parents' ability to visit their children's schools, volunteer in classrooms, participate in campus work sessions, or attend meetings, has been limited. Thus, opportunities for this type of school-based parent involvement have increased simply by returning children to neighborhood schools. Sylvia, a parent activist, described how and why building new schools represents an important step in increasing parental involvement.

> Parents are now closer to the schools…we are asking for parent rooms at each new school, working with principals and superintendents to make sure schools offer resources that parents need…The District knows how important parent involvement in schools is for kids' education to grow.

The inclusion of "parent rooms," or parent centers, on new school campuses represents an important factor in increasing the presence and efficacy of parents on new school campuses. Further, an evolution in the use of such spaces, from small, tucked away social gathering spaces, to centrally located, widely used volunteer work and meeting spaces, has helped to legitimize parent volunteers. Beyond parent center participation and classroom time, some parents have designed and implemented school-based programs that create ways for parents to use their skills to support academic programs. As one parent activist described,

> Parents are seeking out programs to bring to the school. They play a role in bringing what they think they need at their school, and that affects the community as a whole.

Such opportunities for involvement are particularly important in areas like Southeast LA, where many parents are unfamiliar with the educational system and often unwelcome in their children's schools, and hold promise for new schools and the neighborhoods that surround them. Of course, it is not always possible for parents to be present, *at* the school. Many are single parents, work multiple jobs, and/or lack the cultural capital to feel confident entering what they perceive to be a foreign realm with formal rules of engagement. Thus, as researchers learn more about the ways in which culturally diverse families are already involved in their children's education, and how to engage them in new ways (Jordan et al., 2001), it would behoove LAUSD to use such perspectives to help parents and other community members find meaningful and appropriate ways to stay involved in schools.

City–School Connections

In addition to parent involvement, new school construction also has forged opportunities for city–school connections. One example of intra-city and city–District collaboration that emerged in the Southeast around the need for new schools was the Southeast Cities Schools Coalition (SCSC), a quasi-governmental organization comprised of representatives of the six Southeast cities, along with LAUSD representatives. The group coalesced in 2005, out of fear that LA Mayor Villaraigosa's ambition for taking over LAUSD would leave poorer, smaller independent cities increasingly powerless over the timing and location of local school construction. While initially focused on the allocation of school construction dollars, SCSC's broader goals aimed at creating stronger connections between schools and communities, for the sake of LAUSD students, their families, and the neighborhoods in which they live. In short, these communities sorely wanted new schools, but wanted the siting and design of such schools to occur in concert with local community development goals.[8]

As a by-product of the new school construction program, city–school connections also have been enhanced with the increased prevalence of joint-use facilities. LAUSD's joint-use program is just one of a few mechanisms employed by the District to create mutually advantageous external partnerships to leverage District assets that benefit schools, students, and communities. Joint-use funds have been utilized at new schools in the Southeast to enable improvement and maintenance of shared fields and open spaces, install health clinics in schools, and develop joint-use pools. Beyond being a mechanism for cities and schools to share scarce resources, this District initiative also has proven to be a crucial framework for advancing projects and policies that promote schools as centers of community.

Establishing the Foundation for Sustained Community Engagement

Finally, community involvement around new school construction has spawned an expansion of educational activism in Southeast LA, providing a catalyst for some CBOs and a point of expansion for others. One pre-existing school-focused CBO that expanded its reach as a result of new school construction is Parent U-Turn. This parent collaborative was formed by South LA residents who participated in UCLA's Parent Curriculum Project, an initiative intended to inform low-income parents about school reform and encourage them to become school and community leaders and advocates (Oakes et al., 2006). Parents took these basic navigational tools and applied them in their quest for change in the Southeast.

Other organizations, such as Padres Unidos of South Gate, coalesced specifically around school construction, and then expanded their mission to work more broadly for educational quality. This group emerged in the wake of planning for a highly contested site in South Gate, and subsequently broadened its focus to become a prominent force on the local educational scene. As one Southeast principal described,

> They're very active in this area and their focus was just new schools in general for a very long time…I think they're changing their focus from having a nice building to having a quality education. I'm pleased to see that they're really interested in making sure that happens for the children.

Another prominent group in the area, Southeast Parents (Padres del Surestes), formed before the push for school construction, offering classes for parents in the community, but really blossomed with its advocacy for new schools. Members of the group now see their mission as improving the schools, getting parents involved, and improving communication with parents. As one representative recounted,

> This was happening before the district process. Now, we can't stop people...with the campaign to build new schools almost gone, now we are trying to improve education.

Estrella, an LAUSD organizer, attested to the fact that all of the groups involved in school site selection now are active around instruction and educational issues, and noted the foundation for continued activism that appears to have been laid.

> They (community activists) have come into contact with other folks who are in politics, activism, and they have become activists...it doesn't seem like they are going to stop meeting because our process is done. Now these groups meet on a weekly or monthly basis. And it seems like they are going to keep meeting.

Diego, another long-time LAUSD organizer, concurred in his account of the potential for sustained parent and community activism. He also illuminated the uniqueness of Southeast activism, noting that whereas in the City of LA, education is "just one issue on a larger canvas of issues," in the Southeast, "folks are really focused on education." As Luis, another LAUSD organizer put it,

> I think that parents are definitely keyed up about the new school construction program. And, that momentum has been sustained and reinvigorated with the opening of each new school.

Echoing the spirit of Luis's remark, a member of LAUSD's School Board characterized grassroots activism around education in Southeast LA as an evolution, acknowledging a growing awareness of educational issues and an expansion of activism around schools – both of which represent an important step toward meaningful, community-centered reform.

Conclusion

As described herein, outreach and activism around LAUSD's school construction program has helped to deliver new schools to dozens of communities, replace blight with community assets, rebuild community trust, and empower stakeholders to become active in schools and around education more broadly. Yet, as the momentum of new construction stalls, recent and forthcoming changes in District policies and governance structures make the future of District sponsored outreach uncertain.[9] So too is the level and form of continued activism among Southeast community stakeholders. Especially given the lack of community–District affiliation prior to the inception of the new school construction program, the loss of formalized outreach could have the effect of diluting the current enthusiasm around Southeast schools, hence discarding the opportunity for collaborative school improvement that this moment of increased parent and community engagement has inspired. How, then, will LAUSD capitalize on this moment of increased community engagement and enhanced District capacity to build a more collaborative relationship with parents and other community stakeholders and help ensure that communities can harness the benefits that these significant facilities investments have wrought?

One way for LAUSD to leverage these outcomes is to proceed with a more inclusive, democratic governance approach – one that would not only solicit public input, but also empower communities to become more effective District partners. The moment is ripe for such an approach, given the escalation in activism around schools in LA, and the rise nationally in community organizing for education. Such movement demonstrates an interest among community stakeholders in LA and elsewhere – after decades of educational bureaucratization and a parallel decline in public confidence and satisfaction – in returning to a more democratic system, wherein stakeholder empowerment is somehow part of school district process.

Thus, LAUSD would do well to move toward a more democratized model for school governance that emphasizes localism and lay control, and is designed to enable parents to become more effectively involved in the way schools are designed and run. Importantly, such democratic governance will become most effective when *both* institutional *and* community capacity are present, and as with many problems plaguing our society, will require "broad-based community action *with and beyond government*" (Briggs, 2008: 298). In other words, since *neither* civic capacity *nor* government alone can solve such urgent public problems as the need to improve urban schools, part of a District's job must include evolving its governance strategies to empower communities for collaborative action.

By endeavoring to authentically engage communities in school planning, Community Outreach already has nudged LAUSD in a more democratic direction. As described herein, communities in Southeast LA have benefitted most from new neighborhood schools when they have learned through the school development process how to realize their needs by effectively making demands on the District – whether by organizing, by participating in a District-initiated outreach process, or some combination of the two. And, for its part,

LAUSD has governed more effectively where it could develop its own internal capacity to authentically gather and incorporate community input. Yet, with the work of New Construction largely done, LAUSD must find new ways going forward of leveraging community outreach and organizing to build and sustain better schools.

A few potential avenues for such democratic reform exist already within LAUSD's institutional coffers. One is the 2009 Public School Choice Resolution, spearheaded by then School Board Member and Huntington Park native, Yolie Flores, to provide opportunities for community stakeholders with experience in education to work with the District to improve local schools by submitting and implementing governance plans for new (including many in the Southeast) and "troubled" District schools. The resolution's implementation got a rocky start, as early public process left community members and educators feeling as though promises of a transparent, objective, and participatory process had gone unfulfilled. Yet, recent amendments prioritizing in-District applicant teams appear to be pushing reform in the right direction.

LAUSD also could leverage its existing Parent Community Services Branch, which provides tools for parents to stay connected to the latest resources and information needed to support their children's education. It is unclear, however, whether this effort demonstrates a true desire to move beyond information provision toward the work of building parent and community capacity. And, like many school districts in cash-strapped California, LAUSD is at a point where its internal resources must be used wisely. At this crucial juncture, that means not just relying on parents and other community members to augment District services, but legitimizing and building upon the efforts of community stakeholders to improve their local schools.

Regardless of what mechanisms LAUSD chooses to utilize, sustained engagement of key community stakeholders will require a concerted and continuous effort on the part of the District to welcome parent and community involvement, and to create and maintain pathways for it to occur. For, while further research is needed to determine whether the current participatory opening will result in sustained school–community connections, two salient points appear clear at this time: 1) many of the positive outcomes surrounding the District's process may have occurred in spite of it, and 2) without school construction, activist momentum and District incentive may lack a point of focus going forward. Thus, for LAUSD to move toward authentically collaborative, community-centered reform, the District itself must develop an ethos, and policies and practices to support it, that favors inclusive school planning and governance, from conceptual design through high school commencement. Its success or failure to do so will determine whether positive process outcomes will fully be realized, and provide valuable lessons for other urban districts seeking to translate existing or potential civic engagement into school and neighborhood improvement.

Notes

1 This does not include the City of Vernon, for which no city-level census data were available.
2 In 2002, for instance, more than 4,200 children attended South Gate Middle School, a campus designed to serve 800 (Oakes 2003).
3 The Concept 6 calendar provides the maximum increase in the number of students that can attend a school, but limits the number of instructional days to 163 days instead of the traditional 180 days (California Education Code Section 37670).
4 When I began this research, the Community Outreach Department was a department within the New Construction Branch of the Facilities Services Division. I routinely refer to the Facilities Division, or "Facilities" to differentiate between Outreach and the remainder of LAUSD's school planning and construction apparatus.
5 Community Outreach staff members assigned to various communities around the District are called "organizers".
6 Goals are adapted from the "New Construction All Hands Community Outreach" PowerPoint Presentation, presented in October 2005.
7 Beaudry is the street in Downtown LA where LAUSD's main administrative offices are located.
8 In the wake of fiscal crisis and political scandal, at least one of the Southeast cities withdrew from the coalition and, given similar circumstances in other local cities, the future of the organization is at best uncertain.
9 Since the completion of this research, the Facilities Services Division has reorganized to consolidate LAUSD's operating branches as new construction winds down. This reorganization eliminated the previous separation into Existing Facilities, New Construction, and Planning & Development branches, uniting their functions. Under this new structure, Community Outreach staff have been cut substantially, and the role of those remaining has changed to focus primarily on facilitating joint-use of existing facilities by traditional and charter schools and by the school and neighborhood communities.

References

Arnstein, Sherry. 1969. A ladder of citizen participation. *Journal of American Institute of Planners* (35): 216–224.
Baum, Howell S. 2003. *Community organizing for school reform*. New York: State University of New York Press.
Bingler, Steven. 1999. "What if?" New Schools, Better Neighborhoods, nsbn.org.
Blank, Martin et al. 2003. *Making the difference: Research and practice in community schools*. Washington DC: Coalition for Community Schools, Institute for Educational Leadership.
Briggs, Xavier de Souza. 2008. Democracy as Problem Solving: Civic Capacity in Communities Across the Globe. Cambridge, MA: MIT Press.
Dyck, James. 2002. The built environment's effect on learning: Applying current research. *Montessori LIFE*, Winter 2002.
Forester, John. 1999. *The deliberative practitioner: Encouraging participatory processes*. Cambridge: MIT Press.
Henderson, Anne T. and Mapp, Karen L. 2002. A new wave of evidence: The impact of school, family and community connections on student achievement. Southwest Educational Development Laboratory, National Center for Family & Community Connections with Schools. Annual Synthesis 2002.

Hibbard, Michael and Lurie, Susan. 2000. Saving Land but losing ground: Challenges to community planning in the era of participation. *Journal of Planning Education and Research*. 20 (2): 187–195.

Innes, Judith and Booher, David. 2005. *Reframing public participation: Strategies for the 21st century*. UC Berkeley: Institute of Urban and Regional Development.

Jordan, Catherine et al. 2001. *Emerging issues in school, family and community connections*. National Center for Family and Community Connections with Schools, Southwest Educational Development Laboratory. www.sedl.org/connections.

Kennedy, Marie and Tilly, Chris et al. 1990. Transformative Populism and the Development of a Community of Color. In *Dilemmas of Activism: Class, Community, and the Politics of Local Mobilization*, pp. 302–324. Mel King (ed.). Philadelphia: Temple University Press.

LAUSD. 2009. Data Trends Memo 2010. www.laschools.org.

LAUSD. 2011. New Construction Strategic Execution Plan (SEP). http://www.laschools.org/sep/.

Lippman, Peter et al. 2007. Pattern language developed for learning communities of practice. *CAEnet*, Winter 2007. http://info.aia.org/nwsltr_cae.cfm?pagename=cae_a_200701_language.

Noguera, Pedro. 2001. Transforming Urban Schools Through Investments in the Social Capital of Parents, in Susan Saegert, J. Phillip Thompson, and Mark R. Warren, *Social Capital and Poor Communities*. New York: Russell Sage Foundation, 2001: 189–212.

Oakes, Jeannie. 2003. Multi-track, year-round calendar (Concept 6) and busing to address overcrowding. *Williams v. State of California Plaintiff's Expert Reports*. http://justschools.gseis.ucla.edu.

Oakes, Jeannie et al. 2006. *Learning Power*. New York: Teachers College Press.

Shirley, Dennis. 1997. *Community Organizing for School Reform*. Austin: University of Texas.

UC Berkeley Center for Cities and Schools. 2012. California's K-12 infrastructure investments. http://citiesandschools.berkeley.edu/reports/CCS2012CAK12facilities.pdf.

UCLA/IDEA. 2003. Overcrowding in California's Schools, justschools.gseis.ucla.edu/crisis/pdfs/Overcrowding-n1.pdf

Warren, Mark. 2007. Partners for change: Public schools and community-based organizations. Annenberg Institute for School Reform.

INDEX